Minimizing Harm

Minimizing Harm

A New Crime Policy for Modern America

EDITED BY

Edward L. Rubin

Westview Press
A Member of the Perseus Books Group

Copyright © 1999 by Westview Press, A Member of the Perseus Books Group

Published in 1999 in the United States of America by Westview Press, 5500 Central Avenue, Boulder, Colorado 80301-2877, and in the United Kingdom by Westview Press, 12 Hid's Copse Road, Cumnor Hill, Oxford OX2 9JJ

Library of Congress Cataloging-in-Publication Data
Minimizing harm : a new crime policy for modern America / edited by
    Edward L. Rubin; contributors, John J. Dilulio Jr ... [et al.].
      p.   cm.
    Includes bibliographical references.
    ISBN 0-8133-3536-1 (hc.)
    ISBN 0-8133-6804-9 (pbk.)
    1. Crime prevention—United States.   2. Crime—United States—
Public opinion.   3. Public opinion—United States.   I. Rubin,
Edward L., 1948–   . II. Dilulio, John J.
HV7431.M56   1999
364.4'0973—dc21   98-27899
                                                                                                            CIP

The paper used in this publication meets the requirements of the American National Standard of Permanence of Paper for Printed Library Materials Z39.48-1984.

10   9   8   7   6   5   4   3   2   1

Contents

Tables and Figures

Tables

Figures

Preface and Acknowledgments

This book has an interesting history, but that history is part of the book itself, and it is recounted in the Introduction.

Ordinarily, one does not think of a book's origins as being part of its substance, but that is the result of a somewhat old-fashioned theory of knowledge. It is widely recognized these days that one's conclusions depend, at least in part, upon one's context; this is sometimes called the social construction of reality. In the case of this book, the connection between process and substance is more specific. The book is about social policy; unlike most such books, it does not present optimal policy recommendations, but rather the best policy recommendations that are viable in the particular political context of the present day. To frame such recommendations, the authors not only drew upon their own knowledge and analysis but also placed themselves in the context of elected and appointed officials to whom their recommendations are addressed. They met with these officials, took their advice about the design of the project, met with the crime victims' groups that are creating so much of the political climate on this issue, and then presented their conclusions to both groups. That is the reason why the origins and substance of the book are intertwined. The hope is that the recommendations it advances can be used by real-world officials in formulating crime policy in America.

I would like to thank the many people who helped me organize this project. The California Policy Seminar, a program of the University of California, provided the funding; Andres Jimenez and Holly Brown were the seminar administrators who shepherded the original proposal through the process and organized all my meetings with California State officials; Joan Lichterman was the indefatigable editor who prepared the entire manuscript for publication. A number of officials took time from busy schedules to meet with me and the authors of the studies in this book; I particularly want to thank Craig Brown, Greg Harding, Craig Cornett, Elisabeth Kersten, Jim Lewis, Melissa Nappan, and David Panush. Sharon English of the California Office of Prevention and Victim's Services provided invaluable help in contacting crime victims' groups; I want to thank her and also the many representatives of these groups who overcame their initial doubts about Berkeley to meet with us.

My colleagues were of enormous help to me, as they have been throughout my entire career. Franklin Zimring not only contributed one of the book's principal studies but also helped greatly in reviewing my contribution and preparing the entire work for publication. Malcolm Feeley, my coauthor on *Judicial Policy Making and the Modern State*, also helped me with all aspects of the project. Jerome Skolnick agreed to contribute his study on short notice, after the topic of narcotics was identified as a critical concern by the state officials and crime victims' groups. My assistant, Sheila John, was assiduous and infinitely tolerant in transforming thirteen separate contributions into a single manuscript.

Although it is not traditional to acknowledge abstract entities, I also want to thank the University of California. It is truly a great institution, a public university that provides the very best quality education at a price (taking tuition and financial aid into account) that every citizen of California can afford. Perhaps the reason that Californians seem more fun-loving and present-oriented than other Americans—apart from the climate—is that they don't need to save large sums of money to provide their children with an absolutely first-rate education. The university also supports world-leading research in every academic field, and this book is the product of that support. Financial and administrative support came from a university-wide program, and intellectual participation and support came from the vast reservoir of talent in my own department, Boalt Hall School of Law. This is primarily a work of social science, not law, but Boalt Hall has a unique, interdisciplinary program—Jurisprudence and Social Policy—that the university established twenty years ago. Zimring, Feeley, and Skolnick are all members of this program, and the latter two would not have been my colleagues without it.

Finally, it is certainly traditional to end by thanking one's family for tolerating the author as he or she struggled to complete the book. I am as intolerable at home as most people are, but I can't attribute my irritability to this book, which has been a pleasure to work on from beginning to end. So, although it is a bit of an aside, I would simply like to thank my family—Ilene, Greg, Tim, Juliette, and Alex—for being my family.

Edward L. Rubin

1

Introduction: Minimizing Harm as a Solution to the Crime Policy Conundrum

EDWARD L. RUBIN

"That's the effect of living backwards," the Queen said kindly . . . "For instance, now," she went on, . . . "there's the King's Messenger. He's in prison now, being punished: and the trial doesn't even begin till next Wednesday: and of course the crime comes last of all."
"Suppose he never commits the crime?" said Alice.
"That would be all the better, wouldn't it?' the Queen said . . .
Alice felt there was no denying that. "Of course it would be all the better," she said: "but it wouldn't be all the better his being punished."
"You're wrong there, at any rate," said the Queen. "Were you ever punished?"
"Only for faults," said Alice.
"And you were all the better for it, I know!" the Queen said triumphantly.
"Yes, but then I had done the things I was punished for," said Alice: "that makes all the difference."
"But if you hadn't done them," the Queen said, "that would have been better still; better, and better, and better!"
—Lewis Carroll, *Through the Looking Glass*

This book represents an effort by a number of leading criminologists to articulate a pragmatic crime policy for America—a policy that combines academic insights about crime prevention with the realities of contemporary politics. It consists of four principal studies, focusing on public attitudes toward crime, prevention, alternative sanctions, and drug policy, plus two commentaries on each paper. Taken collectively, the studies outline a coherent policy that centers on minimizing harm, as opposed to retribution, eliminating crime, or solving the social problems that generate criminal behavior. The commentaries provide ramifications of—and in some cases, disagreements with—the principal studies. But the general theme is clear: Even in today's politically charged environment, minimizing harm is a pragmatic and effective approach to crime policy in America. Policymakers need not succumb to the naive belief that more prisons and harsher punishments are, as Carroll's White Queen believes, better, and better, and better.

The Conundrum of Crime Policy Analysis

In terms of its impact on people's lives and the level of concern that it engenders crime may be the leading social problem in the United States today. Its impact is felt at both the individual and the collective levels. For individuals, crime affects most aspects of their daily lives: where they choose to live, where they shop, where they go to the movies, and where they walk or drive. It determines whether they feel safe in their homes or going to and from their place of work and, more subtly but perhaps more profoundly, the extent to which they perceive themselves as members of a neighborhood or a community. It causes property loss, trauma, injury, or death for the individuals who are its victims, and in its severe forms, grief and trauma for the victim's family, friends, and workmates.

At the collective level, the crime rate often determines the value of homes, the location of businesses, the extent of tourism, and indeed, the entire pattern of local commerce and development. Expenditures to prevent, deter, or punish crime now make up large portions of state and local budgets, and the geometric increase in these expenditures during the last decade has begun cutting into other governmental services and threatening the fiscal stability of many jurisdictions. Crime prevention efforts, in their turn, produce profound effects on people's attitudes in neighborhoods where crime is prevalent, and, at the individual level again, on the lives of those whose family members have been apprehended and incarcerated.

The amount of concern about crime is fully commensurate with its effects. Crime has become a major issue in national, state, and local elections. Politicians vie with each other to define more crimes, impose harsher sentences, and render the conditions of those sentences increasingly severe. In popular culture, crime now functions as our collective bête noire, the way Communism did in the 1950s. Just as the villains of many 1950s science fiction movies (cold-eyed aliens who conquered earth and took over people's bodies) were projections of our fear of Communism (Sontag 1986), the villains of contemporary films are drug lords or psychopathic serial killers—more obvious, perhaps, but just as emblematic of our deepest fears.

It is to be expected, of course, that the level of concern about crime would be roughly proportional to its social impact. One explanation for this relationship is the obvious one—the effects of crime are real and apparent. At the same time, the relationship functions in reverse: Public concern creates, or constructs, crime as a social problem. Income distribution was more unequal in the thirteenth century than in the twentieth, but only during the latter period do people's political attitudes lead them to perceive this inequality as a social problem; differences in religious beliefs are much greater in the twentieth century than they were in the thirteenth, but this no longer seems to be a problem for the people of most Western nations. Concern with crime is not only a response to crime itself but also a product of independent forces, such as many Americans' dismay about increasing social permissiveness, their smoldering dissatisfaction with their economic situation, and the continued disaggregation of local communities brought about by urban blight, mobility, television, VCRs, and the Internet. Overarching all these factors is race, America's most tragic issue. The criminal is a convenient proxy for minority groups that have won civil rights in the last forty years but continue to be objects of fear and loathing, in Hunter Thompson's phrase (Thompson 1982). This is not to suggest that concern with crime is imaginary but rather that this concern is generated by both real and symbolic forces. Anyone who treats the public's current attitudes toward crime as a direct reflection of the crime rate will severely underestimate the depth and the complexity with which these forces operate.

The interaction between the social impact of crime and people' s concern about it creates a severe problem for public policymakers. All our prescriptive theories about public policy are based on a model of rational analysis. The classic formula is to define the problem, list the alternative responses, select the most effective response, and implement it as the solution (Patton and Sauicki 1986, 26–38; Stokey and Zeckhauser 1978, 5–6). Doubts about the abilities of human decisionmakers to process so much information have led observers such as Charles Lindblom (1959), Herbert Simon (1957), and Oliver Williamson (1985), to propose incremental or heuristic approaches, which Simon characterizes as "bounded rationality." The concerns of the citizenry, however, do not appear in either formulation; the decisionmaker is supposed to devise a policy on the basis of the problem as defined and the data as presented, using a process of rational analysis, whether bounded or comprehensive.

Scholars have not ignored the effects of citizen attitudes on public policymakers, of course. Political scientists have studied the electoral process at every level of government, the manner in which interest groups influence the chief executive, lobby the legislature, and capture administrative agencies, the efforts of elected officials to secure votes by campaigning or doing favors for constituents, and the general sensitiv-ity of politicians at all levels to public opinion polls. But this work has been essentially descriptive, not prescriptive in nature; it focuses on the way government officials are observed to behave, not the way that they ought to behave in formulating and implementing public policy. When scholars produce prescriptive work they generally ignore these phe-nomena and address their recommendations to hypothetical, rational decisionmakers who are free from political influences when reaching their decisions.

To be sure, the depth of the opposition between descriptive and pre-scriptive discourse depends upon one's model of elected representatives, whether one views them as implementing the mandate of their con-stituents, or whether one views them as trustees selected by their con-stituents but deciding on the basis of their own best judgment (Burke 1949, 115; Pitkin 1967, 144–167). If they are trustees, then their task is to carry out the entire policymaking process, including the definition of the problem, according to their individual assessment of the situation, and any post-election influence is necessarily disruptive. If they are supposed to obey a public mandate, they should look to their constituents for the definition of the problem to be solved but should still proceed to solve it by a rational, apolitical process. Administrative agents are generally supposed to func-tion as trustees, and those in independent agencies are explicitly expected to do so; that is the whole point of their independence. Whichever model one adopts, however, it seems clear that political influence is antithetical to our prescriptive theories of public policymaking; once politics takes over, recommendations based on rational policy analysis seem to be precluded.

If rational policymaking occurs in the space left clear of political influ-ence, the size of that space will be of great concern to academic public policy analysts. Their general position, more frequently assumed than ar-gued for, is that there remain some areas in which government officials can function as rational decisionmakers, using instrumental reason to de-vise the best solution to a given problem. In recent years, public choice analysis has come to the lugubrious conclusion, on the basis of its analy-sis of public officials' motivations (Ferejohn 1974; Fiorina 1974; Fiorina 1977; Mayhew 1974), that there is no space at all for rational decision-making. But even if one adopts the more plausible idea that these offi-cials are sometimes motivated to act in the public's interest, rather than their own (Fenno 1973; Kingdon 1989; Rubin 1991), they must still live in a real world of political pressure and interest group activity. These can vary in their intensity, but they are never absent and rarely insignificant.

There are few areas where the conflict between rational policy analysis and political reality has been more intense than in crime policy. The pub-lic has translated its concern about crime into a demand for increased criminalization, longer sentences, and harsher prison conditions. Policy analysts are virtually unanimous in their belief that these are often inef-fective and excessively expensive measures and that other strategies would achieve the agreed-upon goal in a more effective manner. For ex-ample, virtually all observers agree that incarcerating small-time drug dealers is a waste of funds and prison space; these people are employees, not sociopaths, and when they are arrested someone else inevitably takes their job. Similarly, enhanced sentencing provisions, like the "three strikes and you're out" laws for repeat offenders, garner enormous popu-lar support, and elected officials have responded by enacting these provi-sions with unprecedented alacrity. But it is widely agreed among crime policy analysts that criminal behavior is very powerfully correlated with age across gender, social groups, geographic areas, and types of crime; indeed, this is one of the strongest correlations in all of social science (Blumstein and Cohen 1978; Blumstein and Cohen 1979; Gotfredson and Hirschi 1990; Matza 1964; Tittle 1980). Incarceration is expensive, and the incarceration of the elderly is particularly so because of their increasing health care needs. The result of the public demand for increased sen-tences is thus the expenditure of extensive social resources on a popula-tion that crime policy analysts regard as posing relatively low risks of committing crime (Zimring and Hawkins 1991). To put the matter most starkly (and ignoring civil liberties considerations for the moment) most criminologists would regard a "two strikes and you're out till you're forty" law as much more effective than the current three-strikes provi-sions.

This is the conundrum of crime policy analysis. On the one hand, the en-tire conceptual framework of policy analysis depends on the ability of pub-lic decisionmakers to respond to rational arguments, to adopt strategies that achieve a given social goal in the most effective and efficient manner possible. On the other hand, the audience for these recommendations con-sists of real-world government officials, subject to the forces of popular opinion, and the populace has exerted enormous pressure upon these offi-cials that seems to preclude any independent exercise of judgment. This leaves academic policy analysts with two equally unattractive options. The first is to abandon the aspiration of rational analysis and either recommend political strategies to these officials or work in the small interstices of crime policy that for the time being have escaped public notice. The second is to continue using their existing methodology and address rational decision-makers who no longer exist in the real world of American politics.

Surprisingly, current social science methodology offers no solution to this distressing, but far from uncommon, conundrum. Despite the pio-neering work of Aaron Wildavsky (Wildavsky 1979), there is no estab-lished theory that combines descriptive and prescriptive discourse. It is easy enough to find models, based on public choice or related, less mono-valent theories, to describe the way that citizen concern is expressed and that elected and appointed officials respond to it. It is equally easy to find models for the rational analysis of public policy problems. But there is no comprehensive model that tells policy analysts how to address real-world decisionmakers who must operate in the midst of demanding, highly charged political environment. Without such a model, however, no realistic and yet meaningful policy analysis of crime can be articulated.

The chapters and comments in this volume are designed to provide a solution that combines prescriptive and descriptive discourse. They offer recommendations, but these recommendations are not rational abstractions addressed to hypothetical policymakers who operate without political constraints. Rather, they are directed to real decisionmakers, in the real political environment. The general theme of the book, that crime policy should strive to minimize harm, is not a radical departure from existing policy, but it represents both a different substantive emphasis and a different way of characterizing those elements of crime policy that remain unchanged. Neither a new emphasis nor a new characterization may appear as valuable as a dramatic new solution, but dramatic solutions belong to the realm of abstract prescriptive theory, divorced from the descriptive discourse that captures the political reality of public decisionmakers. It is in the more subtle, incremental variations upon existing policy that the joinder of the two discourses resides.

The next section of this introduction discusses the conceptual approach to public policy that allows for prescriptive discourse to be combined with a descriptively accurate account of public policymakers. This is followed by a section that discusses the way this approach was implemented in generating the studies and comments that make up this volume. The last section discusses the results and summarizes the chapters that follow.

The Unification of Descriptive and Prescriptive Discourse

Everyone recognizes that public policy analysis is a multivalent process. Even the most reductionist methodology, cost-benefit analysis, involves an assessment of both the costs of government programs and the benefits that they confer. Devotees of this methodology, in their effort to place both costs and benefits within a common monetary metric, often restrict the range of the program's consequences, but the concepts open out into a potentially vast realm of social considerations. The costs of a regulatory program are not only the size of the budgetary appropriation necessary to implement it but also whatever disadvantages result from its implementation. Thus, many critics of social welfare programs believe that these programs decrease the willingness of the recipients to accept available low-wage employment, a deadweight loss that is measurable in economic terms. The benefits of a regulatory program will generally be even more far-reaching. Welfare, it is argued, not only improves the economic well-being of the recipients by an amount roughly equal to its total cost less the cost of administration but also yields measurable economic benefits by decreasing the crime rate and the demands on public health facilities.

Moreover, policy analysts often recognize other factors that are beyond the reach of cost-benefit analysis in its entirety. A recent criticism of welfare programs, for example, is that they encourage teenage pregnancy. Some people find teenage pregnancy undesirable per se, others emphasize its deleterious impact on other values, arguing that immature, unprepared parents have children who are less likely to lead successful lives. Claus Offe argues that the welfare state subverts the capitalist economy by decreasing people's general motivation to strive for economic rewards (Offe 1984). The analogous arguments in favor of welfare are that it is undesirable, per se, to permit American citizens to suffer from indigence and that indigence leads to a variety of other social problems. Moreover, it is virtually a consensus position among historians and political scientists that the modern welfare state defused revolutionary Marxism and preserved liberal democracy.

Thus, policy analysis involves an enormous range of considerations operating at different levels of generality and with different degrees of precision. These considerations must be balanced against one another, whether by cost-benefit analysis, "softer" sociologically oriented methods, or, to use Lindblom's phrase, just "muddling through" (Lindblom 1959). There is no reason the concerns of the citizenry should not be added to this already complex mixture. After all, people's satisfaction with their government is a positive good for them, a consumption product in economic terms. It is vague and difficult to measure, of course, but so are the effects of social welfare programs on political legitimacy, or the impact of environmental policies on future generations. There is no a priori reason to exclude this one factor from consideration, particularly since so many closely allied considerations, such as the motivation, loyalty, and demoralization of the populace are willingly factored in to the analysis.

The reluctance to include citizen concerns among the relevant factors for policy analysis probably stems from the overlap between these concerns and outright political influence. There is, however, a subtle but essential distinction between the two. Political influence stands outside policy analysis and operates as a constraint on it, limiting its scope of operation. Citizen concerns, on the other hand, can be regarded as an element of policy analysis, one of the many considerations that must be balanced against each other in order to devise a realistic course of action. The distinction may seem to be a mere matter of terminology, and a suspect terminology at that, since decisionmakers may be all too eager to clothe their subservience to politics in the raiment of public policy. But describing citizen concern as an element of policy as opposed to brute political influence yields results that can be operationalized in real-world terms. It means that the policymaker must think comprehensively, balancing optimal policy and citizen concerns in fashioning a single program that will be both beneficial and acceptable. It also means that the public policy analyst must incorporate this same range of considerations into any recommendation. In contrast, describing citizen concerns as merely politics implies an irreconcilable conflict between these concerns and rational decisionmaking, a conflict that seems to compel policymakers to choose between self-destruction or supine surrender, while academic analysts stand on the sidelines, wringing their hands and bewailing the decline of civic virtue.

This balancing process is illustrated by a familiar story about Franklin Roosevelt and the first social security act. Roosevelt's advisors urged him to fund the benefits out of general taxes, rather than employee contributions, using arguments that have become staples of public finance literature (Musgrave and Musgrave 1989). "[T]hose taxes were never a problem of economics," Roosevelt responded. "They are politics all the way through. We put those payroll contributions there so as to give the contributors a legal, moral, and political right to collect their pensions and their unemployment benefits. With those taxes in there, no damn politician can ever scrap my social security program." (Leuchtenberg 1963, 132–133; Perkins 1946, 188–189, 282–285; Schlesinger 1959, 308–309). Roosevelt's advisors were playing the standard role of policy analysts, informing him about the most efficient and rational way to implement a stated goal. When Roosevelt responded that the issue was "politics all the way through," he did not mean that he was responding solely to the demands of the electorate. Social security, after all, was based on his genuine beliefs about the good of the country. What he did, however, was to compromise between optimal policy and citizen attitudes, blending the two into a coherent program that met his goals and achieved long-term acceptability. His social security plan was a combination of politics and policy, "all the way through."

The process of incorporating citizen concerns into public policy analysis not only requires compromise with those concerns but also emphasizes the importance of the way public policies are characterized. This can be readily dismissed as mere symbolism, or window dressing—the very antithesis of true policymaking. In fact, it possesses both theoretical and pragmatic justifications. At the theoretical level, the social construction of policy problems precludes a dismissive stance toward citizen concerns. Policymakers must recognize that their efforts can only be as good as their agenda and that their agenda is formulated by a complex interaction between the governmental institutions and the public. At the pragmatic level, public policy, no matter how well conceived, must be implemented, a process that requires public understanding and support. Even if a policy could be enacted in isolation from prevailing political forces, which is unlikely, it cannot be implemented in isolation. Thus, the incorporation of citizen concerns into public policymaking suggests two separate steps. First, policymakers must compromise between their own best judgment and citizens concerns, not merely in obtaining approval for their program but in formulating their program from the outset. Second, they must find a way to characterize, or package, their program so it will be comprehensible and convincing to the general populace.

One possible objection to this approach is that citizen concerns are not always communicated to public policymakers in an accurate or reliable manner. As our long-standing theory of interest groups asserts, and as public choice affirms, narrowly focused, well-organized interests often dominate political discourse (Olson 1965). But it is simply false, as an empirical matter, that special interests are the only voices heard; mass movements dealing with the environment, consumer rights, and abortion have flourished in recent years, despite the diffuse concerns they represent, their lack of clear economic incentives, and the free rider problems that supposedly bedevil their organizational efforts (Luker 1984; Wilson, 1980, 364–394). Moreover, interest groups should not be viewed exclusively as a mechanism that distorts citizen concerns. Although they generally do not represent the general populace, they often register the intensity of political opinion rather accurately. One-person-one-vote is the rule for elections, but one cannot assume that the mild preferences of larger groups should always prevail over the intensely felt beliefs of smaller ones. Finally, the point of the proposed approach to public policy is to take citizen views into account in a realistic manner, not to uncritically succumb to any views that happen to be presented to the decisionmaker. The fact that interest groups often present a distorted view of citizen concerns is well known to public officials. They are fully capable of evaluating expressions of concern and deciding which ones are appropriate to incorporate into their decisionmaking process. They may not do so, of course, but they would then be doing a poor job, just as a policymaker who failed to consider a plausible alternative would be doing a poor job of using the rational decisionmaking model.

A deeper difficulty with the proposed approach is that it abandons the deeply felt aspiration to purely *rational policymaking*, as that term is generally understood. Rational decisionmakers take a variety of factors into account, including the needs of citizens, but they analyze the options by means of an independent, theoretically justified process. To incorporate citizen concerns, and not merely citizen needs, into the process means that those concerns operate at the same level as the policymakers' rational analysis. Because they stand apart from that analysis, however, their inclusion introduces an element of irrationality; the policymakers are no longer functioning as pure trustees. To be sure, they are not simply following a mandate either, that is, acting according to the predictions of public choice, or they would not be engaging in any policy analysis at all. Instead, they are compromising—balancing their sense of rational policy against their knowledge of public sentiment. This may seem like a perfectly realistic approach, but it is not an entirely *rational* process as we generally use that term.

There are at least four reasons why abandoning the process of rational public policymaking is not as serious as it sounds, despite the popularity of rationality and rational discourse among modern political philosophers. These reasons are pragmatic, methodological, philosophical, and moral. The pragmatic reason is that no one has ever successfully explained how rational discourse would become institutionalized as a democratic society's exclusive mode of decisionmaking. For Bruce Ackerman, such discourse is simply an imagined process used to construct his political morality (Ackerman 1980). Theodore Lowi treats it as a real-world aspiration, but his description of its implementation is so jejune as to be completely discontinuous with his analysis of the prevailing political situation (Lowi 1974).

A much more formidable effort to propose an institutional setting for rational discourse is Jurgen Habermas's most recent book, *Between Facts and Norms* (1996). Habermas provides a wonderfully complex and subtle discussion of popular opinion and the forms of interaction between the populace or civil society and governmental institutions, but he still fails to close the yawning gap that appears in his previous work, *The Theory of Communicative Action* (1981, 1987), between rational discourse and political reality. Indeed, his new book is really a partial admission of defeat. Habermas now recognizes that government decisionmaking in a modern democracy is necessarily affected by citizen concerns, and indeed should be affected by those concerns. To achieve rational policymaking therefore, the citizens themselves must engage in rational discourse. As an empirical matter, this seems unlikely in any foreseeable future. One need not go so far as Murray Edelman (1974) who regards all popular opinion as the product of manipulation and distortion. Citizens can certainly think rationally, they are capable of learning, and they are probably becoming more civilized over time, as Norbert Elias suggests (1994).

But public discourse remains led by emotion, symbolism, prejudice, both profound and casual, half-baked notions, and fugitive impressions. The major source of improvement during the course of the last of several centuries, if there has indeed been an improvement, is probably attributable to a change in sensibility, rather than any increase in rationality. And there is simply no plausible account of any mechanism by which decisionmakers in a democratic state can insulate themselves from these less-than-admirable public attitudes.

The second reason why abandoning the exclusive reliance on rationality in policymaking is not a particularly serious defeat is methodological. Citizen attitudes are not rude intrusions into an otherwise self-sustaining intellectual discipline, the way they might be for quantum mechanics or even medical research. The methodology of public policy analysis is simply not sufficiently developed so that we can be confident that it would produce desirable results if isolated from the political process by which citizens express their feelings to government decisionmakers. Many political thinkers who believe that isolation can be partially achieved, including Max Weber (1978), Robert Michels (1962), and Joseph Schumpeter (1942), regard this possibility as a disastrous one. Without the constraint of a definitive and generally accepted methodology such as that of natural science, decisionmakers are likely to use their independence to serve personal or narrowly defined class interests. In other words, freedom from the irrationality of citizens is purchased with exposure to the irrationality of the decisionmakers, a danger that the modern methods of policy analysis are too weak to combat. The point is not simply that decisionmakers are likely to be self-interested, in some self-conscious, cynical fashion, although that may well be the case. Rather, the real problem is that even conscientious policymakers will not be able to generate definitive answers and are thus likely to be misled by their less explicit prejudices and predilections. Nor will listening to external, disinterested observers provide a solution for these conscientious policymakers, because the observers, however disinterested, do not know the answers either.

This methodological problem with the concept of purely rational public policymaking might appear to be an unfortunate but temporary situation, to be resolved once policy analysis advances to the state of normal science, in Thomas Kuhn's terminology (1970). Some modern epistemologists, however, argue that "human sciences" such as policymaking can never reach this vaunted state (Gadamer, 1988). Even if one rejects this view, there may well be a third, philosophical reason why policy analysis in particular could never develop a self-contained methodology. The whole purpose of modern public policy analysis is to maximize the welfare of the citizenry, whether this is measured in economic, that is, utilitarian terms, or by some more equity-based process such as Rawls's theory of justice (1971). But it may well be just as beneficial to the welfare of citizens to satisfy their irrational desires as to satisfy their rational ones. A policy that reduces the crime rate in an economically efficient manner would be regarded as beneficial because it increases citizen welfare. One might also increase citizen welfare, however, by responding directly to their concerns, even if that response has no additional consequences. When people feel safer, their welfare has been increased, despite the fact that the actual level of danger to them remains unchanged. In other words, people's feelings about current social problems, however irrational they may appear to the policymakers, are part of their welfare function, and there are no persuasive grounds on which they can be excluded from consideration.

The final reason why the concept of purely rational public policymaking should be abandoned involves political morality and has been explored in the works of Hannah Arendt (1958a, 1958b, 1968). Even if we could insulate the policymaking process from expressions of citizen concern, and even if we could devise a methodology that was robust enough to avoid distortion by policymaking elites, and even if that methodology could take account of citizens' subjective and deeply felt concerns, we might find the result objectionable because an administrative system so insulated from its citizens seems inconsistent with our notions of democratic government. One need not subscribe to the self-congratulatory myths of popular sovereignty that festoon political stump speeches and high school civics textbooks to recognize that the interaction between the citizens and the administrative apparatus is a crucial element of our democracy. However irrational the voice of the citizens, that voice should be heard by those who govern, and not just on election day. For nearly 100 years, the Roman Empire was ruled by a succession of five absolute monarchs whose wisdom and fairness are rivaled by few democratically elected regimes. Gibbon called this the period in the history of the world during which "the condition of the human race was most happy and prosperous." (1932, 70). Of the fourth of these emperors, Antoninus Pius, he wrote: "His reign is marked by the rare advantage of furnishing few materials for history; which is, indeed, little more than the register of the crimes, follies and misfortunes of mankind." (1932, 69). The fifth emperor, Marcus Aurelius, was more admirable still, a true philosopher king. And yet this halcyon era further infantilized the once self-reliant citizens of the Roman state and left them lacking either the will or wherewithal to resist the depredations of the various perverted monsters who succeeded Marcus. The agonies of third-century Rome may be regarded as an instrumental argument for maintaining the citizenry's political skills as an antidote against the tyrannies of an unforeseen future. But they are also an illustration of a moral lapse on the part of the Roman citizenry. Even those people who were fortunate enough to live their lives under the five good emperors were denied the experience of political responsibility.

None of these issues, abstract though they may seem, are at all remote from day-to-day crime policy; in fact the pragmatic, methodological, philosophical, and moral considerations for abandoning the concept of purely rational public policy are all directly applicable. To begin with, it is clear, as a pragmatic matter, that there is no longer any insulation between the formulation of crime policy by public officials and the political concerns of the populace. David Garland (1990) and Franklin Zimring and Gordon Hawkins (1986) have observed that crime policy has become increasingly politicized in recent years. Although public concern about crime has always been present, people were generally content to leave the mechanics of policing, prosecution, sentencing, and punishment in the hands of bureaucratic elites. During the last two decades, these issues have moved to the center of public debate. Political campaigns are won or lost over details of crime policy, lobbyists organize to lengthen sentences and restrict parole, and letters and phone calls precipitate out of the vast, and previously empty firmament of public opinion when it becomes known that prisoners are lifting weights or watching television in their cells. As a result, law enforcement and correctional administrators sense that they have little room to maneuver. The legislature, responding to citizen demands, prescribes increasingly specific rules to govern their decisions, while their remaining exercises of discretion threaten to elicit additional citizen demands.

Second, the methodological difficulty for rational policymaking is particularly acute in the area of crime since so few answers seem to be forthcoming from the academic establishment or from government researchers. The problem is not a lack of research, or even a lack of consensus (the volume of research grows along with the size of everything else, and consensus has long been foreign to this field) but a lack of enthusiasm for the proposals being advanced. Prior aspirations for rehabilitation, behavioral conditioning, deterrence, or sociologically based prevention have foundered on the adamantine intractability of the crime problem; even incapacitation, the principle that seems to guide the bulk of current policy (Zimring and Hawkins 1995), is generally regarded as an unfortunate second-best, rather than a comprehensive solution. The entire field of criminology lacks the sense of forward motion that characterizes nuclear physics, macroeconomics, or even post-structuralist anthropology; it no longer possesses what Thomas Kuhn has called a paradigm (1970), or what Lakatos refers to, less grandly, as a research program (1978). Moreover, as Robert Weisberg observes, "the best empirical studies in contemporary criminology tend to be intellectually and politically paralyzing, tending to show that most law enforcement or crime prevention policies are counter-productive or counter-intuitively irrelevant (1992, 525)." Much valuable work continues to be done, but criminology, in its current rate of disarray, cannot serve as the basis of an argument for expert decisionmaking.

At the same time, the rise in citizen concern about crime has far outpaced both the crime rate and the ability of government officials to make sense of it. Traditional policy analysis treats this as a problem for the officials, but in terms of political philosophy, it is properly regarded as a problem for the citizens as well. Fear of crime is now a social problem in its own right, imprisoning people in their houses, banishing them from the center city, the beach, or the amusement park, taxing them with expenditures for home alarms, car alarms, and cans of pepper spray, and alienating them from their fellow citizens. Undoubtedly, the enthusiasm of elected officials for enacting draconian criminal laws stems from their desire for political survival, but it could also be interpreted as a conscientious response to a level of fear that has passed beyond the reach of more moderate remedies. In other words, government officials must now address people's fear of crime, as well as their victimization by it, and there is no obvious reason why the latter set of issues are any more compelling than the former.

Finally, the only moral way to address both crime and the fear of crime in a democratic regime is by means of an interaction between the government and its citizens. There is a great deal of expertise among the crime control professionals in the state and federal governments, far more than most people realize or are willing to acknowledge. But the crime problem has become too big to be solved by expertise alone. Any government that could persuade people to rely on its rational decisionmaking process to solve the crime problem would be too powerful to remain within the confines of a democratic, pluralist regime. It could persuade people of almost anything and advance a claim of expertise that would disable, if not eradicate, dissent. In the final analysis, it would deprive them of the experience of governance.

The Crime Policy Project

The studies and comments that make up this volume were generated by the California Crime Policy Project, which was specifically designed to address the conundrum of crime policy analysis by integrating prescriptive and descriptive discourse about crime. Thus, this volume speaks to real-world decisionmakers who must exist, and survive, in the highly charged environment of contemporary politics. But it does not offer strategic advice on political survival; government officials generally know at least as much about the topic as academics do, and besides, there is no reason to assume that the continued political survival of the officials in power at a given moment has any particular value for society as a whole. The purpose of the volume, rather, is the traditional academic goal of recommending desired public policy but to do so with full recognition of the situation that real decisionmakers face and of their understandable desire to remain in office. Thus this volume combines rational discourse and practical politics, as described in the previous section.

The California Crime Policy Project was sponsored by the California Policy Seminar, itself an effort to combine these two modes of discourse. Established by the University of California in 1977, the seminar provides a liaison between the University and the state and local governments of California. Part of this task is achieved simply by acting as a "broker"; the seminar puts government officials who want information in contact with academics working in that field or puts academics with particular concerns in contact with the relevant officials. The seminar also designs and funds its own projects to bring academic expertise to bear on current social issues. Given the current public mood, in both California and the nation generally, crime policy was a natural choice and constituted one of the seminar's two major projects for the 1994–1995 academic year. Although the project focused on California, it was formulated in general terms. Moreover, although California crime policy has a few peculiarities, such as the inclusion of residential burglars in its "three strikes" law, there is no reason to think that the patterns we observed would not be applicable throughout the United States.

Once the issue of crime policy was selected, the first step was to meet with a small group of state legislative and administrative staff to determine specific topics for investigation. We wanted to know, at the very outset, what the front-line decisionmakers regarded as the crucial aspects of the crime problem. It immediately became apparent that the integration of citizen concerns with rational policy analysis would be crucial, because the staff members informed us that the political pressure for increased sentences and harsher punishments was overwhelming all other considerations. The recently enacted three-strikes-law had "sailed through both houses of the legislature faster than any statute we've even seen," they said. Even legislators who were centrally concerned with the state's ever-worsening financial situation had not dared to raise objections against this enormously expensive piece of legislation. There was a palpable sense, at this first meeting, that rational policy analysis, focusing on costs, on effectiveness, or on other alternatives, had been ground into the dust by the juggernaut of public concern about crime.

The source of this heightened public concern was somewhat difficult for the legislative and administrative staff to fathom, since there had been no corresponding increase in the crime rate. Their best guess was that it stemmed from the "democratization" of crime—the increasing occurrence of crime, especially violent crime, in "nice" urban neighborhoods and relatively bucolic rural settings. Middle-class people were beginning to feel that no place was safe, that, in Genet's words, "their daily lives are grazed by enchanting murderers, cunningly elevated to their sleep, which they will cross by some back stairway that had abetted them by not creaking"(1964, 51). There is an element of classism, or worse, in this attitude, since the poor in general, and poor minorities in particular, have always lived in high-crime neighborhoods. But government officials do not have the luxury of dismissing middle-class concerns they find distasteful, nor can they afford to treat these concerns as products of a false consciousness from which people will emerge in some unspecified but exalted future. The middle class votes, the middle class contributes, and the middle class constitutes the public to which politicians must respond.

The event that galvanized public concern, in California and elsewhere, was the murder of Polly Klaas following her abduction from her home in Petaluma. Although stranger abduction is a relatively infrequent crime, its senselessness and the implication of sexual abuse that accompanies it has made it an emblematic felony in these senseless, sexually conscious times, much like a child kidnapping for money was emblematic of the Great Depression. Parents who read newspaper accounts of an abduction, however, can often distance themselves from its horror by noting some element of parental negligence that they would never commit. They would never lose sight of a toddler in the supermarket or leave a baby alone in a parked vehicle. But Polly Klaas was twelve years old, kidnapped at knife-point while she was at home with two friends and her mother was upstairs. There is simply no definition of parental negligence that includes leaving a twelve-year-old girl alone in her room with two of her friends, particularly in Petaluma, and there was no way for members of the anxious middle class to distance themselves from the horror of Polly Klaas's murder.

As noted above, concern about crime is socially constructed to a certain extent, and this particular crime was no exception. The perpetrator, Richard Alan Davis, drove his car into a ditch several hours after the abduction, and apparently hid Polly, bound and gagged but still alive, in some nearby woods. Two police officers sent to investigate helped him pull his car out of the ditch and let him go on his way because the bulletins about the crime had failed to reach them. Davis's background, moreover, was filled with the usual social miseries that characterize habitual offenders. The public, in a different mood, could have drawn the lesson that the police need to be more competent, or that endemic social problems needed to be addressed. Instead, encouraged by the enormous media coverage of the event, it concluded that everyone is vulnerable to horrid crimes, that harsh penalties were the only justifiable response, and that criminals like Davis, who was on parole after a third offense, should be imprisoned for the remainder of their lives.

The staff members we consulted felt that topics for crime policy analysis must be structured to incorporate these intensely felt public concerns. The age-old questions about the nature of crime, the possibility of prevention, and the effectiveness of punishment all remained but had to be reinterpreted in this new context. Thus, the first topic that was suggested was to assess the origin and nature of citizen concern—to determine precisely what it was that was driving the unprecedented outpouring of public fury about crime. A second topic was to explore the possibility of prevention efforts in an environment where people were demanding only increased punishment. Were there prevention programs that worked, and could these be presented in a way that answered people's concerns, as opposed to appearing as social welfare efforts that used crime prevention as a disguise for the reformist agenda of a political elite? The final topic was whether alternative modes of punishment that were less expensive or more effective than state prison could be developed, given the public demand for harsher punishment that only prison seemed to satisfy.

The goal of the Crime Policy Project was to survey existing research, identify studies that seemed to address these issues, and relate them to the political context that prevailed in the area. To this end, three researchers were identified: Franklin Zimring, of the University of California–Berkeley Law School (Boalt Hall), who worked with his collaborator, Gordon Hawkins, director of the Institute of Criminology at the University of Sydney, to explore the sources of citizen concern; Peter Greenwood, of the RAND Corporation, to assess prevention programs; and Joan Petersilia, of the University of California, Irvine Department of Criminology, Law, and Society, to assess alternative modes of punishment. Work on the surveys began in the summer of 1994 and ultimately lead to three of the four principal chapters in this volume.

In the fall of 1994, we convened a meeting with a larger group of state legislative and administrative staff to deliver a progress report on the three research papers. Although the reaction was generally positive, the state officials were even more emphatic about the intensity of public opinion and the resulting pressure on state decisionmakers. They also provided some further insights on the nature of this phenomenon. The concept of the public, or public opinion, that had been invoked so frequently in the project's first meeting, is an abstraction, of course. People communicate with government officials in a variety of ways, such as opinion polls, letters, e-mail, phone calls, lobbying, and direct contracts. In the case of crime policy, public opinion was being represented, and focused upon state decisionmakers with a tremendous intensity, by the lobbying efforts of the crime victims groups. These groups operated both as special interests and as lenses for a generalized but diffuse political majority. Some of them were funded by the California Correctional Officers Association, which has an obvious economic stake in the construction of new prisons, and thus conformed to the public choice model of lobbying organizations (Ferejohn 1974; Olson 1965). Yet it is equally clear that many ordinary citizens were gratefully free riding on the efforts of these groups, which contradicts public choice and conforms to James Q. Wilson's model of entrepreneurial politics (1980). Moreover, the impact of these groups, as both special-interest lobbyists and popular representatives, was further strengthened by the fact that few lobbyists are as tragic—or as photogenic—as a genuine crime victim. The result, as one of the participants in the meeting bluntly summarized the situation, was that the crime victims' groups were now "in charge" of crime policy in California.

Based on this information, we decided to convene a meeting between the researchers and representatives of crime victims groups. We obtained a list of the most politically active groups from state officials. As academics, we were aware that we tended to demonize these groups, viewing them as responsible for the increasing irrationality of crime policy and its increasing blindness to the available information about crime prevention. The purpose of this meeting was to find out whether our beliefs were justified and also to sensitize ourselves to the forces that were acting upon the decisionmakers to whom our recommendations would ultimately be addressed. The crime victims groups, we quickly learned, tended in their turn to demonize academics, viewing them as a coterie of ultra-liberals who believe that crime is a justifiable response to social inequality and that it should be treated exclusively through social programs aimed at eradicating its underlying causes. But they also realized that academics tended to demonize them and were thus surprised, and somewhat gratified, to receive an invitation to a meeting sponsored by the University of California. Some ten separate groups attended, with a total of twenty-two individual representatives.

This meeting yielded a number of important insights. To begin with, it confirmed our belief that *rational discourse* with these groups, in the sense that political philosophers use this term, would not be possible. This is not to suggest that the group representatives were in any sense illogical or crazed; in fact, they turned out to be knowledgeable, articulate, and obviously effective advocates. But it was equally apparent that many of the representatives had become involved in their organizations as a means of reintegrating their lives and overcoming their personal grief. This was particularly true for the groups (the majority of those attending) composed of murder victims' family members. The representatives described themselves as "murder victims;" during the introductions, they would declare, very much like the participants in a classic Alcoholics Anonymous meeting, "I'm Jane Doe and I'm a murder victim." For them, the commitment to victims' rights and the harsh punishment of criminals were clearly starting premises that could not be altered by rational discourse. They were thus a classic instance of the ground-level citizen concerns that impact public policymaking.

A second feature of the victims' groups was that they were almost exclusively middle class and white. Of the twenty-two individual representatives, there was only one person of color. This is obviously unrepresentative of America's general population and even more unrepresentative of the demographics of crime victims. (National Center for Health Statistics 1989; Ropp et al. 1992). Although no overt racism was observable among the groups that were present at the meeting, race remains a sensitive and polarizing issue in American society, and the skewed composition of these groups creates a number of disturbing possibilities for coded messages and divisive political practices. To their credit, the representatives at the meeting acknowledged the need for outreach among minority communities; to their discredit, their groups have apparently failed to do so. Their acknowledgment, at least, suggests that overt racism is not a citizen attitude that must be factored in to crime policy analysis the way concern about crime seems to be. In any event, policymakers should certainly assume this to be so, since the contrary would confront them with a genuine crisis of political morality. Harsh punishments, though distasteful to many civil libertarians, are generally regarded as constitutional and morally acceptable. Racism is neither and thus represents a limit on the extent to which citizen attitudes can properly be integrated into the policymaking process.

Beyond these basic attitudes about crime and race, the various victims' groups at the meeting were by no means monolithic in their views. For example, they split on the issue of gun control, some taking the position that citizens needed guns in order to protect themselves, others regarding guns as increasing the lethality of criminal attacks. On the issue of prisons, many, but not all, of the murder victims' groups favored harsh conditions, but a few, plus the one rape victims' group, took the position that public safety would be increased if convicts were educated, rather than being brutalized, in prison. Attitudes toward the three-strikes legislation ranged from enthusiastic to reluctant; ironically, California's version of this law was opposed by Mark Klaas, of the Polly Klaas Foundation, on the ground that it would expend limited resources on nondangerous offenders.

One area of unanimity among the groups—and probably the easiest to integrate with an academic's sense of effective public policy—involves the treatment of victims and their families in the criminal justice system. The crime victims' groups referred to their treatment as "the second victimization" and focused more comments on it than they did on sentencing or punishment. This is a criminal procedure issue, however, and its resolution, by itself, would do little to address crime policy issues. On those issues, the divergence between most academic criminologists and the crime victims' groups was rather wide. There did appear to be some room to maneuver, however, not only because the victims' groups vary in their views but also because they are genuinely concerned about reducing crime. Clearly, none of them will tolerate long-range sociological approaches. Crime policy must speak to their grief and to their sense of justice if it is to be tolerable to them and to the public that they represent. Once it does so, however, there is at least a possibility that alternative approaches can be considered and assessed.

Following the meeting with the crime victims' groups, the first drafts of the three studies that had been commissioned were completed, and a conference was organized to present them. Two commentators were selected for each paper to provide alternative perspectives. The concept was to present the papers and the comments, but then to engage the audience in discussions that would function as collective problem-solving sessions. Invitations were sent to staff level crime policy officials in the California legislature and administrative agencies, mainly the Department of Corrections and the Youth Authority, as well as to a selection of crime victims' groups who had attended the previous meeting. Although forty people were invited, approximately fifty attended, which indicates the level of interest in the subject matter.

The response to the papers was again quite positive, and the tone of the discussions generally congenial, but the gap between politics and policy remained. The victims' groups did not seem particularly gleeful over their recent political victories and expressed continuing concern about the crime rate and the government's perceived inability to deal with it. The state officials conveyed, once more, a sense of being increasingly constrained by political forces, so that they could no longer use their own best judgment. Discussion revealed that both sets of views have considerable justification. Elected officials are eager to respond to public concern about crime by passing laws but reluctant to implement those laws by the necessary but painful process of appropriating funds. A number of the state administrators observed that without receiving increased resources, there was relatively little they could do. Implementing three strikes, for example, clearly will involve more trials, since a person charged with a third-strike offense has little reason to plead guilty. But most urban counties simply do not have the resources to try more cases and consequently have not done so; it seemed clear that some of the discretion that the law had eliminated at the plea bargaining stage had simply been shifted back to the charging stage (Tonry 1987). Similarly, prison administrators felt that even the current increases in the prison budgets would not keep pace with the burgeoning population that longer sentences would produce. They envisioned decreases in discipline and ultimately administrative or court-ordered releases of equally dangerous, non-three-strike offenders.

At the same time, it seemed clear that the administrators' ability to develop programs that they believe will be effective has been displaced by the politicization of crime policy, or what might be called the public micro management of criminal justice. The state officials felt that even one visible failure of any program that removed convicted felons from maximum permissible confinement could readily become a political disaster for the existing administration. Opposing politicians would seize upon it the way George Bush did with Willie Horton and the Massachusetts furlough program, or the press would publicize it to feed the public's appetite for news about the failure of the criminal justice system. Since everyone who gives any serious thought to public policy recognizes that no social program functions perfectly and that success can only be measured in statistical terms, this reaction seems to preclude any innovative effort. For programs designed to save costs, or produce more beneficial overall results through less restrictive means, this low tolerance for failure represents death by anecdote.

Apart from these general points about the relationship of policy and politics, there was extensive discussion at the conference of particular issues and programs. One theme had direct relevance for the design of the Crime Policy Project. Participants responded to each of the three papers by emphasizing the enormous role that illegal drugs play in the crime problem and the government response to it. With respect to the Zimring and Hawkins study, crime in general and violent crime in particular is often generated by drug use, even excluding those convictions obtained for possession or sale of the drug itself. With respect to the Greenwood study, prevention often means prevention of drug use, since use of these substances leads so predictably to criminal activity. And with respect to the Petersilia study, alternative models of incarceration, or alternatives to incarceration, are likely to fail without drug treatment; their greatest promise lies in increased availability of treatment programs.

Based on these comments and related observations in the papers themselves, the California Policy Seminar decided to sponsor a fourth paper, devoted to the relationship between drugs and crime policy. Jerome Skolnick, currently of New York University Law School, was commissioned to write this paper; like the other three, it was designed to survey current knowledge in the field and relate this to the existing political environment of public policymakers. Two commentators were selected to provide differing perspectives, even though the paper was not being presented in a conference format.

The Policy of Minimizing Harm

The policy recommendations that emerged from the four principal studies, the comments, and the various discussions in the Crime Policy Project can be described as minimizing harm. In other words, the organizing goal of crime policy should not be viewed as the elimination of crime (an obvious impossibility) or even the reduction of the crime rate but a minimization of the amount of harm that crime imposes. This recommendation represents a combination of prescriptive and descriptive discourse. It is meant to improve crime policy, but it is also meant to respond to citizen concerns and thus be politically feasible for real-world decisionmakers. To some extent, this combination of discourses emerges from the individual studies, for each one frames its policy recommendations in light of prevailing political realities. To some extent, the combination results from the effort to characterize the conclusions of these four complex analyses in a simplified, readily comprehensible form. This section will consider the four studies first and discuss the nature of the characterization. It will then specify the concept of minimizing harm at greater length and consider some of the countervailing considerations that are raised by the commentaries.

Franklin Zimring's and Gordon Hawkins's study suggests that the public's main concern is not with crime per se but with violent crime. The two are not directly related; in some nations, such as the Netherlands, the crime rate is relatively high, but very little of this crime is violent; in others, such as Finland, the crime rate is low, but the rate of violent crime is relatively high. The United States has a high crime rate but an astronomical violence rate, probably because of the violent nature of our society in general. It is violence that people fear, and that has generated the public demand for increasingly severe criminal laws. Similarly, it is violent crime that generates victims. Some nonviolent crimes, such as narcotics use, are truly victimless; others, such as receiving stolen property, are functionally victimless. Even when there is a victim, as in the case of embezzlement or residential burglary, the victim generally regards the event as a misfortune, unpleasant though it may be, rather than as a life-transforming experience. Rape, assault, or murder of a family member are the crimes that bring people to perceive themselves as crime victims and are the source of fear among those who have not been personally affected.

It is certainly true that the public has been demanding heavy sanctions for nonviolent crime, such as burglary and drug dealing, as well as for violent crimes, such as murder, robbery, and rape. But Zimring and Hawkins argue that this is the result of "category contagion"; citizen fear about violent crime has become so intense that it expands beyond the boundaries of the crimes that people are intensely concerned about and hovers over the entire subject. When Americans think about criminals of any kind, they imagine violent people; the residential burglar is pictured as someone who will kill if he is surprised by the home's occupant, and the minor drug dealer as someone who regularly slaughters passersby. These images overwhelm reality and produce demands for heavy punishment of burglars and drug dealers who are convicted of nonviolent crimes.

Peter Greenwood's study indicates that certain types of prevention programs lead to measurable and significant decreases in the crime rate and, more importantly, the victim rate. These include (1) early childhood programs such as weekly home visits to at-risk families at the prenatal and early childhood stage, combined with early childhood education; (2) parent training of ten to twenty sessions with a therapist for at-risk families with school-aged children; (3) school-based intervention; and (4) early intervention with delinquents. The problem is that costs tend to be substantial, and the results, particularly for early childhood programs, are not achieved until many years later. These liabilities can be reduced by selecting programs that focus on school-aged children who are at high risk of becoming violent offenders. Thus, early childhood and school-based intervention would be rejected as too broadly directed, with the former suffering from the additional disadvantage of being too delayed in its effects. Parent training and early intervention with delinquents are more promising, because they can be directed at the violence-prone, a point underscored by John Reid and J. Mark Eddy in their comment. In addition, because they deal with children who are seven to fourteen years old, their impact will be felt in a reasonably short time. Greenwood reports that properly-run parent intervention programs have been shown to cost approximately $390 per serious felony prevented thirty years after implementation. Early intervention for delinquents is more expensive, costing about $2,555 per serious felony prevented. But California's three-strikes law costs $16,000 per serious felony prevented, according to a separate RAND analysis. Another contrast is that someone permanently incapacitated by means of the three-strikes law has necessarily created at least three victims before the preventive impact of the law takes effect; since not all crimes are reported, and not all reported crimes are solved, the actual figure is probably anywhere from five to fifty victims. An effective prevention program achieves its effects before any victims at all have been created. Proponents of three strikes argue that the law will prevent crime through its deterrent effects, a claim that has been challenged by criminologists. Even if it is true, however, that effect would necessarily be weak before the first conviction and perhaps before the second. By then, the felon has already left a trail of victims behind.

Just as prevention programs should focus on the potentially violent, incapacitation should focus on the actually violent. This means that alternative modes of punishment need to be found for those offenders who are unlikely to create victims or who will only create victims of property crimes. Joan Petersilia's study summarizes what we know about the cost and potential risks of alternative prison programs. At present, California spends about 13 percent of its correctional budget on technical parole violators and those convicted of minor property crimes and another 17 percent on those convicted of drug use or possession. Thus, fully 30 percent of the budget is devoted to incarcerating those who commit essentially victimless crimes, since the property offenses in this category involve shoplifting, receiving stolen merchandise, and the like. In addition, 9 percent of the budget is spent on drug sellers and another 11 percent on medium-level property offenders. Of course, these individuals have all violated the law, and it is state policy to punish them in some fashion. Prison, however, is the most expensive way of doing so, costing nearly $22,000 per year. County jail, at nearly $20,000 per year, is not far behind. A one-year program consisting of boot camp and intensively supervised parole costs about $11,500, whereas house arrest with electronic monitoring costs between $3,500 and $8,500. Thus, the state could save over 15 percent of its costs, that is, over 50 percent per prisoner for 30 percent of its prisoner population, by using these alternatives for offenders who have not created any real victims. If offenders whose victims are not as seriously affected as others, namely drug sellers and medium-level property offenders, are included in these alternative programs, the savings increase to 25 percent.

Prevention programs and imprisonment alternatives can be combined through the use of drug treatment programs. As Petersilia reports, research indicates that well-managed treatment programs produce significant decreases in criminal activity. Thus, residential treatment programs, even though they are as expensive as prison, would be cost effective because of their crime reduction effects. Of course, it is easier to escape from such facilities, so a harm-minimization approach would restrict the program to nonviolent drug offenders. Further savings could be achieved by using less-restrictive treatment settings, such as the social model—drug-free group homes—or outpatient services. If all nonviolent drug offenders were placed in programs of this nature, the state would save over 13 percent of its prison budget, that is, at least 50 percent of prison costs for 26 percent of offenders. In addition, the recidivism rate would be lower because of the demonstrated effectiveness of these programs, leading to further economic savings and fewer victims.

These considerations lead to the general issue of drug policy. Jerome Skolnick's study notes that a society can adopt three different approaches to drug use: that it is acceptable private conduct, that it is undesirable conduct that should be discouraged, or that it is morally repugnant conduct that should be eliminated. The U. S. government, backed by powerful public support, has adopted the third approach; it has declared a "war on drugs," with the primary weapon being the criminal justice system. Skolnick argues that this strategy has produced unfortunate, even disastrous results. Although it has not significantly reduced the level of drug consumption, it has engendered new sources of supply, more ruthless suppliers, and more potent drugs. At the same time, it has led to the corruption of law enforcement agencies and to such high levels of imprisonment in some communities that prison no longer carries any sense of stigma. Most seriously of all, the current strategy increases violent crime; addicts must commit crimes to obtain money for their illegal and thus exorbitantly priced drugs, and suppliers must use violence to carry on their illegal and thus otherwise unenforceable enterprises.

Given these well-recognized failures, many policy analysts argue that drug use should be treated as acceptable private conduct, just as alcohol use is. But legalization is not a realistic option in the present political context; even the most modest movement in that direction, like decriminalizing marijuana, would encounter such intense public opposition that it would be political suicide for a public official to endorse it. A possible alternative however, is to design approaches that discourage drug use without trying to extirpate it or treat it as the embodiment of evil. Skolnick discusses needle exchanges, methadone maintenance, drug courts, and the supervised probation and parole that Petersilia describes. These programs are designed to reduce the enormous harm that current policy produces—to prevent addicts from contracting AIDS, to provide them with a pharmacological substitute so that they do not need to commit crimes to support their addiction, and to provide treatment so that they will stop harming themselves and others. At the same time, it maintains the criminal status of all currently illegal drugs and thus represents a politically feasible approach.

In short, all four of the principal studies speak simultaneously to the need for rational public policy and the need to address citizen concerns.

Zimring and Hawkins argue that criminal justice resources should be directed toward violent crime, because that is the real source of citizen concern, even if the citizens themselves displace that concern to other areas; Greenwood argues that we should focus on prevention programs that are directed at potentially violent individuals and that produce reasonably fast results; Petersilia argues that alternative sanctions should be explored only for those offenders who have not committed violent crimes that anger citizens, and that even these criminals must be subjected to a regime that citizens regard as punitive; Skolnick argues that we should seek ways to treat addicts, decreasing the harm they do to themselves and others, within the current framework of criminal sanctions for drug selling and drug use.

As stated, the conclusions of these four studies can be described as a politically realistic policy of minimizing harm. This policy represents a compromise between the best current research and the concerns of citizens. Research suggests that prevention is generally more effective than punishment, that alternative modes of punishment are generally more effective than incarceration, and that mild sanctions or treatment for drug offenders are more effective than harsh punishment. But the public fears victimization and demands punishment for the perpetrators of its fears, a sentiment expressed most powerfully and effectively through the crime victims' groups. Consequently, any policy that moves toward prevention, treatment, and alternative modes of punishment must simultaneously move toward reducing the level of victimization in a direct and readily comprehensible manner. It is from the compromise between these two demands that the policy of minimizing harm emerges. The most important features of this policy are that it represents a second-best approach, that it focuses on the incremental allocation of enforcement resources, and that it characterizes that allocation process in a manner intended to appeal to the general populace.

A second-best approach is compelled by the unfortunate but obvious fact that we will never eradicate crime in its entirety; people will always be killed, raped, and deprived of property by those who violate the law. The question, then, is how the resources allocated to criminal justice can be used in the most effective manner. It should be emphasized that this question does not imply a policy of reducing those resources; in fact, it is entirely neutral with respect to resource level. No matter how many resources are expended on the problem, we would still want those resources used effectively to achieve our policy goals. To put this another way, each incremental dollar spent on crime should be used to achieve the maximum possible effect. Only if resources are infinite—an obviously pointless assumption—can the incremental effectiveness of additional expenditures be ignored.

Much attention has been devoted to the issue of victimless crimes; arguments for decriminalizing gambling, prostitution, and, as Skolnick discusses, the use of drugs, have been part of the crime policy debate for many years. The emphasis on minimizing harm is narrower in some ways, but broader in others. It is narrower because it concerns only the allocation of enforcement resources, not the policy decisions about criminalization or the complex moral questions that underlie those decisions. To reiterate, we will never achieve full compliance with our criminal laws. Thus, even if a law is enacted, and even if it represents a policy that is fully supported by the populace, the question will remain whether an incremental dollar should be spent on enforcing that law or enforcing a different one. At the same time, the concept of minimizing harm is broader than decriminalization because it recommends that enforcement resources should be shifted away from a much larger group of offenders than decriminalization could conceivably cover. As Zimring and Hawkins indicate, violent crime is the principal source of citizen concern; thus, nearly all nonviolent crimes would fall into the lower priority grouping.

Minimizing harm is not only a second-best but also nothing more than an incremental enforcement strategy; unlike many policy proposals, it does not attempt to explain the underlying causes of crime or reconceptualize crime policy. This incremental approach emerges from the joinder of prescriptive and descriptive discourse, both in the general design of the project and in the particular recommendations of the research papers. Since public policy invariably bears the imprint of an uneven and contested process of development, it will almost always be optimal to level the edifice to its foundations and begin again. For exactly the same reason, it will almost always be politically impossible to do so. Thus, change in general must be incremental; if it is informed by public policy analysis, however, it will move in a particular direction. The individual studies in the project emphasize that incrementalism is required with respect to their particular recommendations. Prevention programs can be more effective than incarceration, as Greenwood suggests, but the shift in resources can only be gradual and will need to be implemented largely by the decrease in prison population that effective prevention will produce. Public safety can be increased, as Petersilia suggests, by concentrating resources on violent offenders, but the public would never tolerate the outright release of burglars, car thieves, or drug dealers.

There are, of course, a number of questions that can be raised about the strategy of minimizing harm, and many of these are explored by the commentaries to the principal studies in this volume. To begin with, Albert Reiss, Mark Kleiman, and Robert MacCoun all observe that there are many different types of social harm and that a strategy that reduces one may well lead to an increase in another. This is true at a very general level, as John DiIulio notes, because otherwise unrelated programs are linked by their dependence on the same limited resources; increased funding to combat air pollution may result in decreased resources for re-medial reading programs. It is even more true within a specific area of public policy, such as crime control, where different approaches compete for portions of preestablished allocations. Reiss argues that property of-fenses, even minor property offenses like defacement of buildings and the now-paradigmatic "broken windows," produce harm by degrading urban neighborhoods. Kleiman argues that drug use, whether the drug is legal or illegal, is a serious harm that should be prevented whenever pos-sible.

The strategy of harm minimization presented by the principal studies is that the primary harm to be prevented is that which results from vio-lent crime. There are two reasons for this, one that can be recognized within the framework of rational policy analysis and one that involves the integration of policy analysis with political practicality. In policy terms, violent crime has a devastating, life-transforming effect that is ab-sent from other forms of criminal activity. People obviously do not like to have their homes burglarized, their cars stolen, or their bank accounts depleted by embezzlement. But the losses from these crimes can gener-ally be compensated by money and, even if the loss is not insured and no compensation is forthcoming, these losses are generally viewed in eco-nomic terms. A conscientious policymaker, therefore, might well treat these harms as presenting a less urgent demand on limited crime control resources.

In terms of political practicality, the public demand for security is dri-ven by violent crime, as Zimring and Hawkins point out. Again, no one is pleased about the proliferation of property offenses, the widespread use of drugs, or the deterioration of urban neighborhoods. But major po-litical developments, like the current spate of three-strikes laws, seem to result from public concern about violence. It is true that California's ver-sion of this legal strategy included those who burglarize a residence or sell drugs to a minor among its three-strike offenses. These added cate-gories, which will probably double the number of felons subject to the law's increased prison terms, appear to be the result of legislative inad-vertence rather than conscious policy. When asked directly about this as-pect of the law, however, most of the crime victims' groups expressed support and pointed out that a burglar with two previous felony convic-tions indeed merits serious punishment. It appears, however, that these groups were motivated largely by their desire to present a united front and obtain passage of the law and the corresponding referendum mea-sure, because of its treatment of violent offenders. None of them ever mentioned property offenses or narcotics offenses when describing their positions, and there do not appear to be any organized groups of property or narcotic offense victims. Indeed, the very concept readily lends itself to satire ("My name is Richard Roe and someone stole my BMW") and underscores the validity of the Zimring and Hawkins analysis.

Of course; as Mark Kleiman points out, every priority, no matter how intensely felt, must ultimately be balanced against other, less-insistent priorities. At some point, even national defense against nuclear destruction becomes too expensive and takes too much money away from other programs. Although the public is more concerned about violent crime than property offenses, small decreases in the level of violent crime that were accompanied by massive increases in residential burglary would probably engender public opposition. But at present, and for nearly the last two decades, the problem with crime policy in America has been exactly the reverse. Concern about violent crime, combined with existing, steady-state condemnation of drug use and nonviolent crime, has led to massive increases in the incarceration of nonviolent offenders. This fails to minimize harm because it diverts crime control dollars from the most dangerous individuals, and because it diverts those dollars from other approaches that might produce better results than incarceration. It is certainly true that a policy of minimizing harm might reach an aggregate effects boundary—that the concern with preventing and punishing violent criminals might give too much license to property offenders, drug dealers, and drug users for public tolerance. But the current problem with the U. S. crime policy, and one that seems likely to persist for some time, is that it fails to focus on preventing and punishing violent crime and thus fails to minimize the primary harm that Americans are now concerned about.

This leads to a second question about harm minimization that the comments raise. The whole approach is based on integrating rational public policy with public opinion, but public opinion is not a preexisting, static, or self-evident entity. Whereas the punitive character of the public mood is unmistakable, the stance that an observer or a decisionmaker adopts in response to that mood can vary substantially. Among the commentators, John DiIulio notes, with some enthusiasm, that the public knows what it wants, and what it wants is severe punishment for wrongdoers; people are angry about having these desires mediated or diverted by public officials and have responded with an electorial fury that has compelled both political parties to comply. Mark Moore agrees, with some regret, that public attitudes are predominantly retributivist and are largely insensitive to counterarguments based on either cost or the potential effectiveness of prevention. In a democracy, he observes, such views are entitled to respect and will in any case command respect from politicians. Robert

Weisburg, in contrast, argues that voters greatly exaggerate their risk of being victimized by crime; their increasingly punitive mood results from the cultural demons that haunt them and the opportunistic politicians who exploit these paranormal fears (see Tonry 1995). A natural implication of this view is that a conscientious politician should strive to counteract the false consciousness of the electorate.

The harm minimization strategy that emerges from the principal studies takes public attitudes as a basic framework but not necessarily as a detailed prescription. It acknowledges, as do DiIulio and Moore, that people know what they want and that public officials must respond to such clearly indicated desires. As the issues become more technical and detailed, however, public opinion, even if its direction is clear, becomes less reliable and less compelling. The process of aggregating and transmitting public views necessarily produces distortions. Although broadly based views on major issues cannot, and should not, be dismissed on this ground, more specific expressions of the public mood may be properly regarded with a certain skepticism. The basis of this skepticism—the reason why it would be leveled at some public attitudes but not at others—is rational policy analysis.

People really want criminals, particularly violent criminals, imprisoned (Kahan 1996), and they really want drugs to remain illegal. But do they really want prison cells to be filled by sickly old men who are unlikely to commit any further crimes and with minor drug dealers who will inevitably be replaced by other dealers after their arrest? Do they really insist that treatment programs for drug users be implemented only within prisons, when their greater effectiveness in nonprison settings has been demonstrated? (Morris and Tonry 1990). Public opinion can do little more than bring a general attitude to bear upon these issues; it cannot make fine distinctions. But, as Robert MacCoun suggests, public officials, acting within the general framework of these attitudes, can develop more effective approaches in such specific cases and can probably persuade the populace that these are preferable. Thus, all the principal studies in this volume treat public attitudes as a basic framework, meriting and demanding respect, but recommend that policymakers make distinctions based on expertise and present those distinctions to the public as a better strategy for achieving its primary goals. People fear crime, but they can be convinced that some crime is not quite as fearsome; they want criminals punished, but they can be convinced that prevention programs will divert nonblameless individuals before they become criminals and that not all criminals need be punished with equivalent severity; they want drugs outlawed, but they can be convinced that less-punitive treatment of some violators will lead to less drug use and less harm to the users and the general population.

The third question, raised by Mark Moore and Norval Morris, is whether alternative approaches can be implemented under real-world conditions. A short answer is that all government programs were innovations at one time or another. Prisons, at least in Britain and the United States, were introduced in the early nineteenth century as an alternative to corporal punishment (Ignatieff 1978; Rothman 1990). This may not be particularly reassuring to present-day public officials, who do not know which innovations will ultimately succeed, or which will succeed only after grinding up the careers of innumerable public officials. A better answer then, is in the inherently incremental nature of the harm minimizing strategy that is suggested in the studies. The programs recommended by Greenwood, Petersilia, and Skolnick, and also by John Reid and J. Mark Eddy in their comment, are all designed to be implemented piecemeal precisely because they are addressed to real-world decision-makers.

Norval Morris argues a seemingly opposite but in fact related point— that public officials are obligated to try alternative approaches in order to reach coherent assessments about which programs are superior to others. Taken to extremes, this could lead to the most thorough-going version of Weberian rationality or to the managerial excesses of zero-base budgeting. But at a more modest, incremental level, Morris's implicit suggestion seems incontrovertible. Surely, it is time to begin testing alternative strategies for minimizing harm, given the widely recognized failures of the existing approach. The principal studies in this volume present a series of quite specific programs that could be readily implemented on a tentative or experimental basis. Once these programs were evaluated, we would know whether they indeed serve a purpose of minimizing harm.

In terms of the political viability of such experiments, there remains the problem of the fatal anecdote, described above and exemplified by George Bush's use of Willie Horton. The problem, in essence, is that even a single failure of an innovative program can become a cause célèbre and a political liability for anyone connected with the program. A program that reformed and released 100 rapists, with only a single failure, would be a great success in social science terms, but the twisted visage of that one failure, displayed on the evening news or in an electoral campaign, could have disastrous effects for those in charge of this successful program. Given the current mood of the populace, such fatal anecdotes may preclude our efforts to develop alternative approaches. If these approaches are to survive, they must be supported by a positive characterization of the larger strategy that motivates them. Michael Dukakis had no answer to Bush other than abstruse cost-benefit analysis or appeals to standard correctional practice. One possible response regarding the programs favored in this book is that the government is minimizing harm, that each prisoner moved to a less-restrictive environment makes room for a more dangerous one. That response at least offers the possibility that these programs can be defended in the real world of political debate.

Fatal anecdotes are something of a political "cheap shot," since most public officials understand the inevitability of occasional failures, but they lead back to the general issue that cannot be underestimated. Many officials, and most crime policy experts, have been distressed, if not aghast, at the increasingly punitive mood of the citizenry. But the conflict between general public opinion and the views of policy elites is not restricted to crime policy or, indeed, to electoral democracies. It is one of the basic issues in the governance of society. Democracy has not solved this conflict, of course—the conflict may not be soluble—but it provides a fairly successful means of mediating it. In essence, the political dynamics of democracy demand that public officials respond to widely held public views, particularly when those views are stable over a significant period of time, but these dynamics also permit a considerable amount of discretion in the way officials respond and create limited, but important, opportunities to persuade the citizenry that particular exercises of discretion are desirable. It is in the balance between response and discretionary initiative that the secret of good democratic governance resides. The studies in this volume suggest that a strategy focused on minimizing the harm can achieve that balance in the field of crime policy.

References

Ackerman, Bruce. 1980. *Social Justice and the Liberal State.*

Arendt, Hannah. 1958a. *The Human Condition.*

_____. 1958b. *The Origins of Totalitarianism.* 2d ed.

_____. 1968. *Between Past and Future.*

Blumstein, Alfred, and Jacqueline Cohen. 1978. *Deterrence and Incapacitation: Estimating the Effects of Criminal Sanctions on Crime Rates.*

_____. 1979. Estimation of Individual Crime Rates from Arrest Records. *Journal of Criminal Law and Criminology* 70:561–585.

Burke, Edmund. 1949. "Speech to the Electors of Bristol." In *Burke's Politics,* edited by J. Hoffman and P. Levack.

California Penal Code §1170.12 (1995).

California Proposition 184 (Increased Sentences: Repeat Offenders) approved November 8, 1994.

Edelman, Murray. 1974. *The Symbolic Uses of Politics.*

_____. 1988. *Constructing the Political Spectacle.*

Elias, Norbert. 1994. *The Civilizing Process.*

Farrington, David. 1989. "Early Precursors of Frequent Offending." In *Families, Schools and Delinquency Prevention,* edited by J. Wilson and G. Loury.

———. 1991. "Childhood Aggression and Adult Violence: Early Precursors and Later Life Outcomes." In *The Development and Treatment of Childhood Aggression*, edited by D. Pepler and K. Rubin.

Fenno, Richard. 1973. *Congressmen in Committees.*

Ferejohn, John. 1974. *Pork Barrel Politics.*

Fiorina, Morris. 1974. *Representatives, Roll Calls and Constituencies.*

———. 1977. *Congress: Keystone of the Washington Establishment.*

Gadamer, Hans-Georg. 1988. *Truth and Method.*

Garland, David. 1990. *Punishment and Modern Society.*

Genet, Jean. 1964. *Our Lady of the Flowers.* Translated by B. Frechtman.

Gibbon, Edward. 1932. *The Decline and Fall of the Roman Empire.* Modern Library.

Gotfredson, Michael, and Travis Hirschi. 1990. *A General Theory of Crime.*

Habermas, Jurgen. 1981, 1987. *The Theory of Communicative Action.* Translated by T. McCarthy.

———. 1996. *Between Facts and Norms: Contributions to a Discourse Theory of Law and Democracy.* Translated by W. Rehg.

Ignatieff, Michael. 1978. *A Just Measure of Pain: The Penitentiary in the Industrial Revolution, 1750–1850.*

Kahan, Daniel. 1996. What Do Alternative Sanctions Mean? *Univ. of Chicago Law Rev.* 63:591.

Kingdon, John. 1989. *Congressmen's Voting Decisions.*

Kuhn, Thomas. 1970. *The Structure of Scientific Revolutions.* 2d ed.

Lakatos, Imre. 1978. *The Methodology of Scientific Research Programmes.*

Leuchtenberg, William. 1963. *Franklin D. Roosevelt and the New Deal 1932–1940.*

Lindbolm, Charles. 1959. The Science of Muddling Through. *Public Administration Review* 19:79–88.

Lowi, Theodore. 1974. *The End of Liberalism.* 2d ed.

Luker, Kristen. 1984. *Abortion and the Politics of Motherhood.*

Matza, David. 1964. *Delinquency and Drift.*

Mayhew, David. 1974. *Congress: The Electoral Connection.*

Michels, Robert. 1962. *Political Parties.*

Morris, Norval, and Michael Tonry. 1990. *Between Prison and Probation: Intermediate Punishments in a Rational Sentencing System.*

Musgrave, Richard, and Peggy Musgrave. 1989. *Public Finance in Theory and Practice.* 5th ed.

National Center for Health Statistics. 1989. *Prevention Profile: Health, United States.*

Offe, Claus. 1984. "Some Contradictions of the Modern Welfare State." In *Contradictions of the Welfare State*, edited by J. Keane, 147–161.

Olson, Mancur. 1965. *The Logic of Collective Action.*

Patton, Carol, and David Sauicki. 1986. *The Policy Analysis Process: Basic Methods of Policy Analysis and Planning.*

Perkins, France. 1946. *The Roosevelt I Knew.*

Pitkin, Hanna. 1967. *The Concept of Representation.*

Rawls, John. 1971. *A Theory of Justice.*

Ropp, L., Visintainer, P., Uman, J., and Treloar, D. 1992. Death in an American City: An American Childhood Tragedy. *JAMA* 267:2905–2910.

Rothman, David J. 1990. *The Discovery of the Asylum.*

Rubin, Edward. 1991. Beyond Public Choice: Comprehensive Rationality in the Reading and Writing of Statutes. *New York University Law Review* 66:1–64.

Schlesinger, Arthur. 1959. *The Coming of the New Deal.*

Schumpeter, Joseph. 1942. *Capitalism, Socialism, and Democracy.*

Simon, Herbert. 1957. *Administrative Behavior.*

Sontag, Susan. 1986. "The Imagination of Disaster." In *Against Interpretation.*

Stokey, Edith, and Richard Zeckhauser. 1978. *Thinking About Policy Choices: A Primer for Policy Analysis.*

Thompson, Hunter. 1982. *Fear and Loathing in Las Vegas: A Savage Journey to the Heart of the American Dream.*

Tittle, Charles. 1980. *Sanctions and Social Deviance.*

Tonry, Michael. 1987. *Sentencing Reform Impacts.*

———. 1995. Intermediate Sanctions in Sentencing Reform. *Univ. Of Chicago Law School Roundtable* 2:391.

Weber, Max. 1978. In *Economy and Society,* edited by G. Roth and C. Wittich, 956–1002, 1381–1462.

Weisberg, Robert. 1992. Criminal Law, Criminology, and the Small World of Legal Scholars. *University of Colorado Law Review* 63:521–568.

Wildavsky, Aaron. 1979. *Speaking Truth to Power.*

Williamson, Oliver. 1985. *The Economic Institutions of Capitalism.*

Wilson, James Q. 1980. *The Politics of Regulation.*

Zimring, Franklin, and Gordon Hawkins. 1986. *Capital Punishment and the American Agenda.*

———. 1991. *The Scale of Imprisonment.*

———. 1995. *Incapacitation: Penal Confinement and the Restraint of Crime.*

2

Public Attitudes Toward Crime

Is American Violence a Crime Problem?

FRANKLIN E. ZIMRING
AND GORDON HAWKINS

By longstanding habit, Americans use the terms *crime* and *violence* interchangeably. When expressing concern about urban conditions we commonly talk about "the crime problem" or "the violence problem" as if they were the same thing. When drive-by shootings create newspaper headlines, we demand that our elected officials do something about crime.

As a matter of strict definition, the equation of crime and violence is incorrect. Criminal violence is the intentional and unjustified infliction or threatened infliction of physical injury to a human being. Crime is a much broader category, referring to all violations of the criminal law. The question we consider in these pages is whether there is actual harm in confusing the categories of crime and violence when making policy; whether it is an error to address violence in the United States as a crime problem.

The standard of judgment we propose for this question is a pragmatic one. We are not here concerned with definitional niceties; only with the sorts of mistakes that waste material resources and opportunities to save lives and alleviate public fears. We will demonstrate in these pages that regarding crime and violence as interchangeable social problems is a policy mistake of substantial significance.

The empirical justification for regarding American violence as a crime problem can be simply stated. Almost all of the serious intentionally inflicted personal injuries in the United States are also violations of the criminal law. Because such serious violence violates the standards of our criminal code, our violence problem is a crime problem as well. It is, however, an elementary mistake to assume that because most violence is criminal it is also true that most crime is violent.

There is no reason to assume that the more than 80 percent of felony crime in the United States that does not involve the threat or the actuality of force is similar to the less than 20 percent that is violent (Federal Bureau of Investigation 1992). There is no reason to believe that the sorts of people who commit violent acts that are criminal are indistinguishable from the sorts of people who commit nonviolent acts that are criminal. There is also no reason to assume that the same conditions function as the proximate causes of violent and nonviolent incidents. There is finally no reason to assume that countermeasures that succeed in reducing nonviolent crime will have equivalent success in reducing the incidence and seriousness of violence. Yet those who regard American violence as a crime problem all too frequently do assume that unjustified intentional personal injuries involve the same protagonists, the same causes, and the same effective solutions as other forms of criminal behavior.

This chapter is divided into four parts. The first part provides a context for the consideration of American violence with a series of international comparisons. The second part presents a sustained analysis of robbery, an offense that combines elements of theft and violence and that results in thousands of homicides each year in the United States. The third part discusses the degree to which public fear, which we usually think of as fear of all sorts of crime, is more narrowly focused on the threat of lethal violence. The last part addresses the errors of policy analysis that are likely when crime and violence are regarded as interchangeable categories.

Published scholarship on the specific topics covered in this analysis is not yet extensive. Cross-national comparisons of crime are a recent phenomenon (Bennet and Lynch 1990; Lynch 1995), although international comparisons of homicide have a slightly longer history (Archer and Gartner 1984). The first multinational crime victim survey was executed in the late 1980s (van Dijk and Mayhew 1993). The purpose of this chapter is to use existing data on violence and crime and to shape future research on violence, crime, public fear, and public policy.

Crime and Violence in International Perspective

Los Angeles and Sydney

Los Angeles is the second largest city in the United States with a 1992 population estimated at 3.6 million for its crime statistics reporting unit. It is a multiracial, multicultural city on the Pacific coast with a crime rate

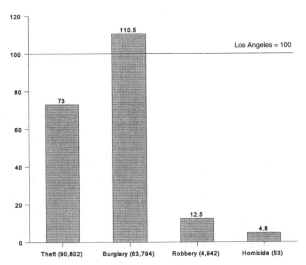

FIGURE 2.1   Sydney Crime Volume Compared with Los Angeles, 1992
SOURCE U.S. Department of Justice Federal Bureau of Investigation, Uniform
Crime Reports (1992); New South Wales Bureau of Criminal Statistics (1992)

that by most accounts is its most serious civic problem. Sydney, Australia is also a city of 3.6 million located on the Pacific coast of the continent. Although multicultural by Australian standards, the ethnic and language mixture of Sydney falls far short of that in Los Angeles. Crime in Sydney is a serious annoyance but not a major threat to the continued viability of the city or to the health and welfare of its citizens.

Figure 2.1 compares the volume of four crimes reported by the police in Sydney and Los Angeles by expressing the number of offenses in Sydney as a percentage of the Los Angeles crime volume. Since the population of the two cities is the same, the crime volume comparison is also a crime rate comparison.

The theft category reported at the far left of Figure 2.1 includes most forms of stealing that are unaggravated by elements that the law regards as increasing the gravity of the offense. This is the most common offense reported in all cities and the two jurisdictions under review are no exception. Sydney reports just over 90,000 theft incidents, roughly three-quarters of the volume reported in Los Angeles.

Burglary is an aggravated form of theft where the offender breaks and enters private property in order to steal. The crime statistics for Sydney, Australia, report the offense under two headings: breaking and entering a dwelling and breaking and entering a building that is not a dwelling. The volume of such crimes in Sydney during 1992 exceeded 63,000, about 10 percent more than the number of burglaries reported in Los Angeles.

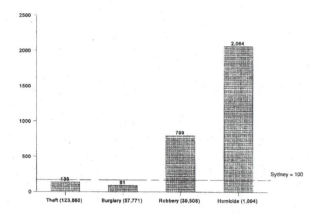

FIGURE 2.2   Los Angeles Crime Volume Compared with Sydney, 1992
SOURCE U.S. Department of Justice, Federal Bureau of Investigation, Uniform
Crime Reports (1992); New South Wales Bureau of Criminal Statistics (1992)

The pattern noted for burglary contrasts sharply with that of robbery, the other major category of aggravated property crime. Robbery is defined as the taking of property from the person of another by force or by the threat of force. In 1992 Los Angeles reported 39,508 robberies, whereas Sydney reported 4,942, one-eighth the Los Angeles rate. The ratio of burglaries to robberies in Los Angeles is just under 3:2; the ratio of burglaries to robberies in Sydney is greater than 12:1.

The final crime category reported in Figure 2.1 is for homicides resulting from intentional injury. There were fifty-three such offenses reported by the police in Sydney during 1992, a crime volume equal to 5 percent of the 1,094 homicides reported by the Los Angeles police that same year. The difference between the two cities in rates of criminal homicide exceeds an order of magnitude. The citizens of Sydney can thus live with their high crime rate in relative comfort because they are not dying from it in large numbers.

Figure 2.2 reorders the same data used in Figure 2.1 so that Los Angeles is depicted using Sydney rates as a base.

Figures 2.1 and 2.2 carry visual, statistical, and substantive lessons about crime and violence in the two cities. Visually the use of Sydney rates as the basis of comparison means that the scale of the figure must be expanded. The theft and burglary representations are dwarfed by the distended bar values necessary to show Los Angeles violent offenses on a Sydney scale.

The statistical conclusion one draws from an inspection of Figures 2.1 and 2.2 is that the nature of the comparison between Sydney and Los An-

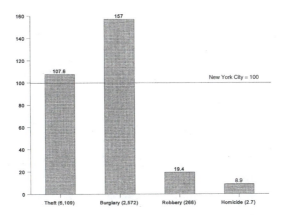

FIGURE 2.3   London Crime Rates (per 100,000) Compared with New York City, 1990
SOURCE U.S. Department of Justice, Federal Bureau of Investigation, Uniform Crime Reports (1990); Home Office (1990)

geles depends on what is being compared. For theft and burglary the two cities are quite similar. For robbery, they are vastly dissimilar; for homicide, the 20:1 difference is huge.

The substantive conclusion to be drawn from the statistical pattern can be stated in two ways. First, it seems beyond dispute that what separates the two cities is not the amount of crime they experience but the character of the crime they experience. Second, we think the point can be put more sharply than that: What is distinctive and threatening in Los Angeles is not a crime problem but a problem of lethal violence.

New York and London

New York is the largest city in the United States with a population just past 7 million. London has a city population of 6.6 million. Figure 2.3 shows London crime rates per 100,000 using New York rates as a standard for comparison.

The statistical comparison in Figure 2.3 is even more surprising than that concerning Los Angeles and Sydney, and to the same effect. London has slightly more theft than New York and a rate of burglary 57 percent higher. But the robbery rate in London is less than one-fifth the robbery rate in New York, and the homicide rate in London is less than one-tenth the New York figure. Figure 2.4 shows us New York rates compared with London.

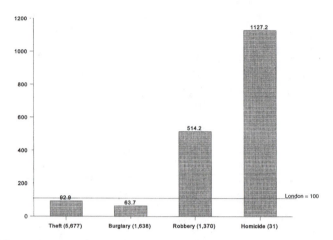

FIGURE 2.4   New York City Crime Rates (per 100,000) Compared with London, 1990
SOURCE U. S. Department of Justice, Federal Bureau of Investigation, Uniform Crime Reports (1990)

The total number of offenses per 100,000 citizens in Figure 2.4 is slightly higher in London than in New York. If crime rates were the problem, Londoners should live in fear or New Yorkers in relative complacency. They have the same magnitude of crime. But with robbery rates five times those of London and death rates eleven times as high, the population of New York is far from comfortable. Violence is their problem, not crime, and lower rates of general theft are no consolation for huge death toll differences.

If readers are wondering if these data are selective and misleading or the numbers are produced by the peculiarities of different reporting systems, the next set of comparisons should provide some reassurance that our city comparisons are part of a broad and consistent pattern.

Twenty Countries

We can show clearly that America's special problem is violence and not crime by comparing the results of a twenty-nation survey of citizens about the rate at which they were victims of crime with World Health Organization data on death from assaults for the same nations. Figure 2.5 shows the violent death rates for the five nations with the highest crime levels, then the next highest, then the next highest victimization rate, and finally the lowest crime categories.

There are several indications that a country's crime rate is substantially independent of its violence rate. First, the variation in violent death rate

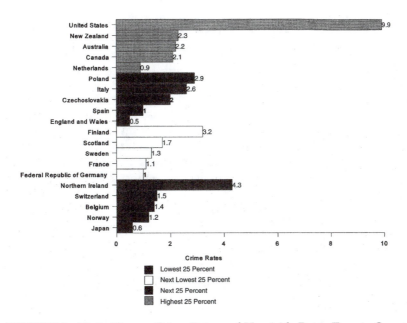

FIGURE 2.5   Victim Survey Crime Rates and Homicide Rates, Twenty Countries

SOURCES Jan van Dijk and Pat Mayhew, *Criminal Victimization in the Industrialized World: Key Findings of the 1989 and 1992 International Crime Surveys* (1993) (victim survey crime rates); World Health Organization, World Health Statistics (1990) (homicide rates)

is quite large within the separate crime rate categories. Within the group of highest crime nations, the homicide rates vary by a factor of ten, in the next group, by a factor of five, in the third group, by a factor of three, and in the lowest crime group, by a factor of eight. In contrast, the median homicide rates for the different crime categories are clustered between 1.3 and 2.2. So knowing which crime rate category a country belongs in does not tell you anything much about what rate of violent death that country suffers.

And knowing a country's death rate does not predict much about its crime rate. The lowest death rate country (England) has a crime rate just over average. The next lowest violence nation is Japan, which has the lowest crime rate also. Tied for third lowest death rate country are the Netherlands and Spain, which are in the highest and second highest crime rate group. The pattern is just as opaque at the top of the violence distribution. The most violent country, the United States, has a high crime rate as well. The next most violent country, Northern Ireland, is in the lowest crime rate group.

This data set provides a multinational example of the central point that lethal violence is the problem in the United States. It shows the United States clustered with other industrial countries in crime rate, but head and shoulders above the rest in violent death.

It also shows us why violence should be the best predictor of citizen fear on a transnational basis. Where would you rather live when examining the map of Figure 2.5? In England with its high crime rate and 0.5 deaths per 100,000 or in Northern Ireland with a much lower crime rate and eight times the death rate? Your money or your life?

Judging from Figure 2.5, the United States has about the same rate of crime and prevalence of criminality as the Netherlands and Australia. But ours is by far the more dangerous country to live in. We currently have a Netherlands-size crime problem and a king-size violence problem that threatens the social organization of our cities. Which problem should we try to solve?

American Robbery: Crime or Violence?

Robbery is both a very important part of American violence and also representative of most violence in the United States. Indeed, it is not possible to comprehend violence in America without understanding the motivation and outcomes of American robbery. And it is not possible to understand robbery in America—why it occurs so often, why it kills so frequently—without coming to terms with violence as a phenomenon separate from the motivations and conduct norms that govern most forms of crime.

The standard legal definition of robbery is the taking of property by force or by threat of force. It is thus both a property crime and a crime of violence. It is a property crime, unlike theft and burglary, that threatens the physical security of its victims. It is a crime of violence that in all its heterogeneous forms occurs more than half a million times a year in the United States, striking many more victims than rape[1] (U.S. Department of Justice 1992) and reaching across boundaries of social distance far more often than does aggravated assault, which typically involves victims and offenders who are acquainted. Robbery is the stranger-to-stranger crime that most frequently results in victim death and injury in the United States, accounting for over 2,000 deaths per year, nearly 50 percent of all the killings that are classified by the Federal Bureau of Investigation as "felony murders."[2]

If any category of life-threatening behavior would appear to support the conclusion that American violence is a natural outgrowth of high levels of American crime, robbery is the prime candidate. Material gain is the objective of this behavior, unlike with most violence, so it is proper to think of the behavior that leads to the risk of bodily injury in robbery as the means used by the actor rather than as his end. There is thus continuity between robbery as an instrumental behavior and other criminal conduct designed to achieve the unauthorized taking of property. Yet two puzzling features of robbery in the United States point to the conclusion that the injury and death associated with American robbery should not be considered a natural consequence of the high volume of crime in the United States.

The first puzzle associated with robbery in the United States is why it is the crime of choice for so many offenders when other forms of property crime are more lucrative and less dangerous. The second puzzle is why robbery events so frequently lead to injury and death. This high death rate is a mystery because a dispassionate analysis of failure to obtain property from a stranger who refused to cooperate should lead an unthreatened robber to disengage and seek another victim.

An Irrational Crime?

Those who believe that criminal behavior is governed by rational principles would find it hard to explain the persistence of high rates of robbery in the United States. The muggings and armed robberies that alarm city dwellers also turn out to be a terrible way to make a living. Only a minority of American robberies are directed at commercial establishments with relatively large amounts of cash (Federal Bureau of Investigation 1992, table 3.143). Even the rewards for such hard-target robberies are far from commensurate with the risks involved. Many commercial establishments are well-defended against robbery with alarm systems and guards with weapons. The arrest rate for commercial robberies is relatively high (Zimring and Zuehl 1986, 27 [table 18]); and the more lucrative the robbery target, the greater the chance of detection. At the top end of the scale, a majority of bank robberies are cleared by arrest even in cities where the clearance rate for burglaries is no more than 5 percent. Further down the scale, the twice-a-week robbery of convenience stores is a career that ends quickly in arrest and would not earn more than the minimum wage prior to apprehension.

At the bottom of the scale, the unplanned street robberies, which constitute the majority of all robbery victimization, generate a risk of apprehension or injury that is smaller than that for commercial robbery but much larger than the risks associated with larceny or burglary. And those who persist in robbery are always eventually caught and are usually imprisoned. Moreover, the cash rewards for street robbery are usually pitifully small—under $200 on average.

Occasional armed robberies in convenience stores are statistically as foolhardy as going over Niagara Falls in a barrel. Repetitive street robbery is a low-wage occupation with a virtual guarantee of ultimate imprisonment. When California prisoners were asked to compare crimes they committed with crimes they were punished for, 90 percent of the inmates who admitted to committing any robberies had been sent to prison for robbery; by contrast, 35 percent of those who reported selling drugs were in prison for that crime (Peterson and Braiker 1980). On a risk-reward basis, no crime against property makes less sense in the United States than robbery.

Yet it is precisely the $200 armed robbery that kills thousands of victims a year, that causes prisons to overflow, that makes us appoint blue-ribbon commissions to study the crime problem. Why then does this behavior persist in the streets of urban America?

The high volume of robbery in the United States certainly seems irrational if we think of potential offenders as motivated only by the desire to acquire property in making choices among the various possible criminal means of acquisition. This model of choice assumes no skill requirement on the part of the potential offenders for either violent or nonviolent means of acquisition. It further assumes that there is no special utility or enjoyment associated with a particular criminal means of acquisition.

But what if the domination of another human being by threat has positive utility for a potential offender (Katz 1988)? Or what if an offender's habits and skills render him better prepared to acquire property by intimidation than by stealth? Only in these circumstances—the greater ease of committing robbery and its noninstrumental satisfaction for the offender—does the election to commit robbery approach rational behavior under current conditions.

But if either the possession of assaultive habits and skills or the enjoyment of intimidation are necessary to explain the American tendency toward robbery, then high levels of robbery should best be seen as a spillover from general tendencies toward violence and not as a separate behavioral system operating independently of other factors that condition violent behavior in a social system. On this view, robbery should be regarded as the violent man's property crime; and the best predictor of the level of robbery in a particular setting may not be the general level of property crime but rather the general level of violence.

The Mystery of Robbery Killings

The second puzzle that we noted concerned the high rate of injury and death associated with robbery in the United States, particularly when the robbery victim is unwilling to hand over money or property. The injury or death of a robbery victim is not difficult to explain when there is resistance of a kind that puts the robber in jeopardy. And studies have shown the rates of victim injury and death are high in such circumstances (Zimring and Zuehl 1986, 18). But rates of victim injury or death are also high when the person threatened simply refuses to provide money or property, or tries to escape. Since both the risk of apprehension and the potential punishment escalate when the victim is killed, the rational robber would be well advised to meet flight or refusal by avoiding conflict and seeking another victim.

Yet frequently a frustrated robber uses lethal force in response to noncooperation by a victim whose resistance poses no immediate threat whatever to the robber. In the Zimring and Zuehl study of urban robbery in Chicago, the most significant predictor of death in urban robbery was whether the victim was active in not cooperating with his or her assailant (Zimring and Zuehl 1986, 18 [table 10]). "Active noncooperation" cases included refusal and flight as well as resistance with physical force. These cases had a death rate fourteen times as great as robberies where there was no resistance. Cases where victim denied having any money were twice as likely to result in the death of the victim as the nonresistance cases but only one-seventh as lethal as refusals (Zimring and Zuehl 1986, 10).

Why would a robber shoot a stranger who refused to hand over property when a killing increases the offender's chances of being caught by a factor of four and moreover threatens the law's maximum punishment? We think that one fruitful approach to this problem would be to regard all attempted robberies as potential social conflicts. Even if the offender and victim are strangers initially, the victim's refusal to cooperate in the robbery creates a contest of wills that may explain the high rate of lethal violence in cases of refusal. The robber experiences refusal as a challenge to his or her authority and credibility. All too often this challenge is met with life-threatening violence. The most plausible reason why refusal to cooperate with a robber generates a high risk of the use of lethal force is that the offender takes refusal personally.

If the foregoing analysis is an accurate explanation of the death rate from robbery, the common theme in robbery assaults and conflict-motivated assaults between acquaintances is apparent. Violent assault in the United States is very often a matter of maintaining status, combatting disrespect, and standing up to challenges to manhood and personal authority. The same motivation and the same kind of conflict are found in a high proportion of the robbery attempts that result in serious injury and death.

This background permits us to specify in some detail what we mean when we say that the death rate from robbery in the United States should not be regarded as a crime problem. The acquisition of property by criminal means is as widespread in London and Sydney as it is in New York and Los Angeles. London has just as much crime as New York and just as many criminals. But the public heath consequences of crime in other developed nations are relatively trivial; the crime problem in most industrial nations is criminal acquisition of property not danger to life. In Sydney, Australia, the chance of being killed by a robber, burglar, or purse snatcher in 1992 was 1 in 500,000.[3]

In the United States, however, it is the overlap of the tendency to favor the use of personal force with the desire to acquire property by criminal means that results in a high rate of robbery, robbery injury, and robbery killing. The preference for robbery by those who choose it is not a matter of either lower risk or greater material rewards than other forms of property crime. Thus, it is more appropriate to regard violent robbery as an aspect of a larger propensity toward violence than it is to view it as a part of a broader pattern of crimes against property. Given the considerable risks involved, and the relatively modest rewards, robbery is the violent man's property crime. A high volume of robbery therefore must reflect the character and tastes of the offenders who perpetrate it.

Crime, Violence, and Citizen Fear

One sharp contrast between Sydney and Los Angeles invites us to consider the relationship between rates of life-threatening personal violence and public perceptions of the seriousness of crime as a problem. As measured by the political importance of crime as an election issue, or the degree to which fear of crime is mentioned as a major disorganizing influence on urban life, Sydney does not seem to have a significant crime problem. To be sure, housebreakers are not popular figures in New South Wales and complaints about crime are quite common, but terror is not.

Los Angeles is a city where fear of crime and of criminals is arguably the single most important social and political issue for the majority of citizens. Scientific surveys of public opinion reflect this difference to some degree, but they do not capture the palpable difference between crime as an annoyance in Australia and crime as a fundamental threat to social life in Los Angeles. The statewide Field polling organization in California finds crime to be the number one problem reported in the state; and concern about policy toward criminals dominated the 1994 California elections to an extent that would be unthinkable at any level of government in Australia. The intensity of citizen concern in California is also reflected in the demand for substantial changes in criminal justice policy. The prison population in California grew 400 percent in the fifteen years prior to the 1994 elections, but California voters nevertheless overwhelmingly supported a referendum in 1994 that required a twenty-five-years-to-life sentence for anyone convicted of a third felony if the offender's previous convictions had been as serious as housebreaking.

Since general levels of nonviolent crime in Sydney and Los Angeles are closely similar, why not conclude that it is levels of lethal violence rather than of crime generally that determine the degree of public fear? Why else would similar numbers of criminals and rates of crime lead to such a sharp cleavage in public response? The question is an important one, but far from easy to answer with confidence. Evidence regarding the relationship between rates of different types of crime and public attitudes is surprisingly sparse, and the specific question of the influence on attitudes of rates of violence rather than rates of crime generally has not been systematically addressed.

There are two different issues involved in determining the relationship between rates of violence and public fear: the salience of violence as a focal point for citizen fear and the influence of rates of violence on levels of public concern about violence. On the first issue the answer seems clear: When citizens are afraid of crime it is life-threatening personal violence that dominates their attention. On the second issue, the evidence is far from clear. Although the objective risks of violence undoubtedly influence the level of public fear, so also do many other variables. And the extent to which differential levels of public concern can be explained by differences in objective risk is not known.

To characterize concern about serious personal violence as the dominant image in public fear of crime may seem like an overstatement. Earlier sections of this chapter have documented the relatively low levels of danger to life associated with residential burglary as a crime, but residential burglary is a crime that citizens greatly fear in California. Indeed, including residential burglary as a triggering felony in the California "three strikes" sentencing proposal was vigorously supported by the public even though it tripled the cost of the program (Zimring 1994). Is not this evidence that nonviolent threats are as salient to individuals as violent ones?

Probably not. Public fear of burglary is probably associated with images of the worst thing that could happen in the course of a housebreaking, rather that the kind of things that usually do happen when burglars appear. The majority of burglarized dwellings are unoccupied at the time of the invasion. But the image of burglary that provokes public fear is of the burglary of an occupied dwelling. The great majority of burglars would react nonviolently in any interaction with household members. But the image of burglary that produces high levels of citizen fear finds the victim defenseless in bed and at risk of murder. It is the worst-case burglar that provokes those citizens who express high levels of fear regarding residential burglary. This is an issue that could be explored by carefully constructed survey research. To date, however, the question of what images preoccupy citizens with high levels of fear regarding particular types of crime has not been investigated.

But the worst-case burglar does not explain the contrast between Sydney and Los Angeles. Why would housebreakers provoke much more fear in Los Angeles than in Sydney? One reason might be the fact that many people have homogeneous images of "the criminal." That is to say that they do not think of robbers and burglars as different sorts of people but rather imagine the criminal offender who threatens their sense of security as a composite of the personal characteristics of the criminal offenders that they have heard about. If this homogeneity of image phenomenon is operative, citizens who live in environments where homicidal attacks are common will fear all kinds of contact with criminal offenders much more than citizens whose composite image of the criminal offender derives from a general environment that experiences less lethal violence.

In an urban environment where armed robbery frequently leads to the death of victims, the purse snatcher and the burglar will acquire much of the threatening character of the robber because the composite generalized image of the criminal that conditions public fear acquires the characteristics of the lethal armed robber. The fear generated by the kidnap and murder of Polly Klaas provokes long sentences for residential burglars because the burglar in the citizen's scenario has acquired the characteristics of Polly Klaas's killer.

High levels of interpersonal violence could thus generate a process we call categorical contagion. This is the agency whereby citizens come to fear many forms of criminal behavior because they imagine them all committed by extremely violent protagonists. Lower general levels of violence may be associated with less pressure toward categorical contagion because there is less in the way of frightening violence to condition the citizen's image of the criminal threat.

Processes of categorical contagion may operate in social life well beyond the frontiers of the criminal code. Just as personal safety and bodily security are the core concerns of fear of crime, concern about vulnerability to assault can produce fear of a wide variety of social encounters that include rudeness and incivility and even face-to-face contact with strangers in the streets if those strangers are seen as threatening. If a person carries profound feelings of physical vulnerability into a social setting, even ambiguous or innocuous behavior can produce substantial levels of anxiety.

It is also important to recognize that this process of categorical contagion may be a two-way street in which a high level of anxiety about strangers or face-to-face interaction may express itself as a fear of becoming a victim of a violent crime. Just as substantial anxieties about being robbed or attacked may make a person apprehensive about encountering strangers, an intense but nonspecific fear of strangers or foreigners or black people may produce more specific concerns that the subjects of our apprehension intend to assault us.

When arguing for physical vulnerability as a citizen's core concern, we do not want to suggest that this preoccupation will be found to the same degree at all stages of social and economic development. It is ironic that modern industrial nations do a better job of protecting their citizen's property interests from potential criminal threats than of protecting their bodily security; in large part because insurance can provide commensurate compensation for most property interests. Citizens in a modern state do not keep all their money under their mattresses, so that the totality of a person's property interests is not vulnerable to trespassory taking. Citizens can keep their money in banks and government can provide depositors with insurance that will repay them if the bank fails. The private sector provides mechanisms of insurance to purchase replacements for automobiles that are stolen or personal property that is carried away by burglars.

But even where it exists, financial compensation for the victims of violence cannot restore what is lost in the same sense that the insurance company can enable one to purchase a new Chevrolet. Life insurance can provide financial benefits to the family or dependents of the deceased, and this is important; but it cannot give him his life back. For this reason, the more successful a society is in providing its members with security of property, the greater will be the concentration of concern with violence.

But what predicts variations in citizen concern about safety in a modern industrial society? This is a complicated question and one that has not been squarely addressed in the social science literature on the fear of crime. We would expect at least three major influences on the level of fear regarding serious crime: 1) The amount and seriousness of violent crime; 2) The level of fear-arousing social conditions in the immediate physical environment of the subject; and 3) the amount and perceived seriousness of fear-arousing cues in the mass media and the personal social universe of the subject.

How important are variations in actual risk in the mix of cues that produce levels of citizen fear of violence? We would expect variations in the risk of serious violence to be a major determinant of levels of fear that exert influence in a variety of ways. The higher the rate of serious violence, the larger the chance that the average citizen will have personal experience as a crime victim or in some social relationship to a violence victim. The larger the risk of serious violence, the stronger the associations between fear of violence and various fear-arousing cues in the citizen's immediate social environment. The higher the number of people who get shot, stabbed, or mugged, the more fear arousing will be citizen contact with boom boxes, broken windows, or threatening-looking strangers. Finally, we would expect both that the number of social cues and the amount of media attention to violence would be directly influenced by the rate and seriousness of violence; although we are more confident of this relationship in the contacts of the citizen than in the quantum of media cues about violence.

We would expect to find a positive association over time and cross-sectionally between risks of life-threatening violence and the mix of cues that determine levels of public fear. But variations in risk are by no means the only influences on levels of public consciousness in mass society. Processes of categorical contagion will link levels of public fear of violence to fluctuations in other social conditions that make people anxious and insecure. Further, to the extent that the character and quantity of media attention to violence is a variable that fluctuates independently of trends in risk, this will also influence levels of fear, particularly when citizens lack more direct experience. It thus seems probable that fear of violence in the 1990s is a media event independent of changes in other social conditions. We would also expect that variations in media coverage will be of larger importance in determining levels of concern and fear among groups that lack significant first- and second-hand experience of violence than among persons with more direct experience.

What we do not know is the maximum level of public fear that can be produced and sustained in an environment of general social anxiety but low levels of lethal interpersonal violence. An attempt to import an American-style "law and order" campaign into the electoral politics of a nation with low death rates from violence might tell us whether fear can be sustained without high rates of death.

A similar issue concerns the generality of fear induced by incivility and disorder. James Q. Wilson and George Kelling argue persuasively in *Broken Windows* that indications of incivility and disorder produce citizen fear and the demand for law enforcement and social control (Wilson and Kelling 1982). One reason such indications could arouse fear is that they convey to many persons the message that they are vulnerable to more direct and more violent predation. But will the level of fear produced by disorder and incivility be as great where rates of lethal violence are low as they will where those rates are high? The context in which the broken window argument was made was urban conditions with high rates of lethal violence. The extent to which fear of lethal violence and fear of concentrated threats to public order feed off each other should be a priority concern in the social psychology of crime.

Crime Policy as Violence Policy

Life-threatening violence is, of course, against the public policy of the modern state in all but exceptional cases, but so are a wide variety of acts that range from larceny to illegal drug taking to sexual exploitation of the immature. What then is wrong with public policy that treats violence as one of the many crime problems that are best addressed by police, prosecutors, and prisons?

This section discusses some of the difficulties associated with misdefining American violence as solely a crime problem. In pursuing this analysis we do not deny that crime in the United States is destructive, costly, and disorganizing. Rather, we argue that it is the violent strain in American social life that causes the special destruction and disorganization produced by American crime.

There are three hazards associated with making general crime control policy the dominant governmental and social policy with respect to violence: the narrowness of a crime policy perspective, the failure to address noncriminal sources of potential violence, and the diffusion and loss of priority that result when violence is principally addressed as part of the U.S. crime problem. The section will provide a general outline of these objections and then illustrate many of these problems from the historical record of recent American crime wars.

Three Objections

The first problem we encounter when violence is regarded as a crime problem is that it tends then to be regarded as only a crime problem properly to be addressed with the usual tools and processes of the criminal justice system. The first difficulty with this narrow view of violence prevention is that current criminal justice processes do not seem to be very successful in combating any form of crime so that limiting the campaign against violence to available anti-crime mechanisms is not a hopeful emphasis.

Assuming that the rate and seriousness of our life-threatening violence is a natural outgrowth of a high volume of crime and criminals is also a false diagnosis of the problem. It is widely believed that the reason the United States suffers particularly from violent crime is that America has so many criminals. If it is a crime problem, the most natural and obvious cause is an excess supply of criminals and whatever social processes may be responsible for that surplus. The only problem with this diagnosis is its demonstrable falsity. Recall the comparative incidence of theft, burglary, and robbery in Sydney and Los Angeles. For every ten theft offenses reported in Sydney, Los Angeles reports just over thirteen such offenses.

The supply of thieves in the two communities would seem to be at rough parity. The distribution of one form of aggravated theft, burglary, lends further support to the hypothesis of equivalent criminogenesis: For every ten burglaries reported in Sydney, Los Angeles counts nine. But for every ten robberies reported in Sydney there are eighty in Los Angeles. The significant contrast between the two cities will not concern the number of offenders any more than it will involve the number of offenses. It is only the kind of crime that differentiates the cities, so that any search for the causes of crime generally as an explanation of the particular problem in Los Angeles is barking up the wrong tree.

It is not helpful to respond that the reason other countries have similar crime rates and much lower rates of violence is that cities in the United States have different types of criminals and crime. This merely begs the question of *why* United States crime is so much more likely to include life-threatening violence. The central fact that regarding violence as principally a crime problem obscures is that rates of lethal violence cannot be implied, predicted, or explained as a consequence of our general level of crime or population of criminals.

A related problem is that searching for the sources of violence only in the caseload of the criminal courts would be to miss many processes of great importance in generating violence. A propensity for violence is characteristic not only of American crime, but also of many other aspects of American social life. The reader will recall that for every homicide reported in Sydney, twenty bodies are added to the count in Los Angeles. Only a minority of Los Angeles homicides grow out of criminal encounters like robbery and rape. A far greater proportion of Los Angeles homicides grow out of arguments and other social encounters between acquaintances. Only those arguments that produce great injury and come to the attention of the police and are regarded as criminal. Most of the processes that generate the risk of lethal violence are not analyzed.

Why should arguments in Los Angeles lead to so much more loss of life than in Sydney? It is likely that the same social tendencies that make crime more dangerous in Los Angeles also make barroom fights and arguments among coworkers more likely to be life-threatening. The tendency toward life-threatening violence in the United States is neither limited to a discrete criminal class nor confined to criminal patterns of behavior. The same social tendencies that predispose American offenders to robbery more often than their foreign counterparts also make arguments more lethal in California than in New South Wales.

Violence in the United States is both a broader and a different problem from merely the life-threatening forms of criminal offenses. The social values and processes that require study to understand American violence are unlikely to be confined to the criminal classes. To confine the search for explanations of American violence to criminal behavior and offenders is grossly underinclusive.

If violence in the United States is a much broader problem than crime, it is also the case that the range of criminal behavior in America is much broader than that of violence. Most offenses and most offenders are not violent. In Los Angeles for example, only 26 percent of index crimes in 1992 involved the use or threat of personal violence (Federal Bureau of Investigation 1992). When nonindex offenses such as drug sales and possession are added, the proportion of crimes involving violence declines to under 15 percent.

If this small portion of crime involves violence, the first concern with using a general anticrime policy to combat violence is that the policy will miss the target (if violence should be the target) 85 percent of the time. A related problem of a crime-driven orientation is the lack of any explicit priority given to punishing and controlling violence. The best illustration of the practical impact of unfocused anticrime crusades is found in recent American history.

The Paradoxical Priority Impacts of Crime Wars

The dramatic increase in resources devoted to the punishment of crime in recent years provides a clinical case study of the impact of a general crackdown on crime on policy toward violent crime. The paradox of the crime crackdown is this: When penal resources are scarce, the priority given to more serious offenses means that violence will receive a large share of the most serious punishments. No matter how small the prison, we tend to make room for Charles Manson and Willie Horton. But expanding punishment resources will have more effect on cases of marginal seriousness than on those that provoke the greatest degree of citizen fear. The result is that as fear of violence is translated into a general campaign against crime, the share of extra resources that is directed to violent crime will tend to decrease.

Serious crimes of violence result in prison sentences when offenders are apprehended under most criminal justice policies. Armed robbery, attempted murder, and offenses of equivalent magnitude are seriously punished even before special efforts to increase penal severity are introduced. This pattern of serious punishment means that there is less room left in the system to get tough with this sort of offense.

Instead, crime crackdowns have their most dramatic impact on less serious offenses that are close to the margin between incarceration and more lenient penal sanctions. This pattern of nonviolent offenses absorbing the

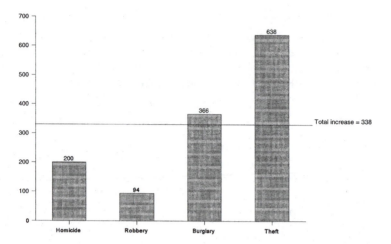

FIGURE 2.6   Percentage Change in Prisoners by Offense of Conviction, California, 1980–1990

SOURCE California Department of Corrections (1991)

overwhelming majority of resources in crime crackdowns can be clearly illustrated in the recent history of criminal justice policy in the United States. During the decade 1980–1990, for example, the state of California experienced what might be described as the mother of all crime crackdowns. In ten years, the number of persons imprisoned in California quadrupled, and the population of those incarcerated in the state's prisons and jails increased by over 100,000 (Zimring and Hawkins 1992).

Figure 2.6 shows the impact of this unparalleled "get tough" policy on the growth in the population confined in the California prison system as a result of conviction for the four offenses that were profiled in Figures 2.1 and 2.2.

The relative growth in prison population for the two nonviolent offenses is greatly in excess of the growth experienced for robbery and homicide. The relative growth of the number of burglars in prison was over three times that of the number of robbers, and the growth rate of prisoners convicted of theft was over six times the rate for robbers.

The relatively modest impact of California's crime crackdown on violent offenders is not a result of lenient attitudes toward robbery and murder in California. Quite the opposite. Since robbery and murder were always seriously punished in California, there was a smaller number of leniently treated robbers and killers who had been spared by the previous regime and were thus available to be swept up by the crackdown.

This tendency for changes in criminal justice policy to have the most profound effect in marginal cases produced a sharp contrast in California's prison system over the decade of its unprecedented expansion. Sixty percent of all California prison inmates in 1980 had been committed for offenses of violence; but only 27 percent of the additional prison space added between 1980 and 1990 increased the number of inmates who had been convicted of violent offenses. If one imagines that the efficiency of an anticrime policy as a way of combating violence can be measured by the proportion of offenders imprisoned for violent offenses, the prison resources available in 1980 had a 60-percent efficiency rating, whereas the additional resources committed to imprisonment during the 1980s were employed with 27 percent efficiency.

The national pattern is less pronounced but also shows shrinking proportions of violent offenders as populations increase. In 1979, 46 percent of the 274,563 persons in state prisons had been convicted of a violent offense. But just under 35 percent of the 429,618 additional prisoners that were present in 1991 had been convicted of crimes of violence. This diminished overlap between imprisonment and violence is in large measure an inevitable consequence of substantial increases in the proportion of felony offenders sentenced to prison. It creates an enormous gap between the motive for crime crackdowns and their effects.

Bait and Switch

For those who wonder why both violence and the rate of imprisonment have been going up, we present the parable of the bait-and-switch advertisement. The practitioner of "bait-and-switch" selling advertises a brand new vacuum cleaner with several attractive features for the unheard of price of $39.95. That advertised product is the "bait" designed to attract customers into the store. When the consumer enters the shop, advertisement in hand, she is either told that the advertised special is no longer available or is shown an obviously defective piece of merchandise and actively discouraged from its purchase. The salesperson then attempts to "switch" the consumer by interesting her in the $300 vacuum cleaner that the whole scheme was designed to promote.

The "bait-and-switch" character of anticrime crusades occurs in the contrast between the kind of crime that is featured in the appeals to "get tough" and the type of offender who is usually on the receiving end of the more severe sanctions. The "bait" for anticrime crusades is citizen fear of violent crime. Willie Horton is the poster boy in the usual law and order campaign. But the number of convicted violent predators who are not already sent to prison is rather small. In the language of "bait-and-switch" merchandising, the advertised special is unavailable when the customer arrives at the store. The only available targets for escalation in imprisonment policy are the marginal offenders and offense categories. If an increase in severity is to be accomplished, the target of the policy must be "switched." Nonviolent offenders go to prison and citizens wonder why rates of violence continue to increase.

Conclusion

Rates of common property crimes in the United States are comparable to those reported in many other Western industrial nations, but rates of lethal violence in the United States are much higher than can be found elsewhere in the developed nations. This penchant for life-threatening violence cannot be a natural result of a high volume of either crime or criminals. If it were, other high-crime-rate developed nations would share our higher rate of violence. The propensity toward life-threatening violence seems independent of general crime rates. That is why violence is not a crime problem.

The international comparisons in the first part of this chapter make plain the independent nature of crime rates and rates of violence. The analysis of robbery in the second part suggests that high rates of robbery do not come only from rational utility maximization on the part of offenders seeking easy ways to make money by lawbreaking. A taste or preference for violence must be a part of why this criminal method is adopted. The third part argues that fear of life-threatening violence is the central concern of those who are afraid of crime. Even levels of fear regarding nonviolent offenses such as housebreaking can increase as a response to higher levels of personal violence as citizens project the murderous intentions they fear most onto a broad range of crime victimization situations. What is not yet known is the relationship between variations in rates of lethal violence and variations in the fear levels experienced about all crime.

The fourth part of this analysis discussed the inadequacies of "getting tough" on crime as an antiviolence strategy. If lethal violence is the priority target of governmental concern, the anticrime crackdown is inefficient, diffuse in focus, and misses the opportunity to look beyond the category of criminal behavior for the sources and control of violence. The inefficiency of anticrime crusades against violence has recently been demonstrated in the diffuse impact of the huge increase in panel confinement in the United States.

There is, however, one linkage between citizen fear and government policy that may systematically broaden anticrime efforts beyond lethal violence. The categorical contagion processes we mention may mean that a murder by robbers generates citizen fear that burglars will murder and is expressed in relation to a broad variety of crime that may involve little objective risk of violence. Unless some discipline is imposed on the policymaking process by analysts, the generality of fear or crime may render law enforcement less effective against the life-threatening acts that are the greatest cause of fear.

References

Archer, Dane, and Rosemary Gartner. 1984. *Violence and Crime in a Cross-National Perspective.*

Bennet, Richard R., and James P. Lynch. 1990. Does a Difference Make a Difference? Comparing Cross-national Crime Indicators. *Criminology* 28 (1).

Bureau of Criminal Statistics, New South Wales. 1992.

Federal Bureau of Investigation, U.S. Department of Justice. 1990. *Uniform Crime Reports.*

_____. 1992. *Crime in the United States.*

Katz, Jack. 1988. *The Seductions of Crime.*

Lynch, James P. 1995. "Crimes in International Perspective." In *Crime*, edited by James Q. Wilson and Joan Petersilia.

Peterson, Mark A., and Harriet B. Braiker with Suzanne M. Polich. 1980. *Who Commits Crimes: A Survey of Prison Inmates.*

Wilson, James Q., and George L. Kelling. 1982. Broken Windows. *Atlantic Monthly* March, 29–38.

World Health Organization. 1990. *World Health Statistics.*

van Dijk, Jan, and Pat Mayhew. 1993. "Criminal Victimization in the Industrialized World: Key Findings of the 1989 and 1992 International Crime Surveys." In *Understanding Crime: Experiences of Crime and Crime Control*, edited by Anne Alvazzi del Frante, Ugljesa Zvedic, and Jan van Dijk.

Zimring, Franklin E. April 11, 1994. 'Three Strikes' Law' Is Political Fool's Gold. *The Christian Science Monitor* 23.

Zimring, Franklin E., and Gordon Hawkins. 1992. "Prison Population and Criminal Justice Policy in California." Paper prepared for California Policy Seminar, Berkeley.

Zimring, Franklin E., and James Zuehl. 1986. Victim Injury and Death in Urban Robbery: A Chicago Study. *Journal of Legal Studies* 15 (1): 27.

Comment: When and for
Whom Is Violence a Crime Problem?

ALBERT J. REISS JR.

It appears mistaken to form public policy in terms of heterogeneous categories like crime or violence. Their diversity makes it difficult to formulate sensible public policy even for a restricted class of crimes such as crimes involving violence toward persons. The history of policy and practice toward "violent person" and "sex offenders" amply illustrates this difficulty. Neither crime policy nor violence policy can satisfactorily address the diversity among crimes or among violent behaviors. Policy issues are obfuscated when they are framed in terms of general categories and debated as general policies or practices.

The relationship of violent actions to citizen perceptions of crime and their own physical vulnerability is complex. By focusing on physical vulnerability as a citizen's core concern Zimring and Hawkins run the risk of oversimplifying this complexity. In the remarks that follow, I present two ways that their focus may distort our understanding and obfuscate public policy debate on crime and violence. I shall first suggest that a citizen's sense of vulnerability extends not only to their being physically harmed but to the destruction of their property as well. I shall follow this by maintaining that the violent destruction of private and public property is perceived as a threat to collective as well as to individual safety and security. Communities and their collective life are as much the victims of violence as are its individual members.

Violence Toward Property

More than a dozen years ago, I published a paper in the *Vanderbilt Law Review* (Reiss 1982) that drew attention to crimes involving the destruction of property. I contended that the intentional destruction of property is a violent act. It may be with malicious intent as in vandalism, arson, and terrorist bombings. Or it may be an instrumental aspect of crime, as in breaking to enter and commit crimes of auto, residential, and business burglary. I noted then that often the cost of the property destruction in burglary exceeded the value of any property taken. Moreover, it is precisely that element of destruction of property that threatens personal safety and generates fear of personal harm. Breaking and entering one's private property is an intrusion into private space and carries the message that one is vulnerable (Reiss 1987). It becomes a major element in generating fear of victimization by crime and is one reason why burglary is regarded as a serious crime.

To have one's home burglarized is to experience the trespass as a personal violation. Women are more likely to regard burglary as a personal trespass than are males; burglary is an assault on their personal domain and may account for the conflation of burglary and the threat of rape.

Recent experiments on spouse assault, disclose that in a substantial minority of cases the offending spouse threatens and intimidates by the destruction of property (Sherman 1992). The TV set, clothing, and dishes are often selected as targets of destruction. Violence does not exhibit itself solely as actual or threatened physical harm to people. Damage to another's property can be symbolic personal destruction as it often appears to be in domestic violence. Parenthetically, I note that we know far too little about threats to private space. Acts that menace the private self such as the many forms of personal harassment (sexual harassment, stalking, anonymous threatening, and obscene phone calls or mailings) are perceived as violent (Reiss 1987). Bias crimes carry similar threats.

I sense that Zimring and Hawkins assume that offenders are not rational choosers, or else they would not commit crimes such as robbery where the income is small relative to the risks. I sense also that they ignore the fact that few criminal careers are specialized by type of crime and that in a career, crimes against property are interspersed with those against persons. At the offender level, person and property crimes are not independent of one another (Blumstein and Cohen 1986). Moreover, offenders normally do not burglarize, rob, or steal to open bank accounts and make routine deposits for withdrawal of cash. The prototypical offender has a diversity of offenses in his (or her) criminal career—crimes against persons as well as against property. It is unusual for an offender to specialize in a type of crime. Typically they commit crimes with others (Reiss 1986a; Reiss and Farrington 1991). This is particularly so for youthful offenders whom we assume may share their profits if not their losses. Additionally, even granted the vagaries of plea bargaining to a lesser offense for adult offenders, the offenses on which conviction and sentencing are based are weighted on average toward the most serious offense on which one can get a guilty plea. The same holds pretty much for sentence bargaining.

Victimizing Communities and Collective Life

In my study of policing the central district of Oakland, California (Reiss 1985), I focused on the importance of what I termed soft crime as a factor in the abandonment of the central business district and other business areas in Oakland neighborhoods. Soft crimes threaten in a number of ways. Crimes like panhandling and the congregation of unruly youths in the public streets—corner boys—are perceived as threats and experienced as harassment by citizens. Others like graffiti and vandalism are *visible signs*—regarded as threatening personal and collective safety and a threat to private property. It is neighborhoods and business streets that are the victims of crimes of violence against property. These offenses, taken individually as less serious crimes, are serious crimes in their collective consequences. They destroy sections of London and Sydney as surely as they destroy them in New York and Los Angeles.

Some crimes are regarded as victimless on the presumption that they are a matter only of private harm and do not bring harm to others. The use of narcotic substances is a common example. Yet so long as their distribution and sale is illegal, they give rise to illegal markets that are governed by violence and intimidation. Not only do the market's entrepreneurs seek market shares by violent means, but their use of violence may result in community residents becoming the victims of violence as by, for example, drive-by shootings and gang warfare. Moreover, the concentration of sales in dwelling as well as on street locations opens residential housing and communities to nonresidential as well as residential users who engage in crimes of prostitution, robbery, burglary, and theft to obtain money to purchase drugs. It seems reasonable to conclude that ordinary citizens in these communities are the victims of so-called victimless crimes.

Wilson and Kelling (1982) contend that the failure to repair vandalized buildings and leaving them unoccupied carries a symbolic message that generates increasing vandalism and destruction. Property damage is not limited to residential housing, however. Public property as streets, parks, playgrounds, and schools are also the targets of vandalism. Research I did in 1967 for the National Crime Commission disclosed that the costs of vandalism to schools, parks, streets, and other public buildings was a substantial part of the public budget for these facilities. Damage to public and private property and the abandonment of buildings are not simply symbols of what is to be feared for one's personal safety. They are an actual loss to a common life and the amenities that make a community. Crime not only induces public fear, but it destroys community life by depredations against public and private property as well as against persons.

Since the eighteenth century we have known that offenders and their crimes are not uniformly distributed in residential space and that the risks of offending and victimization vary enormously in time and space. The underworld of Dickens's day was not an organization but a section of London where predators of all stripes resided and where no respectable person would venture. Cities have always been regarded as varying in their quality of life, and crime and violence along with death, disease, and squalor were primary qualities. It was Shelley who remarked that: "Hell is a city very much like London."

There are sections of most large world cities where an outsider's risk of victimization is substantial. But in all too many U.S. cities the risk of harm to insiders is likewise substantial. Most offenders do not have a long journey to work; their victims are nigh dwellers, often enough, acquaintances, family members, or places where one does business. Such elements are helpful in their apprehension but hardly guarantee public or private safety.

My point in repeating these few well known facts about territorial patterns of crime and violence is to draw our attention to the fact that crime and violence policies often take territorial concentration of risks into account when allocating public resources. They do so, for example, by offering special services in areas of high crime and violence—more police and fire stations, emergency services, outpatient clinics, and so on. It can be regarded as a form of redistribution of income to the poor who reside in those areas. Although the wisdom of territorially based policies to cope with crimes and violence seems firmly established, such policies are often poorly implemented to address the problems of community life.

What I miss in Zimring and Hawkins's treatment of crimes and violence is attention to the territorial concentration of different crimes and forms of violence in territorial space, especially within neighborhoods and communities of cities, and a discussion of the policy implications of that concentration for community living. Crimes and especially violence toward public and private property as well as violence toward residents destroys neighborhoods and community life. A major question that any violence or crime policy prevention program must address is why is there greater vulnerability and risk in some areas than others and what can be done about it? An interesting policy question, for example, is do we enhance the risk of members of a neighborhood by the placement of released offenders in their community, especially high-risk released offenders? Under what circumstances should Willie Horton or sex offenders be released to a residential community? Do the neighbors of a person released on parole have a right to know whom the state is paroling in their midst? Citizens increasingly demand an accounting for such practices. Legislatures, alas, make bad law in responding to their demands for administrative accountability as Megan's Law in New Jersey and Connecticut attest.

References

Blumstein, Alfred, Jacqueline Cohen, Jeffrey A. Roth, and Christy A. Visher, eds. 1986. *Criminal Careers and "Career Criminals."* National Research Council, National Academy of Sciences series, vol. 2.

Bottoms, Anthony E., and Paul Wiles. 1986. "Housing Tenure and Residential Community Crime Careers in Britain." In *Communities and Crime*, edited by Albert J. Reiss Jr. and Michael Tonry, 101–162.

Reiss, Albert J. Jr. 1982. How Serious Is Serious Crime? *Vanderbilt Law Review* 35 (3): 541–585.

Reiss, Albert J. Jr. 1985. "Policing a City's Central District: The Oakland Story." In *U.S. Department of Justice, National Institute of Justice Research Report*.

_____. 1986a. "Co-offending Influences on Criminal Careers." In *Criminal Careers and Career Criminals*, edited by A. Blumstein, J. Cohen, J. Roth, and C. Visher, 121–160.

_____. 1986b. "Why Are Communities Important in Understanding Crime?" In *Communities and Crime*, edited by Albert J. Reiss Jr. and Michael Tonry, 1–33.

_____. 1987. "The Legitimacy of Intrusion into Private Space." In *Private Policing*, edited by Clifford D. Shearing and Philip C. Stenning, 19–44.

Reiss, Albert J. Jr., and David Farrington. 1991. Advancing Knowledge About Co-Offending: Results from a Perspective Longitudinal Study of London Males. *Journal of Criminal Law and Criminology* 82 (Summer): 360–395.

Sherman, Lawrence W. 1992. *Policing Domestic Violence: Experiments and Dilemmas*.

Skogan, Wesley. 1986. "Fear of Crime and Neighborhood Change." In *Communities and Crime*, edited by Albert J. Reiss Jr. and Michael Tonry, 203–229.

Wilson, James Q., and George L. Kelling. 1982. The Police and Neighborhood Safety. *Atlantic Monthly* 249 (3): 29–38.

Comment: Crime, Violence, and
Public Mythology

ROBERT WEISBERG

Zimring's international comparisons are, like typical Zimring work, searingly clarifying. I know of no set of criminological data so fascinatingly counterintuitive as the set that shows that cities like Sydney and London have theft and burglary rates as high as ours and robbery and homicide rates a trifling fraction of ours. Yet he also leaves us in a very unclarified state of mystery.

First, a law professor's brief tangent: Zimring promises that he is not worried about doctrinal niceties here. I pause, however, to note that one classic doctrinal result of the confusion of crime and violence he describes is a criminal law rule on which Zimring himself has written eloquently. The felony murder rules assume some inherent link between certain felonies and the likelihood of homicide or the moral aggravation of homicide and so drastically increases homicide liability when that other felony is present. The categorical statutory linkage of, say, a burglary and a death into a first-degree murder exemplifies Zimring's main point. In addition, the almost comically incoherent California doctrine of second-degree felony murder shows what happens when judges have to tackle this problem without at least the benefit of a work-saving arbitrary statute. Thus, California law students have been tortured for decades with learning to apply the principle that a nonenumerated felony may aggravate a killing to second-degree murder if that felony is "inherently dangerous in the abstract." In parallel, federal criminal law, and in particular the maze of Federal Sentencing Guidelines, often increases punishment when part of a defendant's course of conduct is a "crime of violence," leaving to prosecutors and judges the conceptual problem of discerning the relationship between crime and violence and of determining whether to do so by fact-specificity or category. Though all this is apart from Zimring's main theme, it is more than a matter of nicety, since these doctrinal questions can often have powerful consequences for punishment.

To return to the sharply refocused political landscape Zimring offers us: Zimring is surely right that a key political consequence follows from the misleading confounding of crime and violence. If the polity wishes to greatly expand the numbers of those imprisoned and the length of prison sentences, it may have no choice but to do so largely with the pool of nonviolent offenders, for the simple reason that there simply is not

much room left for increase with violent offenders, who are already punished about as often or as severely as is ever likely to happen in this
country. Hence, we fill the prisons with nonviolent drug offenders not
exactly because we exaggerate their propensity to cause us harm, but because they are the only bodies constitutionally available to us as we, for
independent reasons, express our need to fill the prisons.

But this clarification also leaves us with a sense of mystery. Zimring argues that it is a "general propensity toward violence," rather than a
propensity toward crime, that explains the American obsession with violence—both in terms of the actual rate of violence and the salience of the
fear of violence in American politics. Why? It would be unfair to complain
that Zimring begs the question by speaking of our propensity to violence.
Indeed, I would only urge that he beg the question more explicitly.

Why, for example, are there so many more irrational American robbers
than irrational English or Dutch robbers? Why, if the motive for robbery
is maintenance of ceremonial respect on the streets, is this more important in this country than any other? The bizarre criminal psychological
modeling of Jack Katz in *Seductions of Crime*, despite its overheated exis-
tential fervor, convincingly captures the motivation of many violent non-
rational actors. But why do *we* have so many of them? Is reference to our
having started as a frontier society or a revolutionary movement merely
a question-begging metaphor of its own? Is the lineage through us? Is it
that local militias helped found this country and thereby left us a dual
legacy: an affirmation of guns as a bulwark against threats to autonomy
that is both constitutional right and social catastrophe?

In seeking the unique ingredient of American culture to explain violence, one is tempted to speak of slavery and heterogeneity, but it is not
clear what they have to do with this propensity toward violence. Perhaps
they indicate the absence of some sense of communal social control we
see more of in more "traditional societies." Perhaps it has something to
do with so-called distrust of government. After all, there is a rather obvious sense in which Germany over the last century has shown a much
greater "propensity" toward violence.

I am more concerned with an area that Zimring does not quite leave as a
mystery, and on which he may have the balance slightly off. He suggests
that the fear, and the salience of the fear, of crime depends on three factors:
the actual amount of violent crime; the level of other "fear-arousing conditions" in one's social environment, and media exploitation. Though Zimring does not purport to treat the allocation of these factors systematically, I
would argue that he should greatly emphasize the last and a very specific
version of it—politicians' demagoguery over the crime issue, as opposed
to depiction of crime and violence in entertainment.

I do not deny that actual encounters with crime or related forms of social disorder are relevant. But one thing Zimring does not consider is

whether those factors could come close to explaining the reckless expansion of criminal punishment in recent years through plebiscitary-like elections. I say that because, at least roughly, the chances of one being a victim of crime or living in social disorder in the United States are inversely correlated with likelihood of voting. Those who vote for three-strikes laws are largely voting "on behalf of" crime victims who live in neighborhoods far different from where these voters live.

Why do people exaggerate the risk of being a victim of a crime? Surely there has been enough of a general increase in recent years to explain some of this. And surely Zimring is right that the oddly independent phenomena of much violence and much crime make people susceptible to the Hortonesque contagion of social imagery. But I think far more of the blame goes quite straightforwardly to the Hortonizers. Politicians exploit the tendency of Americans to believe—or to express the belief (an important distinction)—that they fear crime. The problem in relying too much on real changes in rates of crime or social disorder is to assume that even if the public is empirically wrong, it is acting "authentically" on real belief. I do not think it generally is. I believe that most political attitudes on visceral subjects are scripted acts of rationalization—and nowhere so obviously as in the area of crime.

Americans relentlessly purport to believe that theirs is the most dangerous of times, because to believe so is to redeem their general social and economic insecurity. It is a way of dignifying the conventional miseries and constraints of bourgeois life. It is a form of egotism and conceit. Politicians supply voters with scripted phrases and attitudes and voters adopt them. Were this to cause nothing worse than bigoted social interactions, it would be bad enough. Unfortunately, voters and the politicians they elect recklessly pass laws like three-strikes, and we all pay the price.

This collective self-aggrandizement, this tendency of Americans to believe they are so specially suffering, is more important than any undermining it does of American pride on the wonders of our society. And on this score, there is nothing subtle whatsoever about the racist element. A critical mass of Americans basically believe that the society would be better off without black Americans, and, half explicitly, half consciously, it blames black males for messing the society up. It is true that young black males commit a disproportionate amount of violent crime (it is also true that so do whites, as compared with whites in other countries); but it is also true that most of the violence black males commit is on other black males.

This gets us back to the sense of mystery. I do not purport to have solved the larger mystification that I earlier imputed to Zimring. Quite the opposite, I have mystified myself even more on this specific issue. I do not understand why Americans engage in this symbolic projection so inordinately. It may be the convenience of a repressed history of slavery that offers black Americans as such a convenient target of the projection. It may be a perversion of a distinct form of American populism.

Put in more cultural terms, at a certain accidental juncture in our political history, it became necessary for all politicians to take a meaningless religious oath, a gesture toward the superficial principles of antiliberal populism that began animating American politics in the mid-1960s. The political science of this view is simple: This populism basically derived from the Nixon-Goldwater Southern strategy: Nixon and Goldwater swung the electoral balance of power toward the Republicans by persuading middle-class white Southerners that despite their historical tie to the Democratic party, the logic of their ideology and racial attitudes argued for joining the Republicans. The appeal to white Southerners as the prototypes of social anxiety about the loss of moral and social order was linked to a post-1960s reaction among middle-class voters everywhere, including the Rustbelt North.

As a result, it became useful for politicians to focus on this prototypical or even iconic figure—most concretely, a lower-middle-class-male white Southerner. To please that voter was to please lots of other voters, who either identified consciously with our Southern prototype or who just conveniently had developed similar social concerns. Soon, even upper middle class nonwhite Northern women (for example, working-class Catholic "Reagan Democrats") began to share the "ressentiment" of this iconic figure, and the death penalty oath is a gesture toward that figure in all of us. Many economists tell us that the true source of social anxiety for this iconic voter is the decline in real wages over the last two decades, but, given the difficulty we all have in understanding economic forces, the death penalty oath becomes a wonderful way for a politician to express empathy toward those so concerned with the perceived breakdown in social order. In the great words of George Bush, the death penalty oath says everything and nothing: "Message: I care." People are rarely so reckless as when they think of themselves as "the people."

Notes

A different version of Zimring and Hawkins's essay was published as Chapter 1 of Franklin E. Zimring and Gordon H. Hawkins, *Crime is Not the Problem: Lethal Violence in America* (1997).

1. In 1992 more than 672,000 robberies and more than 109,000 rapes occurred.

2. Of the 4,887 felony murders known or suspected by the police in 1992, 2,254 were known robberies (Federal Bureau of Investigation 1992, table 3.125).

3. The New South Wales Bureau of Crime Statistics and Research reported two burglary killings and five robbery killings in the Sydney statistical division, with a population of 3.6 million. (Analysis performed by Roseanne Bonney of the New South Wales Bureau of Crime Statistics and Research, August 1995).

3

Prevention

The Cost-Effectiveness of Early Intervention as a Strategy for Reducing Violent Crime

PETER W. GREENWOOD

The 1990s will go down in history books as the decade when U.S. politicians finally discovered *The Crime Issue* in a big way. The preceding decade had seen the largest growth in prison populations since the penitentiary was invented, as legislatures around the country passed a flurry of new mandatory minimum sentencing bills. In most states the number of prison inmates more than tripled although crime rates remained fairly flat. However, it was not until several foreign tourists were murdered in Florida and Polly Klass was snatched from her bedroom in suburban Petaluma, California, that politicians and their campaign consultants fully realized the significance of the crime issue to voters. "Toughness on crime" became one of the primary litmus tests for political office, whether that office dealt directly with crime or not. Voters were treated to the spectacle of candidates debating, not the merits of alternative crime control approaches, but primarily the issue of who supported the toughest measures first.

From the rhetoric of these recent campaigns one might get the impression that incapacitation and deterrence are the only available means to combat violent crime; that toughness toward criminals was the only reasonable response. Although it is certainly true that locking up repeat offenders for longer periods of time will have some incapacitative effects, these effects are considerably more modest than many of their proponents claim and can be quite costly to achieve. An analysis of California's recently passed Three Strikes and You're Out Law (Greenwood et al. 1994) estimated that, if fully implemented, over the next twenty-five years the Law would:

- Increase the state's criminal justice system operating costs by more than $5 billion dollars a year (or 100 percent);
- Decrease serious and violent crime by about 25 percent

Combining these two findings leads to an estimate of the cost of preventing serious and violent crimes through the Three Strikes sentencing mechanism of around $16,000 per crime prevented. The study went on to predict, however, that the new law would *not* be fully implemented because of its high costs and funding competition from other state programs.

There are certainly ample reasons for the public to be concerned about crime. In recent years, homicide rates among juveniles have been increasing sharply and homicide is now the leading cause of death among young African-American males (Reiss and Roth 1993). Geographic and cultural boundaries that once kept violent crime confined to particular neighborhoods and population groups have given way to a more pervasive spread of crime throughout the population.

However, despite the dominance of the recent "get tough" rhetoric, deterrence and incapacitation are not the only methods available for reducing crime. Preventive and rehabilitative strategies should also be receiving some of our attention as we look for better ways of controlling crime. In fact, the apparent modest impact on crime trends resulting from recent increases in imprisonment (Zimring and Hawkins 1995) should increase our interest in other strategies.

Crime prevention efforts can take many forms from more effective security devises, gun control, and better street lighting to antitruancy programs and efforts to decrease school dropout rates among high-risk youth. One of the problems with various target hardening strategies, such as providing better locks and streetlights, is that a substantial portion of the crimes prevented at the hardened site may simply be displaced to less well protected sites; the offenders will adapt. The advantage of prevention programs that focus on potential offenders is that the crimes prevented are not displaced to others, with the notable exception of market-driven crimes like drug selling and prostitution.

Public discussions of violence prevention programs these days, for instance those concerning the recently passed Federal Crime Bill, emphasize programs that target high-risk youth in the age ranges where violence is most prevalent, around fifteen to twenty years of age. Many of these programs emphasize dispute resolution skills, mentoring, after school activities, and reducing the number of weapons on school campuses; all of which are hoped to reduce the immediate likelihood of violence among youth. Unfortunately, despite the funding of a number of recent programs designed to demonstrate or test the value of such activities and programs, the value of any one or combination of these activities for reducing violence remains a matter of speculation or faith rather than an empirically demonstrated fact (Reiss and Roth 1993).

Rather, it is at the opposite end of the juvenile age spectrum where promising results have been more firmly demonstrated. Home visit programs that target young, single, poor mothers and enriched preschool programs that target the children of such mothers have both been demonstrated to produce substantial benefits to participating families and society in general. At a somewhat later age, programs that increase the parenting skills of parents with troublesome children have also proven to produce positive results (Farrington 1994; Davidson et al. 1990) as have programs designed to provide structure, supervision, and support for young delinquents.

In the next section of this chapter we will review the risk factors and theoretical arguments suggestive of interventions targeted upon 1) high-risk mothers and their very young children; 2) troublesome or disruptive youth and their parents; 3) schools; and 4) young juvenile delinquents. In subsequent sections, we review what is currently known about the effectiveness of such interventions and attempt to estimate the costs and benefits of such programs tailored to the needs of California's youth. The last section summarizes our results and discusses their implications for public policy.

Risk Factors and Individual
Patterns of Criminal Behavior

There is a high degree of continuity between childhood conduct problems, delinquency, and later criminal behavior (Loeber and LeBlanc 1990). The best predictor of any individual's future deviant or antisocial behavior is the amount and severity of similar behaviors in the past (Farrington 1994). Age of onset and severity of juvenile record are two of the best predictors of adult criminality (Greenwood and Abrahamse 1982; Blumstein et al. 1986).

Troublesome and delinquent children are more likely to come from troubled families and neighborhoods. Family factors associated with higher rates of delinquency include: early childbearing or teenage pregnancy, and substance use during pregnancy (Farrington 1994); parent's criminal record or mental health problems, and low birthweight or other types of birth complications (Brennan et al. 1995); poor parental supervision, erratic childrearing behavior, parental disharmony, and parental rejection of the child (Loeber and Stouthamer-Loeber 1986). Being abused or neglected as a child increases the likelihood of arrest for a violent crime by 38 percent (Widom 1992).

Delinquency is not a problem that appears alone. Delinquent youth are also at higher than average risk for drug use, problems in school, school dropout, and teenage pregnancy (Elliott et al. 1989; Greenwood 1993). Research attempting to explain the likely sequence or relationship between these various behaviors now supports an interactional model in which all are interconnected with causality flowing both ways between any two (Thornberry 1987). Given this perspective, any intervention that reduces the incidence of one of these problem behaviors is likely to reduce the others as well.

Opportunities for Intervention in the Developmental Cycle

Prenatal and Early Childhood Interventions with High-Risk Families

Most of us have an intuitive sense that the basic patterns of character and personality are laid down very early in life. Longitudinal studies have demonstrated that inappropriate or inadequate parenting are among the strongest predictors of later delinquency (Loeber and Stouthamer-Loeber 1986). The most obvious and direct means of reducing violent crime by youth raised in such circumstances is to educate high-risk young women about how to avoid unwanted pregnancies and why they should postpone pregnancy; or discourage them from such pregnancies in some other way. I will leave it to others to deal with the moral and programmatic issues related to achieving such goals (Carnegie 1994) and merely assert that, if effective, such measures would reduce crime a great deal. Rather, I will begin with the issue of how to identify women who are at risk of being ineffective parents and what to do about it.

Longitudinal studies consistently identify the following three factors as associated with such risks: poverty, being single or without the aid of a coparent; and, youthfulness. Any woman with one or more of these characteristics is at significantly higher risk of being an ineffective or abusive parent than one who does not (Farrington 1994). Additional risk factors include: substance abuse, mental health problems, or criminality on the part of either parent; birth complications; or residence in a criminogenic neighborhood (Sampson 1995).

Given a pregnancy on the part of any woman with one or more of these characteristics, it can be argued that the community has an interest in helping her overcome potential problems that are likely to interfere with the healthy development of her child. During the past two decades a number of experimental programs have demonstrated the value of home visits and early childhood education in reducing a range of problem behaviors (Farrington 1994; Yoshikawa, 1994).

The Syracuse University Family Development Research Program recruited 108 deprived families to participate in the experimental intervention, which began during the third trimester of pregnancy. All of the families, which were predominantly African-American, had annual incomes under $5,000 (in 1970 dollars). The average age of the mothers was eighteen and 85 percent were single heads of households. The major thrust of the intervention was to support parent strategies that enhanced the development of the child through weekly home visits and day care through the first five years of the child's life. The home visitors were trained to assist families resolve problems in child rearing, family relations, and community functioning.

A ten-year follow-up of the Syracuse sample found 6 percent of the experimental program children had been referred to probation, compared with 22 percent of the matched controls. Program youth also tended to express more positive feelings about themselves and to take a more active approach in dealing with personal problems. Girls who participated in the program showed greater school achievement and higher teacher ratings; and parents of program youth placed more value on prosocial attitudes and behaviors than did the controls (Lally et al. 1988).

Another study in upstate New York randomly assigned at-risk women (young, poor, or single parent), experiencing their first pregnancy, to one of the following four conditions: 1) Sensory and developmental screening for the children at ages twelve and twenty-four months only; 2) Condition 1 plus free transportation to regular prenatal and wellchild visits; 3) Condition 2 plus nurse home visitation during pregnancy; or 4) Condition 3 plus nurse home visitation during child's first two years. Reports of child abuse or neglect during the first two years were substantially less among those receiving the postnatal home visits. Among those most at risk (poor, unmarried, teenagers), the difference between those receiving no services and those receiving the postnatal home visits was 19 percent versus 4 percent (Olds et al. 1986a).

The Houston Parent-Child Development Center randomly assigned one-year-old Mexican-American children and their families, recruited from Houston Barrios to either: 1) a two-year program of biweekly home visits (first year) and four times a week classes and day care (second year) or an "assessment only" condition. Teacher ratings five to eight years after the program's completion show fewer acting-out and aggressive behavior problems with program participants compared with controls (Johnson and Walker 1987).

A study that compared the effects of various levels and timing of home visits for working-class pregnant women in Montreal found that early visits (prenatal through twelve months) resulted in infant accident rates less than half those of the controls and improved home environments (Larson 1980). A study that tested the efficacy of a program of home visits for three years, educational childcare program (years two and three), and bimonthly parent group meetings for low birth-weight children showed significantly higher cognitive scores and lower behavioral problem scores for the intervention group (Brooks-Gunn et al. 1993).

Finally, a long-term follow-up of the Perry Preschool students (who were mostly African-Americans from disadvantaged homes) in Yipsilanti Michigan found that those exposed to a two-year program of enriched preschool and weekly home visits had accumulated only half the arrests of a matched comparison group, up through age twenty-seven (Schweinhart et al. 1993). Earlier follow-up studies had found the Perry group to be more motivated in school, achieving better grades, and more likely to be employed at age nineteen.

Taken together these studies provide strong evidence that early home visits and supportive child care can bring about significant reductions in problem behaviors and increase cognitive functioning, especially for those youth most seriously at risk. The success of this "supportive child care" approach is in marked contrast to a number of educational/cognitive development early interventions that did not produce the hoped for gains in academic performance (Seitz 1990).

Interventions for Acting-Out and At-Risk Youth

The early interventions described in the previous section focus on families that are at risk for having problems with their children because of their socioeconomic status, age, or family composition. The next set of programs target acting-out adolescents and their families.

Gerald Patterson and his colleagues at the Oregon Social Learning Center have developed a program for training parents in how to monitor their child's behavior and respond with appropriate rewards and punishments. A series of small-scale evaluations have shown the training to reduce stealing and antisocial behavior over short periods of time (Patterson, Chamberlain, and Reid 1982; Patterson, Reid, and Dishion 1992).

Another type of parenting intervention, called Functional Family Therapy (FFT), was developed and tested by Alexander and Parsons (1973) in Utah. Their approach focuses on modification of dysfunctional family communication processes and training family members to negotiate effectively and to set clear rules about privileges and responsibilities. A number of evaluations have found that FFT reduced recidivism rates for delinquents by 30 to 50 percent (Barton et al. 1984).

Tremblay et al. (1991) tested a similar program on a group of Montreal boys, who were identified as disruptive by their kindergarten teachers. The experimental program provided assistance in family management to the parents and training in social skills to the boys, who were between seven and nine years of age during the program. In a follow-up evaluation conducted when the boys had reached age twelve, the treated youth were doing better in school and reported less involvement in delinquency than those in the randomly assigned control group (McCord, et al. 1994). Hawkins, von Cleve, and Catalano (1991) found that the combined effects of both parent and teacher training for a sample of Seattle youth identified as disruptive upon entry into the first grade reduced teacher-rated rates of aggressiveness among white boys and self-destructive behavior among white girls but had no observable effects on African-American youth.

More recently, a number of studies have attempted to determine the impact of various kinds of social skills training on delinquency and drug use among middle and high school students. Training in drug-resistance skills and drug education have been shown to reduce or delay initiation into drug use for a limited period following the training (Ellickson and Bell 1990; Pentz et al. 1989). Denise Gottfredson (1990) evaluated several school-based programs designed to reduce delinquency and improve school performance and found the most effective to be a special alternative class that emphasized experiential learning through the use of a limited number of special class projects.

Early Interventions for Delinquent Youth

Somewhere between 30 and 40 percent of all boys growing up in urban areas in the United States will be arrested before their eighteenth birthday (Wolfgang and Tracy 1982). Most of those arrested will not be arrested again. For those that are, each successive arrest will place them at a higher level of risk until after five or six they will have better than a 90 percent chance of being arrested again. Those who reach the five arrest milestone have been labeled as chronic offenders; the 6 percent of all boys who account for more than 50 percent of all arrests (Wolfgang, Figlio, and Sellin 1972). Most criminal careers begin in the juvenile years, and most chronic adult offenders have had multiple contacts with the juvenile justice system (Blumstein et al. 1986).

Since the disposition of juvenile offenders is still supposed to be tailored to the individual needs and circumstances of each case, a wide variety of programs have been developed to meet these needs. For those juveniles whose crimes or records are not very serious and whose family is sufficiently supportive that the youth can continue to reside in their home, there are a variety of programs such as informal or formal probation, intensive supervision, tracking and in-home supervision by private agencies, or after-school and all-day programs in which a youth reports to the program site for part of the day and then returns home to sleep at night.

For those youth who must be placed out of their homes but do not represent such a risk that they must be removed from the community, some jurisdictions provide or contract for a wide variety of group homes and other community living situations. Placements in such facilities are typically in the range of six to twenty-four months, depending on the program and seriousness of the youth's offense. For those youth who represent a more serious risk to the community, or who cannot function appropriately in an open community setting, many states provide a continuum of increasingly restrictive settings ranging from isolated wilderness camps and ranches to very secure fenced and locked facilities. Individual placement decisions are made on the basis of community safety, treatment needs, and amenability to treatment.

Some youth advocates claim that all but a small handful of youth are best served by placing them in small community-based programs. Others will argue that such placements are too expensive and dangerous to the community. They advocate treating youth who commit serious crimes more like adults and keeping them in large, but less expensive to run training schools. Unfortunately, there is little hard evidence to resolve this dispute.

The starting point for any discussion of this issue is the Lipton, Martinson, and Wilks (1975) study of correctional treatment and the National Academy of Sciences' reanalysis of that and other relevant studies (Sechrest et al. 1979). Both reviews concluded that no one method of correctional intervention could be said to be more effective than any other, which was interpreted as saying that "nothing worked." In fact, as many subsequent commentators (Palmer 1978; Ross and Gendreau 1980;) pointed out, Lipton et al. (1975) and the other reviewers identified a number of programs that appeared to have reduced recidivism rates significantly. The problem was that no particular intervention strategy was found to be consistently more effective than any other.

A variety of explanations were offered for this phenomenon. Some argued that the reviewers were not doing an adequate job of distinguishing among various types of programs (Gendreau and Ross 1987). Others argued that reviewers were not paying sufficient attention to the quality with which the intervention models were implemented (Greenwood and Zimring 1985).

Additional insight regarding these issues was provided by a series of meta-analyses that allowed reviewers to combine results across several studies and to control on a variety of program characteristics. The first of these, like the earlier reviews, found little difference between basic correctional strategies and methods (Garrett 1985; Davidson et al. 1990). However, later ones found significant differences. A meta-analysis of eighty program evaluations by Andrews et al. (1990) concluded that appropriate correctional services could reduce recidivism by as much as 50 percent. Appropriate services were defined as those that: target high-risk individuals; address criminogenic needs, such as substance abuse or anger management; and use styles and modes of treatment (e.g., cognitive and behavioral) that are matched with client needs and learning styles.

A meta-analysis of more than 400 juvenile program evaluations by Mark Lipsey (1992) found that behavioral, skill-oriented, and multimodal methods produced the largest effects and that positive effects were larger in community rather than institutional settings. The mean effect of treatment in this study, in comparison with untreated control groups, was to reduce recidivism rates by 5 percentage points—say from 50 percent to 45 percent.

There are several differences between these last two studies that favor the Lipsey analysis as the basis for predicting the potential impacts that might result from improved juvenile correctional programming. First, the Lipsey study was restricted to just juvenile programs, whereas the Andrews study included programs treating both juveniles and adults. Second, the Lipsey study attempted to be comprehensive in identifying studies, and the Andrews study used a small select sample. Finally, the Lipsey study compared programs across a number of objective categories whereas the Andrews study applied a somewhat subjective theoretical classification scheme that could have been biased by the coders' knowledge of the outcomes for individual evaluations.

Unfortunately, many of the youngest delinquents do not appear to be exposed to whatever benefits juvenile corrections programs have to offer until they are well on their way to developing a pattern of serious criminal behavior. In most jurisdictions the juvenile system has little in the way to offer an eleven- or twelve-year-old delinquent youth because they are not yet seen as dangerous (Greenwood et al. 1983), but such youth represent the greatest eventual risk to society of their entire cohort. A number of studies have demonstrated the appropriate community-based interventions work considerably better than regular probation or short-term detention (Davidson et al. 1990).

Estimating the Direct Costs and Benefits of Alternative Approaches

In the preceding section of this chapter we have reviewed a number of studies that demonstrated that effective early intervention could re-

TABLE 3.1   Input Parameter Values

Parameter	Value
Serious crimes per year	1,174,000
Boys per cohort	200,000
Women age 20	230,000
Live births per year	600,000
Incidents of child abuse per year	60,000
Number of school-aged children	9,600,000

duce either the actual incidence of later criminal behavior or at least risk factors (such as child abuse or behavioral problems in school) that are closely associated with future criminality. In this section, we will estimate the direct costs and crime-reduction benefits of implementing such programs in California to address the needs of the appropriate populations at risk. We will consider four generic types of intervention: early childhood home visits and day care; parent training and social skills development for youth; alternate educational curriculum and ways of organizing schools; and correctional interventions for young juvenile delinquents. The basic population and crime incidence parameters assumed in these calculations (based on 1990 census figures, FBI data and national surveys) are shown in Table 3.1.

Early Childhood

According to the 1990 Census, about 8 percent or 367,000 of California's school-age children lived in households headed by a single female who was not in the labor force. In south-central Los Angeles, the only inner city area for which we have assembled the data, this fraction rises to 24 percent (about 26,000 children). The corresponding percentages for pre-school children are about the same. Nationally, about one out of four children live in households with incomes below the poverty line (Carnegie 1994).

We know that nationally there is no father present or willing to provide any kind of economic support for about 30 percent of all births. This fraction is probably somewhat higher in California as a whole and certainly much higher in California's inner cities. These facts support a conservative estimate that about one-quarter of California children can be considered "at risk" for involvement in violent behavior because of their family's characteristics. There were about 600,000 live births in California in 1990.

According to the studies reviewed in the previous section, a generic early childhood program designed to reduce the incidence of child

TABLE 3.2 Program Cost Factors

Intervention	Early Childhood	Parent Training	School-Based	Early Delinquents
Number treated per year	750,000	18,400	9,600,000	7,500
Cost per treatment	$4,800	$15,000	$100	$10,000
Cost per year	$3,600,000,000	$27,600,000	$960,000,000	$75,000,000

abuse, neglect, and delinquent behavior would include as its primary core elements: 1) Weekly home visits beginning by the third trimester of pregnancy and running through the child's second year and 2) full-time day care and early childhood education from ages two through five. Assuming: a fully loaded cost (salary, benefits, and administrative overhead) for each paraprofessional home visitor of $40,000; caseloads of fifteen families per caseworker; average annual day care and early childhood education costs of $6,000 per student; the total cost per child for the generic intervention would be around $4,800 per year or $24,000 for each child's first five years. Assuming around 600,000 births per year, the annual cost of the program that would serve the 25 percent of children most at risk for their first five years would run about $3.6 billion per year (600,000 x .25 x $4,800 x 5). The basic parameters determining the cost for each strategy are shown in Table 3.2.

Recent evaluations suggest that appropriate early childhood intervention may reduce later criminality by high-risk children by as much as 50 percent. Within the general population we can expect about 6 percent of all boys to accumulate at least five arrests and have a very high probability of continuing on into an adult criminal career (Blumstein et al. 1986). Within a high-risk population identified on the basis of family composition and socioeconomic status the percentage would be considerably higher.

Assuming that the 25 percent of the population targeted for this intervention now account for at least half of all crimes by individuals of a similar age, a 25–50 percent reduction in crime by these individuals would produce a 12–25 percent reduction in crime by individuals in their age cohort. Unfortunately, the reduction in propensity to commit crime among youths targeted by this intervention would not become apparent until about thirteen or fourteen years after the first subjects were enrolled. However, within twenty-five to thirty years the intervention would be affecting potential offenders in all age groups.

The intervention would also reduce the incidence of child abuse for the target population (which, we also can assume, accounts for about 50 percent of all such incidents, or about 15,000 per year) by about 50 percent (National Research Council 1993). The average number of crimes pre-

TABLE 3.3   Estimated Serious Crimes Prevented

Time Period	Early Childhood	Parent Training	School-Based	Early Delinquents
Year 1	15,000	NA	11,740	1,468
Year 5	75,000	NA	23,480	7,338
Year 10	75,000	35,220	46,960	14,675
Year 20	148,375	63,396	58,700	26,415
Year 30	221,750	70,440	58,700	29,350

vented in various years after initial implementation are shown in Table 3.3.

In addition to its direct crime prevention benefits, an early childhood intervention is likely to reduce the number of high-risk children to be dealt with in the future by improving the birth-control practices of high-risk girls and improving their interest and ability in caring for their children. The intervention also improves school performance and later employment prospects (Carnegie 1994); benefits not included in our calculations.

Parent Training

The typical parent-training program involves somewhere between ten and twenty sessions of instruction and one-on-one counseling and coaching (Patterson et al. 1992). Assuming that a trained therapist can run about four such sessions per day, training a typical family will require a total of about four days of a therapist's time. This means that a full-time therapist could work with about fifty families per year, at a cost of around $1,500 per family. In 1990, there were 230,000 women aged twenty in California. Assuming that about 10 percent of all families (childbearing women) would qualify for such services at some point in their child-raising years and about 80 percent of all women bear children, the total annual cost of such a program would run about $27 million per year (230,000 x .8 x .1 x $1,500).

There are no follow-up studies that show the long-term effects of parent training on future criminality. The best that we have is the Barton et al. (1984) evaluation of the program applied to delinquents, which found short-term reductions in offending from 30 to 50 percent. For the purposes of this study, we will adopt the lower figure. Since participation in the program is triggered by the acting-out of the child, we can safely assume that children who participate in the program will be at higher risk for delinquency than the general population. In fact, we might assume the same targeting effectiveness as the early childhood programs, where the average amount of criminality is twice that of the general population.

A 30-percent reduction in crime for this 10 percent of the population would result in an overall 6 percent reduction in crime in age groups that are eligible for the intervention. The estimated average number of crimes prevented in various years after initial implementation of the parent training interventions are shown in Table 3.3.

School-Based Intervention

There is no clear evidence that the more progressive forms of experiential education that have been shown to improve the performance of poorer students are more expensive than more traditional forms. However, the evidence does suggest there can be significant costs associated with shifting over from one style of teaching to the other. For the purposes of this analysis, we will assume an annual cost of $100 per student (or $3,000 per classroom) to provide the kind of training and administrative assistance required to support the new methods. With approximately 9.6 million school-aged children, the annual cost for this intervention would run around $960 million per year.

School-based intervention may produce only modest changes in subsequent criminality, but they affect large numbers of youth. For the purposes of this analysis, we will assume that effective educational programs can bring about a 5 percent reduction in criminal behavior across the entire population of youth. The benefits might be considerably higher, but there is no evidence to prove it. In one year, the intervention would reach youth responsible for about 20 percent of all crime; after five years, 40 percent; after ten years, 80 percent; and after twenty years, 100 percent.

Early Intervention with Delinquents

Although early delinquency is a significant predictor for chronic criminality, most young delinquents receive little in the way of services or supervision (Greenwood et al. 1983). Special day treatment programs and home monitoring can cost around $10,000 per year. Assuming about 250,000 boys per new birth cohort, 3 percent of which would qualify for such an intervention at some point in their adolescence, the total annual cost for such an effort would run about $75 million statewide (250,000 x .03 x $10,000).

Although evaluations of experimental programs on average find positive effects of only about 5–10 percent (reduction in recidivism), those that compare the experimental treatment with no intervention at all usually do somewhat better (Davidson et al. 1984). For the purposes of this study we will assume that an appropriate community-based intervention for these young delinquents would reduce their future criminality by 10 percent. Assuming that 6 percent of the most delinquent youth in any cohort account for 50 percent of the cohort's later crimes, we will assume that the 3 percent affected by this intervention account for 25 percent of their cohort's crimes. Therefore, a 10 percent reduction in this crime translates into a 2.5 percent reduction in crime for their entire cohort.

Policy Implications

In preceding sections of this chapter we have reviewed evidence bearing on the effectiveness of early intervention strategies in reducing later criminality and used that information to estimate the costs and crime reduction benefits of four particular strategies: 1) perinatal home visits and enriched preschool programs for children of high-risk families; 2) parent training programs for the families of troublesome children; 3) improved public school programs that better serve high-risk youth; and 4) early interventions for very young delinquents. In this final section we discuss the relative cost-effectiveness of these strategies in comparison with long mandatory sentences and the implications of these findings for public policy.

The format for this particular study was motivated by a recent RAND analysis (Greenwood et al. 1994) that had estimated that each serious crime (homicide, rape, robbery, assault, or residential burglary) prevented by the mandatory sentences imposed under California's new Three Strikes Law will cost approximately $16,000 in additional criminal justice funding, primarily reflected in the costs of constructing and operating additional prison facilities. That study also estimated that more selective sentencing policies could at best reduce the cost per serious crime prevented to about $12,000 but that this was about the most cost-effective sentencing plan that could be designed.

In discussing the implications of these findings, the RAND report went on to observe that the state could spend up to $1 million dollars preventing just one high-risk youth from becoming a serious chronic offender and still be just as cost-effective as Three Strikes in preventing serious crimes. This review and analysis was undertaken to see whether evidence existed regarding the ability of early interventions to prevent violent offending more effectively than the imposition of long mandatory sentences. The findings discussed below suggest that such evidence exists.

The cost-effectiveness measure that will be used to compare crime prevention strategies is the average cost to prevent each serious felony. Serious felonies are explicitly identified by the California Penal Code (Section 1192.7) and include: all homicides, rapes, other violent sex crimes, and sex crimes against children; all robberies; most aggravated assaults including all those involving firearms or great bodily injury to victims; any kidnapping; and all residential burglaries. The inclusion of this latter crime (residential burglary) is one of the factors that makes California's Three Strikes Law much broader than those adopted or being considered in other states.

In 1992, according to the California Department of Justice, there were approximately 346,000 violent felonies and 427,000 burglaries (of which about 60 percent are residential) reported to the police (California Department of Justice 1992), or a total of approximately 600,000 serious felonies. Since it is well documented by victim surveys (Bureau of Justice Statistics 1992) that only about half of all offenses are actually reported to the police, the RAND Three Strikes study estimated that there were in fact approximately 1 million serious felonies committed in California in 1992; a figure that could be expected to grow to 1,219,000 in twenty-five years with currently anticipated population growth rates. The RAND analysis estimated that, if fully implemented, the California Three Strikes Law would reduce the number of serious felonies committed by adults in any one year by approximately 28 percent (or 329,000 crimes) while costing an additional $5.5 billion dollars a year in government costs, or $16,000 per serious felony prevented. These estimates were derived from a mathematical model that estimates the number of offenders among the general population, predicts the number of crimes they will commit in any given year when they are in the community, and tracks their arrests and movement through the criminal justice system on a yearly basis.

The early intervention approaches described earlier in this chapter offer an alternative means of reducing serious crime. Each targets different segments of the population, but all would produce substantial reductions in crime. The estimates of costs and crime prevention benefits derived earlier in this chapter are not based on elaborate models and do not take into account changes in service costs (health, welfare, etc.), criminal justice processing costs (court costs, costs of imprisonment), or any of the other costs associated with a criminal career. Rather, they are simple first approximations of the direct program operational costs and reductions in crime that could be expected from implementing these programs on a statewide basis. Table 3.4 shows the average cost per serious crime prevented for each of these alternatives in various years following their initial implementation ranging from five to thirty years. Their patterns of costs over time are considerably different.

The parent training intervention could be the most cost effective over the long run at a cost of approximately $390 per serious felony prevented thirty years after implementation. For this intervention there is no significant crime prevention effect during the first five years after initial implementation because youth are usually in the seven- to ten-year age range

TABLE 3.4   Cost per Serious Crime Prevented

Time Period	Early Childhood	Parent Training	School-Based	Early Delinquents
In first year	$48,000	NA	$81,772	$51,107
In 5th year	$48,000	NA	$40,886	$10,221
In 10th year	$48,000	$784	$20,443	$5,111
Over 20 years	$24,263	$435	$16,354	$2,839
In 30th year	$16,234	$392	$16,354	$2,555

when this intervention is administered and require another five years or so before their disruptive behavior would result in serious crimes. A more sophisticated cost-effectiveness analysis would amortize the earlier costs over all crimes prevented during the full time period being considered, discounted back to the present. However, the method used here is adequate for a first order approximation. Even if the small number of crimes prevented during the first ten start-up years had to bear the total costs of the program during its first ten years, the cost per crime prevented would still be around $7,800 (ten times the annual cost) or half the cost of preventing crimes by mandatory sentences. Of course, these calculations assume that a large number of parents would be willing to participate in parent training programs, an assumption that cannot be validated without some careful testing. A number of experimental programs have encountered difficulties enrolling parents of high-risk youth (Kumfer and Turner 1990–1991).

The next most cost-effective intervention is the program for early delinquents at a cost of around $2,555 per serious crime prevented, after it has been implemented for thirty years. This is assuming that the short-term reductions in recidivism observed for such programs hold up over time and is due to the fact that the intervention is directed at the start, rather than the end, of the criminal career for a very high-risk group. This particular intervention is also attractive because its impacts are felt almost immediately, as it comes shortly before the peak ages of criminal behavior—sixteen to twenty years of age. However, the number of crimes prevented in the first few years after the program is implemented is not as high as it is in later years because older offenders, who did not receive the program, are not affected in any way.

The early childhood intervention works with high-risk youth and their families during their first five years. Since youth do not begin to commit serious crimes until their early teenage years, there is something like a ten-year delay between when the intervention is applied and when it begins affecting serious street crimes. However, there is one form of crime it affects immediately—child abuse. Recent surveys have indicated that about one in ten children are seriously abused or neglected by their parents (Carnegie 1994). The rate is considerably higher among lower socioeconomic groups. The kind of early childhood intervention considered here has been shown to reduce rates of child abuse by about 50 percent—an impact that is immediately felt. Including this reduction in the count of serious crimes prevented, the early childhood intervention results in a cost of around $48,000 per serious crime prevented over the first five years, which decreases to about $16,000 over a thirty-year time horizon. The high costs per crime prevented for early childhood interventions are due to the fact that the interventions are expensive ($4,800 per child for five years) and the crime reduction benefits are not reaped until many years after the intervention. Of course, in addition to its crime-reduction benefits, this early childhood intervention would also produce considerable savings in the medical and social service costs associated with child abuse and foster care and improve student performance in school.

The school-based intervention results in costs per crime prevented that are very similar to the early childhood intervention—around $16,000 per serious crime prevented, over a thirty-year time horizon. The high costs are due to the fact that all school children are affected equally, whether they are at risk or not and the fact that demonstrated changes in behavior are fairly modest. However, if the kind of changes in school organization and teaching methods considered here result in significant improvements in educational performance, then these, in addition to the reductions in serious crime produced by the intervention might make them considerably more cost effective. Also, if the interventions need only apply to youth in the upper grades, say 7–12, then the costs would be cut in half.

Once again, it should be reiterated that these estimates are only crude approximations of what the real costs and benefits are likely to be when we take into account start-up costs, economies of scale, degradations in effectiveness when we shift from small pilot projects to large-scale public programs, discounting of costs over time, changes in criminal justice system costs and needs for services associated with lower rates of criminal activity on the parts of program participants, and improved school performance. Nevertheless, these initial estimates do provide guidance regarding which interventions are likely to be most effective in reducing crime.

The parent training and early intervention programs for young juvenile offenders are four to five times more cost effective than Three Strike mandatory sentences in preventing serious and violent crimes. Even if the impacts of these programs are only half what we estimated from the literature, they will still be twice as effective as Three Strikes. Furthermore, not only are they less costly ways of achieving the reductions in serious crime, but their impacts are felt fairly soon after their imposition, with only three or four years' delay in the case of early interventions for delinquents and seven to ten years for parent training.

The cost effectiveness of early childhood and broad school-based interventions, in comparison with mandatory sentences, is not nearly as clear cut. These two interventions require very large expenditures to affect large numbers of youth and only begin to produce cost-effective crime reduction benefits fifteen to twenty years after they are implemented. Of course, both of these interventions may have large collateral benefits in terms of improved school performance, lower health care costs, and gains in worker productivity. Justification of either of these large-scale programs on cost-effective grounds is likely to require more careful assessment of these collateral impacts than was attempted here.

The policy implications of these findings are fairly clear. Based on current best estimates of program costs and benefits, investments in appropriate interventions for high-risk youth are several times more cost effective in reducing serious crime than long mandatory sentences for repeat offenders. Furthermore, investments in these interventions are likely to have additional payoffs that do not result from increased use of imprisonment.

An interesting question to ask is why crime control and victim advocate groups are not demanding expansion of parent training and interventions for young delinquents rather than mandatory sentences. One answer must be our society's current faith in the value of "toughness" as opposed to treatment or prevention-oriented approaches. We have seen this clearly illustrated in the so called war on drugs where enforcement has received much greater funding than treatment in spite of clear evidence that the latter is seven times more cost effective than the former (Rydell and Everingham 1994). It is apparently much easier and more satisfying to spend money forcibly restraining misbehavior rather than spending it on programs designed to bring about voluntary changes in behavior, even though the latter are more efficient.

Another reason must be the basic mistrust in government to run complicated programs like those investigated here. A majority of citizens seem to believe that the government is not very good at anything from delivering the mail to running schools. However this skepticism does not appear to extend to state-run prison systems, which have become the fastest growing segment of government. In California, during the last twelve years, corrections' share of the state budget has grown from 3 to 9 percent, without much public concern about how well the prisons are run. The fact that they exist and are filled well beyond capacity appears to be good enough, unless it is possible to squeeze a few more in. As long as the public and responsive politicians continue to place a higher priority on symbolic toughness as a way of dealing with the problems of criminal violence and drug abuse, rather than investing in more cost-effective prevention approaches, the citizens of this state are going to pay the price in higher victimization rates, taxes, and lost productivity.

Although their apparent cost-effectiveness is not as great, this analysis also provides support for those who argue in favor of greater investment in early childhood education and better schools for high-risk youth. The primary problem with these interventions, in addition to their somewhat lower cost-effectiveness, is the lag time of ten to fifteen years between when the intervention is applied and its potential crime-reduction benefits are felt, except for the reduction in child abuse. It appears that the political process demands interventions that promise more rapid apparent results (like incapacitation).

Not that the incapacitation benefits of long mandatory sentences, like those imposed by the Three Strikes Law, are felt immediately. Increasing the length of time that felons convicted of serious crimes must serve does not result in an immediate increase in incapacitation since such felons would probably have been sentenced to prison or jail even without the new law. The additional incapacitation effects do not kick in until the time at which inmates serving time under the previous sentencing law would have been released. But their costs are not incurred until then either, except for the additional prosecution and court-related costs that are incurred because fewer defendants are willing to plead guilty. Prosecutors are estimating that approximately 50 percent of all second strike cases and 90 percent of all third strike cases will go to trial, as opposed to only 5 percent of all other cases.

How to go about convincing policymakers and voters of the crime-control benefits to be derived from investing in early prevention programs appears to be a real problem. It would help considerably to have several pilot programs under way, with rigorous impact evaluations included. In order to detect a 10-percent reduction in recidivism, it is necessary to compare the outcomes for 200 or more participants randomly assigned to the experimental program against a similar sized group randomly assigned to the current pattern of dispositions or treatment, which as we have said before, is usually no treatment or supervision at all. The cost for such an evaluation is likely to be well in excess of $2 million dollars—much more than is currently available from governmental or foundation sources for program development and testing purposes. The Orange County (California) Probation Department has been developing a program for their youngest delinquent youth, which they call "The Eight Percent Problem" (because 8 percent of their youth account for more than half of all repeat offenses by juveniles), but that program is in serious jeopardy because of the county's financial crisis.

Another problem that any effort designed to test parent training or early delinquent programs will face is concerns about the ethics of randomly assigning some youth to services and others to none. Regardless of existing evidence, many practitioners hold strong views regarding the benefits of particular interventions and prefer determining who is assigned to the limited slots on the basis of need or potential benefits, rather than random draw. These funding and research design issues are serious problems that will prevent the development of sounder knowledge without much stronger public support.

This brings us to the final Catch-22 of crime prevention efforts. One of the reasons the public may have more faith in imprisonment than early prevention efforts is that the crime-reduction benefits of prevention are more difficult and expensive to document. Yet, most criminologists would argue that there will not be any substantial reduction in crime rates without significant prevention efforts that seriously address the root causes and risk factors that clearly contribute to the development of criminal behavior.

References

Alexander, J. F., and B. V. Parsons. 1973. Short Term Behavioral Intervention with Delinquent Families: Impact on Family Process and Recidivism. *Journal of Abnormal Psychology* 81(3): 219–225.

Andrews, D. A., Ivan Zinger, R. D. Hoge, James Bonta, Paul Gendreau, and Francis T. Cullen. 1990. Does Correctional Treatment Work? A Clinically Relevant and Psychologically Informed Meta-Analysis. *Criminology* 28(3): 369–404.

Barton, Cole, James F. Alexander, Holly Waldron, Charles W. Turner, and Janet Warburton. 1984. General Treatment Effects of Functional Family Therapy: Three Replications. *Amer. Jour. of Family Therapy* 13(3): 16–26.

Blumstein, Alfred, Jacqueline Cohen, Jeffrey A. Roth, and Christy A. Visher, eds. 1986. *Criminal Careers and "Career Criminals."* National Research Council, National Academy of Sciences series, vol. 2.

Brennan, Patricia A., Sarnoff A. Mednick, and Jan Volavka. 1995. "Biomedical Factors in Crime." In *Crime*, edited by James Q. Wilson and Joan Petersilia.

Brooks-Gunn, Jeanne, Pam Kato Klebanov, Fong-Ruey Liaw, and Donna Spiker. 1993. Enhancing the Development of Low-Birthweight, Premature Infants: Changes in Cognition and Behavior over the First Three Years. *Child Development* 64:736–53.

Bureau of Justice Statistics. 1992. *Crime Victimization in the United States, 1991.* U.S. Department of Justice Office of Justice Programs, National Crime Victimization Survey Report, NCJ-139563.

Carnegie Corporation of New York. 1994. "Starting Points: Meeting the Needs of our Youngest Children." In *The Report of the Carnegie Task Force on Meeting the Needs of Young Children*.

Davidson, William S., L. Gottschalk, L. Gensheimer, and J. Mayer. 1984. *Interventions with Juvenile Delinquents: A Meta-Analysis of Treatment Efficacy.* National Institute of Juvenile Justice and Delinquency Prevention publication.

Davidson, William S., Robin Redner, Richard L. Amdur, and Christina M. Mitchell. 1990. *Alternative Treatments for Troubled Youth: The Case of Diversion From the Justice System.*

DeJong, William. 1994. *Preventing Interpersonal Violence Among Youth: An Introduction to School, Community and Mass Media Strategies.* National Institute of Justice publication, NCJ #150484.

Ellickson, Phyllis L., and Robert M. Bell. 1990. *Prospects for Preventing Drug Use Among Young Adolescents.* RAND publication, R-3896-CHF.

Elliott, Delbert S., David Huizinga, and Scott Menard. 1989. *Multiple Problem Youth: Delinquency, Substance Use, and Mental Health Problems.*

Farrington, David P. 1994. Early Developmental Prevention of Juvenile Delinquency. *Criminal Behaviour and Mental Health* 4:209–27.

Garrett, Carol J. 1985. Effects of Residential Treatment on Adjudicated Delinquents: A Meta-Analysis. *Journal of Research in Crime and Delinquency* 22 (4): 287–308.

Gendreau, Paul, and Robert R. Ross. 1987. Revivification of Rehabilitation: Evidence from the 1980s. *Justice Quarterly* 4 (3): 349–407.

Gottfredson, Denise. 1990. "Changing School Structures to Benefit High-Risk Youth." In *Understanding Troubled and Troubling Youth,* edited by Peter E. Leone, 246–271.

Greenwood, Peter, W. 1993. *Substance Abuse Problems Among High-Risk Youth and Potential Interventions.* RAND publication, RP-182.

Greenwood, Peter W., and Allan F. Abrahamse. 1982. *Selective Incapacitation.* RAND publication, R-2815-NIJ.

Greenwood, Peter W., Albert J. Lipson, Allan Abrahamse, and Franklin Zimring. 1983. *Youth Crime and Juvenile Justice in California.* RAND publication, R-3016-CSA.

Greenwood, Peter W., C. Peter Rydell, Allan F. Abrahamse, Jonathan P. Caulkins, James Chiesa, Karyn E. Model, and Stephen P. Klein. 1994. *Three Strikes and You're Out: Estimated Benefits and Costs of California's New Mandatory Sentencing Law.* RAND publication, MR-509-RC.

Greenwood, Peter W., and Franklin Zimring. 1985. *One More Chance: The Pursuit of Promising Intervention Strategies for Chronic Juvenile Offenders.* RAND publication, R-3214-OJJDP.

Hawkins, J. David, Elizabeth von Cleve, and Richard F. Catalano Jr. 1991. Reducing Early Childhood Aggression: Results of a Primary Prevention Program. *J. Am. Acad. Child Adolesc. Psychiatry* 30(2):208–217.

Johnson, Dale L., and Todd Walker. 1987. Primary Prevention of Behavior Problems in Mexican-American Children. *Amer. Jour. of Community Psychology* 15(4): 375–385.

Kumpfer, Karol L., and Charles W. Turner. 1990–1991. The Social Ecology Model of Adolescent Substance Abuse: Implications for Prevention. *The International Journal of the Addictions* 25:435–63.

Lally, J. Ronald, Peter L. Mangione, and Alice S. Honig. 1988. "The Syracuse University Family Development Research Program: Long-Range Impact on an Early Intervention with Low-Income Children and Their Families." Chapter 5 in *Parent Education as Early Childhood Intervention*, edited by D. R. Powell, 79–104.

Larson, Charles P. 1980. Efficacy of Prenatal and Postpartum Home Visits on Child Health and Development. *Pediatrics* 66(2): 191–197.

Lipsey, Mark W. 1992. "Juvenile Delinquency Treatment: A Meta-Analytic Inquiry into the Variability of Effects." In *Meta-Analysis for Explanation*, edited by Thomas Cook et al., 83–126.

Lipton, Douglas, Robert Martinson, and Judith Wilks. 1975. *The Effectiveness of Correctional Treatment: A Survey of Treatment Evaluation Studies.*

Loeber, R., and M. LeBlanc. 1990. "Toward a Developmental Criminology." In *Crime and Justice*, edited by M. Tonry and N. Morris, 375–473. Vol. 12.

Loeber, Rolf, and Magda Stouthamer-Loeber. 1986. "Family Factors as Correlates and Predictors of Juvenile Conduct Problems and Delinquency." In *Crime and Justice: An Annual Review of Research*, edited by Michael Tonry and Norval Morris. Vol. 7.

McCord, Joan, Richard E. Tremblay, Frank Vitaro, and Lyse Desmarais-Gervais. 1994. Boys' Disruptive Behaviour, School Adjustment, and Delinquency: The Montreal Prevention Experiment. *International Jour. of Behavioral Development* 17(4):739–752.

Mednick, Sarnoff. 1995. *Birth Complications Combined with Early Maternal Rejection at Age One Year Predispose to Violent Crime at Age 18 years.*

National Research Council. 1993. *Understanding Child Abuse and Neglect.*

Olds, David L., Charles R. Henderson Jr., Robert Chamberlin, and Robert Tatelbaum. 1986a. Preventing Child Abuse and Neglect: A Randomized Trial of Nurse Home Visitation. *Pediatrics* 78:65–78.

Olds, David L., Charles R. Henderson, Robert Tatelbaum., and Robert Chamberlain. 1986b. Improving the Delivery of Prenatal Care and a Randomized Trial of Nurse Home Visitation. *Pediatrics* 77:16–28.

Palmer, Ted. 1978. *Correctional Intervention and Research: Current Issues and Future Prospects.*

Patterson, G. R., P. Chamberlain, and J. B. Reid. 1982. A Comparative Evaluation of a Parent Training Programme. *Behavior Therapy* 13:638–50.

Patterson, G. R., J. B. Reid, and T. J. Dishion. 1992. *Antisocial Boys.*

Pentz, Mary Ann, James Dwyer, David MacKinnon, Brian Flay, William Hanse, Eric Wang, and C. Anderson Johnson. 1989. A Multicommunity Trial for Primary Prevention of Adolescent Drug Abuse: Effects on Drug Prevalence. *JAMA* 261: 3259–3266.

Reiss, Albert J. Jr., and J. A. Roth, eds. 1993. *Understanding and Preventing Violence.*

Ross, R. R., E. Fabiano, E. A. Ewles, and C. D. Ewles. 1988. Reasoning and Rehabilitation. *Intern. Jour. of Offender Therapy and Comparative Criminology* 32:29–35.

Ross, Robert R., and Paul Gendreau. 1980. *Effective Correctional Treatment.*

Ross, R. R., and B. D. Ross. 1989. Delinquency Prevention Through Cognitive Training. *Educational Horizon* 67(4): 124–130.

Rydell, C. Peter, and Susan S. Everingham. 1994. *Controlling Cocaine: Supply Versus Demand Programs.* RAND publication, MR-331-ONDCP/A/DPRC.

Sampson, Robert J. 1995. "The Community." In *Crime*, edited by James Q. Wilson and Joan Petersilia, 193–216.

Schweinhart, L. J., H. V. Barnes, and D. P. Weikart. 1993. *Significant Benefits.*

Sechrest, Lee, Susan O. White, and Elizabeth D. Brown, eds. 1979. *The Rehabilitation of Criminal Offenders: Problems and Prospects.*

Seitz, Victoria. 1990. Intervention Programs for Impoverished Children: A Comparison of Educational and Family Support Models. *Annals of Child Development*, 73–103. Vol. 7.

Thornberry, Terence, P. 1987. Toward an Interactional Theory of Delinquency. *Criminology* 25:863–891.

Tremblay, Richard E., Joan McCord, Helene Boileau, Pierre Charlebois, Claude Gagnon, Marc Le Blanc, and Serge Larivee. 1991. Can Disruptive Boys Be Helped to Become Competent? *Psychiatry* 54:148–161.

Widom, Cathy Spatz. 1992. *The Cycle of Violence.* National Institute of Justice Research in Brief publication, NCJ 136607.

Wolfgang, Marvin, R. M. Figlio, and T. Sellin. 1987. *Delinquency in a Birth Cohort.*

Wolfgang, Marvin, and Paul E. Tracy. 1982. *The 1945 and 1958 Birth Cohorts: A Comparison of the Prevalence, Incidence and Severity of Delinquent Behavior.*

Yoshikawa, Hirokazu. 1994. Prevention as Cumulative Protection: Effects of Early Family Support and Education on Chronic Delinquency and its Risks. *Psychological Bulletin* 115(1): 1–26.

Youth and Adult Correctional Agency. 1991. *California Prisoners and Parolees, 1990.* California Department of Corrections publication.

Zimring, Franklin, and Gordon Hawkins 1995. *Incapacitation: Penal Confinement and the Restraint of Crime.*

Comment: Early Intervention: Promising Path to Cost-Effective Crime Control, or Primrose Path to Wasteful Social Spending?

MARK H. MOORE

Peter Greenwood has, once again, done us all a great service by making a bold, "back of the envelope" calculation. This time he has compared the crime reduction cost-effectiveness of longer prison terms with a variety of early intervention, crime-prevention programs. He concludes: "Based on the current best estimates of program costs and benefits, investments in appropriate interventions for high-risk youth are several times more cost effective in reducing serious crime than long mandatory sentences for repeat offenders."

Now, it would be easy to poke holes in many of the technical features of this calculation. For example, the predicted effects of large-scale parent training interventions on crime are extrapolated from the effects of small-scale research interventions—a somewhat dubious enterprise. The predicted effects of school-based programs are simply assumed without any empirical evidence. On the cost side, the estimates are equally speculative and crude.

But these technical quibbles miss the point. The real value of Greenwood's calculation lies not in the reliability of his estimates of the crime-reduction effectiveness of the different interventions or in the precision of his cost estimates. The value lies, instead, in the forceful claim that the results of his calculation make on society's policy imagination. By having the courage to put early intervention programs alongside longer prison terms for repeat offenders and evaluate them in the same hard-nosed, crime control terms, Greenwood forces us to face up to a very important strategic policy question: Has American society struck the right balance between "retributivist" responses to crime on one hand and "preventive" approaches on the other? There is plenty of time for technical refinements in the calculations. What is important now is getting our minds around this tough strategic issue.

That is my central purpose in this review of Greenwood's piece. I want to try to answer the question of whether society is acting foolishly by investing so much of its meager public resources in prisons rather than in early intervention programs. This requires me to look at the form of the argument Greenwood makes as well as the technical content of his esti-

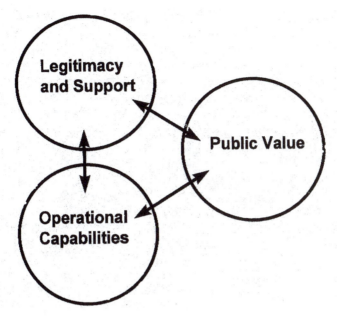

FIGURE 3.1   Strategy in the Public Sector

mates. More specifically, has the framework of his calculation captured the imporant values and concerns that a responsible policymaker should have in mind as he or she considers this question.

I am also curious about why society is acting foolishly, if it is true that it is. Why is it that society has such a tough time weaning itself from reactive responses and committing itself to preventive social interventions even when there are apparently strong arguments for doing so? Greenwood's chapter raises this question at the end and offers some important observations about why it is so hard to switch from one approach to the other. My purpose is simply to refine and expand some of the observations he makes.

A Framework for Strategic Analysis

Let me begin by setting out a very simple framework useful in analyzing strategically important policy questions. The framework is symbolized by a triangle, presented as Figure 3.1. The basic idea that is supposed to be conveyed by this image is that, in order for policy ideas to be useful in democratic systems, they must meet three important tests, symbolized by the three points of the triangle:

First, they have to be designed to achieve states of the world that would be publicly valued; for example, a world in which crime was lower and the money being spent by public agencies to keep it low was less than it is now.

Second, to the extent that the policies depend on the use of public resources (such as tax money or the authority of the state), the policies have to be able to win political support and legitimacy from citizens, their representatives, and others. In this case, that means (crudely) that state legislatures must be persuaded to reallocate funds from prison construction to different forms of intervention programs and to resist using state authority to punish offenders more harshly.

Third, there must be operational capacities to implement the proposed ideas. In this case, it must be possible to imagine that some agency could actually find the at-risk families or children and deliver the proposed service to them in a form that would produce the intended result.

Showing these three tests as different points of an interlocking triangle is supposed to remind us that all three of the tests must be met if a policy idea is to be valuable. It is not enough, for example, that an idea seems substantively valuable, or cost effective. It must also be capable of attracting legitimacy and support and be administratively doable. Moreover, one of the ways that ideas acquire legitimacy and support is through analyses that speak to the values and concerns of citizens and their representatives as well as make accurate predictions about what will happen if a particular policy is adopted. It also helps if evidence exists showing that a policy can be implemented and how that might be done.

This kind of strategic analysis is particularly helpful to us in thinking about whether society is acting foolishly by relying as much as it now does on retributivist crime-control policies emphasizing longer sentences for repeat offenders while refusing to invest more in early intervention programs for two different reasons. First, it may help us uncover some reasons why society might reasonably be reluctant to make this strategic shift in crime-control policy that are obscured by the straightforward cost-effectiveness analysis that Greenwood essays so heroically. This is the normative use of the strategic analysis framework. Second, it may help us understand why more progress has not been made in this direction despite the fact that the basic facts about the efficacy of early intervention programs have long been known. Given that arguments of the type and form that Greenwood makes have long been available, we have to ask why society has not moved more in the indicated direction. This is the descriptive use of the strategic analysis framework.

The Value of Shifting from
Retributivist to Preventive Policies

The starting point for the strategic analysis is in the value circle. Does Greenwood's analysis show clearly that society would be better off if we were to rely more on early intervention programs to control crime? At first glance, the analysis seems substantively compelling (assuming that the estimates are accurate), for it seems to encompass the important values that society either does or should have in mind as it weights alternative policies: It should be looking at how much it can reduce crime (the single measure of effectiveness, or value, used in the analysis) for tax dollars spent in different, competing government programs (the single measure of cost used in the program). Yet, a little reflection suggests two problems with Greenwood's implicit argument.

Risks and Uncertainties

The first is simply that his analysis is only a guess about what society could achieve by investing more in preventive programs. I do not say this to reintroduce technical quibbles about the quality of Greenwood's analysis. The problem is not just that we haven't conducted enough experiments with different kinds of interventions, or that we haven't yet measured the costs of the programs very well, or that Peter has failed to get the arithmetic right. The problem is that even the best analyses, performed several years from now when we have accumulated even more evidence about the cost-effectiveness of different kinds of programs in reducing crimes committed by those exposed to them and figured out how to analyze them, will end up being imperfect guides to this important choice. All prospective analysis is at best a rickety bridge to the future. We do not really know whether something will work until we try it.

This means that the choice about whether to invest more in preventive programs is inevitably a gamble. Moreover, it looks like it is a particularly big gamble. This is partly because the stakes on both sides are pretty high—crimes on one hand, large absolute costs to government on the other. It is also because the evidence is now and will remain thin about the cost-effectiveness of government programs as they will actually be fielded by the government. But it may be that the biggest part of the gamble comes from being confused about how particular kinds of programs should be bundled together in portfolios that constitute strategic policies. Let me explain what I mean.

Greenwood's analysis allows us to compare the relative cost-effectiveness of five generic types of crime control policies (four "early intervention" prevention programs and one retributivist policy increasing prison sentences for repeat offenders) in terms of the cost per crime prevented if one started now and absorbed their effects over the next thirty years. Greenwood is clear that this analysis abstracts from some technical complications having to do with how we should treat costs and benefits that occur in the future. (These technical issues may be related to a real political problem, which is that it is very hard for a democratic political regime to

stay focused on policies that are costly in the short run and produce benefits only in the long run.)

But a potentially more serious problem for his analysis is not the *dy-
namic* issue of how costs and benefits accumulate over time but the *portfo-
lio* question of how his policies interact with one another over both the
short and long run. Presumably, the real world offers not an all or nothing choice of retribution or prevention and one kind of prevention program over another. We would have to decide how much to best invest in
early childhood, parent training, school-based, and early delinquency
programs and in what sequence these policies should be introduced at
what scale. It is quite possible that these different policies interact with
one another in complex ways. For example, it may be that successful
early childhood interventions with at-risk families and kids would substantially reduce the need for subsequent parent training, make it easier
to maintain high-quality schools without special programs, and substantially reduce the need for subsequent early delinquency programs. But it
is also possible that the effects would not be this neat. Perhaps the early
childhood programs would end up missing families that produced later
offenders. Or, it could be that the availability of parent training and good
schools would reduce the effectiveness of early childhood interventions
because the existence of these other programs would reduce the hazards
of having children that could be emphasized as part of early childhood
interventions.

The point is not that any of these speculations are correct or not. The
point is that they could be true, and they signal an important complexity
in the calculation that must be accommodated if we are to see more or
less accurately what is the right path to follow in diversifying our efforts
to control crime in the future. The more complicated the calculation, the
more risky the bet feels. The worry is that we could decide to invest a
great deal in crime prevention programs and still end up having to respond to crimes that were not successfully prevented through retributivist policies, not only in the short run while we were waiting for the
preventive effects to show up but also in the long run when the preventive effects were supposed to appear. Compared with continuing to respond to crime in the traditional manner, the alternative may seem like a
risky gamble that society should not take.

Values at Stake in Retributivist and Preventive Crime Policies

This brings us to the second problem with Greenwood's analysis. One
can reasonably observe that, given the current and future cost of retributivist policies and their apparent ineffectiveness in controlling crime, taking a flyer on prevention policies seems eminently sensible. In short, it
would take only a reasonable prospect of success to decisively beat the

current alternative. And this is the real force behind Greenwood's analysis. He could be way off in his estimate of the effectiveness of prevention policies and still have those be superior to current policies in cost-effectiveness terms.

The difficulty with this position, however, is that this sort of utilitarian calculation is only one of the ways in which society might choose to look at the problem of crime and make normative judgments about what should best be done to deal with it. An alternative perspective would de-emphasize the importance of cost-effectiveness analysis and elevate concerns about what individuals and institutions in society could reasonably expect from one another; that is, it would emphasize ideas associated with justice and the proper ordering of institutions in the society over concerns about cost-effectiveness.

From this vantage point, one might argue that shifting from retributivist crime control policies to preventive measures might be cost effective, but it would not be particularly fair, or just, or supportive of a proper ordering of institutions in the society. Thus, in one conception, one could argue that all citizens owe one another a duty not to commit crimes. Failure to live up to this duty is punishable through the criminal justice system. It is the state's responsibility to administer this punishment. It is not the responsibility of the state to establish conditions that are favorable to individuals growing up not to commit crimes; that is the responsibility of families and of the individuals themselves. It is particularly not just for the state to take money from citizens who can order their lives and use it to create programs for those who cannot. For the state to take on this wider responsibility would be to breach some of the proper boundaries between private and public institutions and between individuals and the state. This would be bad for justice and for the future efficacy of private institutions.

Note that although I have constructed a kind of "justice" argument against shifting from retributivist to preventive policies, one can also construct a "justice" kind of argument supporting this strategic shift. The argument would be one that proceeded from a broad understanding of what children were entitled to and what the state could reasonably hold adults accountable for if they had not received as children the kind of care, investment, and supervision that they were reasonably entitled to. Thus, one would argue that children are owed a decent chance for development, including moral development, and that they cannot have this unless they receive some minimum standard of parenting, schooling, and recreational and job experience. These rights of children are strong enough to authorize and require the state to intervene in family affairs if there is evidence that children are not receiving what they are entitled to from their families. If, for some reason, the children do not receive what they are entitled to, and as a result, their development falters, their crimes must be seen at least partly as the society's crimes, since society has failed to secure their rights.

Obviously, I do not intend to resolve this complex question of justice here. I merely want to point out that it is not entirely obvious that the utilitarian framework of cost-effectiveness analysis captures what society does or should value in thinking through the question of whether it should shift to preventive programs. Such a decision could very well seem to sacrifice some values that society thinks are important in terms of the proper ordering of institutions; such as the idea that most people ought to voluntarily choose to obey the criminal law, that government should punish those who commit crimes, and that it is not obvious that government should, as a matter of justice, assume the responsibility for trying to prevent crime even if it could do so. This seems to violate an important principle of limited government that says that government should not go looking for problems to solve but should instead wait for them to appear and deal with them then. Any other principles would lead to a more entrepreneurial and opportunistic government than is desirable and would undermine the operations of other institutions by unsettling them with the prospect of either unexpected aid or unexpected attacks from the government.

One can reasonably point out (as Greenwood does) that we are paying a very big economic price for maintaining retributivist policies and that we might be missing an important opportunity to reduce crimes by investing in different kinds of governmental activities. But this argument can, in principle, be rebutted by a different kind of argument that makes a great deal of fairness, justice, and a proper ordering of institutions and takes a particular position with respect to these potentially important matters; namely that it is the citizens' duty not to commit crime, the government's duty to punish offenders, and it is wrong for government to be searching for opportunities to prevent problems that are really the responsibility of other institutions.

Political Support and Legitimacy

No doubt, many will think that I have gone on at much too great a length about the "justice" arguments for and against shifting toward preventive policies. I did so for one important reason: The values perceived as being at stake in a particular strategic choice are importantly linked to the all-important question of whether a particular policy can gain the political legitimacy and support it needs to be adopted. I wanted to discuss these values partly because I think they are real and important, but also because it is in these terms that much of the discussion of crime policy proceeds.

Many deplore the fact that the political discussion about crime is approached in terms of "retribution" and "justice." They believe that these are but thin veils masking the primitive, emotional desire for vengeance and that the influence of these primitive desires should be minimized in rational policymaking. They may also believe that the strong interest in retribution really reflects a misguided empirical belief that the reliable ways to control crime are through deterrence and incapacitation rather than prevention. Or, they may believe that principles of retribution and justice are important but they are either indeterminate or misunderstood by those who advocate longer sentences for repeat offenders as a fundamental crime-control policy. Such people long for a "more rational" discussion of crime control in which empirical facts about whether programs do or do not reduce crime have pride of place and where any conceptions of justice that are invoked include notions of mercy, redemption, tolerance, and social obligations to individuals as well as of individuals to the community.

I confess that I am personally attracted to the view that wants to privilege reason and empirical facts in policy debates about crime and that wants to temper demands for justice and accountability with mercy and a keen sense of the role of fortuity in human affairs in discussions of crime control policy. Yet, I am impressed by the extent to which the public as whole wants to talk about crime largely in terms of justice and retribution. I am particularly impressed by how uninterested the public is in any discussion of the costs of imprisonment and the crime-control effectiveness of such policies. It is clear that utilitarian discussions of cost-effectiveness simply do not resonate very powerfully in discussions of crime policy, even in these pragmatic and hard-strapped times; whereas the kind of justice arguments presented previously do.

It is partly for this reason that arguments about the potential economic savings of shifting to preventive policies in the domain of crime control fall on deaf ears; the audience is thinking that people shouldn't have committed the crimes in the first place. As a matter of justice, it doesn't matter that the offenders didn't get what the preventive policies were designed to supply, and that if they had gotten this, they wouldn't have committed the crime.

Moreover, this preference for principled (retributivist) rather than practical arguments about crime seems to be a fairly stable, well-developed position in the American body politic. The feelings about crime are vulnerable to political manipulation, but they are not entirely created by political manipulation. Arguably, in a democracy, such views deserve respect. In any case, as a practical matter, their settled existence makes it difficult to create political support and legitimacy for preventive approaches to crime.

Operational Capabilities

Proposals to shift from retributivist to preventive approaches to crime also face difficulties when we consider the required operational capabilities. The crucial issues here are: (1) how will clients be recruited and treated and (2) from what particular bureaucratic base will such initiatives be launched? The answer differs from one preventive approach to the other, but the discouraging news is that the most promising interventions also seem the most difficult to launch.

The easiest of Greenwood's preventive interventions to implement is the early delinquency programs. A suitable bureaucratic platform exists for this in the juvenile justice system. All that is needed is more resources for such programs and more confidence in using them. These are not small requirements, but they are easier than the other proposed prevention programs.

School-based programs face two difficulties. First, exactly what form they should take is not clear. Second, since schools are under enormous pressure to achieve their primary goal of educating children, they have been increasingly reluctant to take on additional tasks—even though it may be impossible for them to achieve their primary purpose without accepting these new responsibilities. In any case, schools have not shown themselves to be eager innovators or easy to influence in domains other than educational policy.

By far the most difficult to implement are those programs Greenwood estimates to be the most cost effective: early childhood and parent training interventions. In each case, the programs must solve difficult issues of targeting and intervening with targeted families.

With respect to early childhood programs, the favored targeting approach will probably be to provide universal services to young families in high-risk neighborhoods. This eliminates the problem of stigmatizing individual families, but it does contribute to the perception that family problems are confined to people who live in low-income neighborhoods—a perception that is likely to be even less appropriate in the future than it is now. There may also be a problem in persuading reluctant parents that they should accept the publicly financed (but not necessarily publicly provided) services. Despite this problem, it is unlikely that reluctant parents will be coerced to accept the services without evidence of abuse and neglect of their children. The combination of providing universal services to poor neighborhoods and the absence of state coercion will inevitably produce spotty coverage of the families that could use the services. Many will receive services who do not need them; and many who need them will not get them. Given the enormous potential of these programs, these targeting difficulties should be viewed as a minor problem, but they will be there. A greater problem is whether such programs should be based in public health or social service agencies. Neither is particularly well equipped now to take these programs on.

The parent training programs are presented as secondary rather than primary prevention programs; they are designed to wait until some signs of trouble appear rather than act preemptively before the trouble starts, and they make a relatively specific, narrow intervention into family life (though that work can be quite intensive). The principal difficulty with these programs is finding the cases to be treated. Early childhood programs can be targeted by visiting young women in poor neighborhoods, or maternity wards in hospitals. School-based programs can work from well-defined school populations. Early delinquency programs work through the institutions of the juvenile justice system. Parent training programs, designed to help parents of preschool children who are beginning to show signs of aggressive behavior do not have a natural case-finding mechanism. The kids are too old to be in hospitals as infants and too young to be in schools. The only way such families are likely to be identified is by parents volunteering that they are in trouble, or as a result of referrals from social service agencies dealing with troubled families, or families that have abuse and neglect complaints filed against them. Such systems may work well enough, but they will be far from perfect. There will inevitably be both over and under inclusion. And these programs, too, face uncertainty about bureaucratic sponsorship. Will they be housed in social service agencies? Or will they be operated as nonprofits under contract to social service agencies?

Conclusion

Greenwood's calculations have put the case for shifting away from current retributivist approaches to crime control forcefully before us. They force us to explain why his conclusion is not the right one (if it is not the right one).

The use of a strategic analysis that focuses attention on the public values at stake in a particular proposal, its capacity to gain legitimacy and support, and its operational ability helps us understand the difficulties of making this strategic shift in crime control policy and why the shift has not been made despite evidence that preventive intervention programs can work to reduce crime.

Viewed from this particular perspective, the central problems that these proposals face are: (1) that belief in their efficacy requires a substantial leap of faith in the efficacy of large-scale programs that have not really been tested in operation, on a large scale, over a long enough period of time to be sure that they will actually work; (2) that the argument for their value is cast in the utilitarian language of cost-effectiveness, which seems to have less resonance in the political debate than the language of retribution, justice, and the proper assignment of responsibilities to particular social institutions; and (3) that some of the most promising interventions lack operational specifications that detail how they would work to recruit clients and intervene in their lives and that identify bureaucratic hosts.

These problems, combined with the fact that in the short run public officials will still have to respond to crime while waiting for the prevention programs to take effect, make it very difficult for responsible public officials to decide to shift substantial resources to preventive interventions. There is just too great a risk that the funds will be spent, benefits will be produced in many other domains, but the promised crime control benefits will not materialize, and the officials will find themselves paying for both the retributivist system and the new preventive system that, in operation, revealed itself to be less a crime prevention program than a more general social welfare program.

Despite these difficulties, I think it is valuable to continue building the case for the early intervention prevention programs. That can be done by continuing to strengthen the arguments for their cost-effectiveness in controlling crime as Greenwood has done. But my bet is that, over the long run, the best argument for these programs will not be based centrally on their crime-prevention potential. My hunch is that the political support for early childhood and parenting programs can be built more effectively around themes that emphasize the control of child abuse and neglect and the strengthening of the family as a primary social institution. These are important ends in themselves. The programs that are being proposed as effective long-run crime prevention programs contribute directly and sooner to these other objectives. Why not make these the principal arguments for these valuable programs and treat the speculative (but likely) long-term impact on crime as an attractive additional reason to support these programs rather than the main reason?

The only reason for not making this argument that I can think of is that it would reduce the leverage that the argument for the greater cost-effectiveness of early intervention programs has on the public's current enthusiasm for retributivist policies. In essence, what is valuable about the argument for crime prevention is not only that it increases our enthusiasm for prevention programs, but also that it restrains our enthusiasm for retributivist policies. But it is not clear what would happen to our desires for both justice and crime-control effectiveness in the short run if we were now to shift resources from prisons to prevention programs. The worry, of course, is that many criminal offenders would go unpunished and that crimes would increase while we were waiting for the preventive programs to take effect. It is in this sense that these programs are not really competitors in the short run. In the short run, we will continue to have to rely on retributivist policies (though not necessarily our current ones). It is only in the long run that the programs become competitive. And since it is hard for us as a polity to think and act in the long run, it is important that we have some short run reasons for shifting to programs that will produce long-run crime control benefits.

Comment: Can We Afford to Prevent Violence? Can We Afford Not To?

JOHN B. REID AND J. MARK EDDY

As they have done many times in the past, Peter Greenwood and his colleagues (Greenwood, Rydell, and Chiesa 1996) at RAND have succeeded in opening up a brand new discussion of a set of issues that had been prematurely pushed to the side by public and political opinion. In several recent papers and in this current presentation, the RAND group reviewed the history of the Three Strikes legislation in California and conducted analyses of its probable costs and effectiveness (Greenwood, Rydell, Abrahamse, Caulkins, Chiesa, Model and Klein 1994). The researchers concluded that when the program is fully implemented, serious crime will be reduced by up to 25 percent, at a cost of about $16,000 per crime prevented.

Unfortunately, although the projected reduction is significant, even with Three Strikes crime will still be a serious problem. For example, among industrialized countries, the United States ranks first in homicides by males fifteen to twenty-four years of age with a rate that is over four times that of the runner-up. Of even more concern is that half of the arrests for violence involve persons age twenty-one years and younger (Cairns and Cairns 1994; Fingerhut and Kleinman 1990; World Health Organization 1992). In accord with others at this conference, Greenwood forecasted that the financial costs of Three Strikes would have devastating effects on other state programs, including the sorts of family and child services that have been shown to have some preventive impact on the development of antisocial and criminal life trajectories.

Aside from the prevention of violent crime, there are numerous good reasons for the investment of public funds in services for family and children. The future of any society is solidly in the hands of its young, and it is simple self-interest to make sure that they are healthy, well-fed, well-educated, and well-socialized in its values. It makes sense to help disadvantaged families to raise their children. It is also the case that failure to help families in need leads to large costs further down the line. For example, child neglect and physical abuse are associated not only with future serious crime but with more immediate increases in the utilization of pediatric emergency medical services and special education services. However, in California, as in many other states, public fear and concern about youth violence has shoved such usual concerns to the side.

The work of the RAND group has the potential of becoming a bench-mark in our development of a comprehensive policy to reduce violence in this country. Rather than evaluate early preventive interventions on al-truistic or philosophical grounds, their chapter deals directly with the is-sue of fiscal responsibility, conservative usage of resources, and long-term planning. In the current reality of dwindling resources for all aspects of state government, each expenditure proposed must be judged against others in terms of objective costs and benefits. Specifically, in this chapter, various preventive interventions were compared with adult in-carceration in terms of both their effectiveness in reducing serious crime and their financial costs.

The RAND group's strategy in this chapter is similar to the one used previously to estimate the costs and benefits of the Three Strikes program (Greenwood et al. 1994). The first step is to estimate, based on what back-ground characteristics have been shown to place a child at risk, the num-ber of children who are at risk for the development of serious criminal ac-tivity. The next step is to calculate the costs of offering the intervention to all the children/families in the designated risk group. The third step is to use published studies to estimate the average reduction in crimes that one can expect from the intervention. From these data, the researchers es-timated both the number of crimes that could be prevented, given full implementation, and the average cost per crime prevented. In general, their parameter estimates make sense, and when the available data were sparse or questionable, they used appropriately conservative values.

This paper represents a significant first step in developing a straight-forward methodology that links dollars-spent to crimes-prevented across the most reasonable currently available strategies for crime prevention. The value of such procedures cannot be overestimated in informing the allocation of tight resources among competing social needs. As is often the case with real breakthroughs, Greenwood and colleagues substantive findings are only the first installment. Critical gaps in our knowledge base are brought into focus, and a whole set of important methodological and conceptual issues are put on the table. The focus of the following comments will be on five key points pertinent to Greenwood's discus-sion.

Prevention Is a Long-Term Investment

The RAND group present strong empirical evidence that preventive in-terventions directed at parents and/or children during childhood and adolescence can significantly reduce subsequent rates of serious crime. They also present evidence to show that the very early interventions (i.e., prenatal care, home visits) had the potential to effect twice the reduction in serious crime compared with Three Strikes (i.e., 50 percent compared with 25 percent). However, the earlier the intervention, the longer the wait before its impact on crime rates is evident. In the case of large-scale early childhood and school-based interventions, the first noticeable impact would not occur until ten to twenty years after implementation. The impacts of large-scale parent training efforts during middle childhood would occur seven to ten years after implementation. In contrast, impacts of programs for delinquents take "only" three to four years. Of course, the big "immediate impact" winner is incarceration via Three Strikes, which is evident immediately. Thus, even though the Three Strikes solution is extremely costly, it could reduce violent crime by as much as 25 percent, and it is a highly visible quick-fix for a problem that is of central public and political importance.

Three Strikes is aimed at those criminals who are active now. However, it does little to anticipate the new and large cohort of four- to seven-year olds currently in the developmental pipeline (Bell and Bennett 1996). If we are to take a serious look at prevention as an additional and potentially powerful tool in a comprehensive program to reduce violent crime, it will take the type of commitment shown by automotive and aeronautical designers and pharmaceutical developers, who often make investments of time and resources over decades to produce consistent, effective, and ultimately profitable products. Frankly, it will take no less of an investment to build prevention programs that produce consistent and effective results. Given the relatively short tenure of most shapers of public policy and the demands for quick solutions by a nervous and angry citizenry, it will take considerable resolve as well as ingenious budgeting to maintain early prevention services as a high priority in the context of escalating corrections costs.

Early Preventive Interventions
Do Not Have to Break the Bank

Greenwood and colleagues concluded that early preventive interventions are extremely expensive for a number of reasons. First, they assumed that 25 percent of children (i.e., 150,000 per year) were at risk for abuse, neglect, and violence on the basis of a single risk factor: poverty. Second, they assumed a program cost of $25,000 per child over the first five years of life. This included home visits starting during the third trimester of pregnancy and continuing through the second year, as well as full-time day care and early childhood education during ages two to five years. Third, they compared the costs of the program with zero spending if the program had not been delivered. Although their assumptions are not unreasonable, several modifications that would significantly reduce the overall cost of the program may be in order.

In terms of the percentage of children at risk, using several other clear risk factors as selection criteria for the program would reduce program costs substantially. For example, although the risk for boys exhibiting violent crime is sizeable, the risk is almost nonexistent for girls. The overall price tag for the program could be halved by focusing only on mothers expecting boys (which, of course, would add the cost of a prenatal test to determine the sex of the child). Second, other known risk factors could be incorporated to reduce the number of boys considered "at risk," such as maternal youth, history of substance abuse, and marital status.

In terms of the program itself, the researcher's hypothetical program would be quite intensive relative to those that are currently in use. Each component has been shown to affect the relevant outcomes (i.e., abuse, neglect, delinquency) in at least one scientifically sound preventive intervention trial, and combining the components seems like a reasonable strategy. Despite the appeal of such a comprehensive program, powerful and long-lasting effects have been demonstrated with much simpler and less expensive programs.

For example, in an ongoing series of carefully assessed randomized intervention trials, David Olds of the University of Colorado Health Sciences Center trained public health nurses to provide support for risk samples of poor mothers, beginning in the third trimester and continuing through the second year of life. The mothers were not only given support and advice about child rearing but were encouraged not to smoke during pregnancy, to locate and use medical and social services, and to seek out social supports and job training. Follow-up assessments of the children participating in the intervention (the nurse-visited group) and of a randomized control group who did not participate indicate that the program had significant and dramatic effects on a number of powerful early antecedents of serious delinquency. Compared with the control mothers, the nurse-visited mothers had 75 percent fewer premature deliveries, and on average, their babies were 400 grams heavier at birth (Olds, Henderson, Tatelbaum, and Chamberlin 1986). Further, by the time the children were age four years, 19 percent of the control mothers compared with 4 percent of the nurse-visited mothers had abused or neglected their children, according to state registry records (Olds, Henderson, Chamberlin, and Tatelbaum 1986). At three and four years of age, the children of the nurse-visited mothers averaged four to five points higher on standardized intelligence tests. Finally, compared with the control group, the nurse-visited mothers had 42 percent less subsequent pregnancies, had 26 percent lower enrollment in AFDC, were significantly less likely to visit either a physician or a hospital emergency room for child injuries or ingestion, and were 84 percent more likely to participate in the work force (Olds, Henderson, Chamberlin, and Tatelbaum 1986; Olds, Henderson, and Kitzman 1994).

Finally, in terms of the base value against which to compare program costs, the researchers took a very conservative approach by comparing the cost of preventive services against zero spending (i.e., no services provided). However, without preventive services for "at-risk" families, intervention costs due to factors such as abuse, neglect, academic problems and their aftermath (e.g., health care needs, special education costs, foster care) will accrue for a significant proportion of the population, and most of these costs will be shouldered by the state and federal governments. Thus, a more accurate estimate of the costs of prevention would account for such anticipated costs and use these as the base value against which to compare. For example, Olds's prevention program averaged $3,173 (in 1980 U.S. dollars) per family over the first two and one-half years of the child's life. In contrast, by the time children in the control group had reached the age of four years, average governmental expenditures for their families were actually $3,313 *higher* than for nurse-visited families (Olds, Henderson, Phelps, Kitzman, and Hanks 1993). Thus, Olds's prevention program clearly paid for itself in a relatively "immediate" span of time due to a *decrease* in the total service costs that would have been incurred if the prevention program had not been delivered. Of even greater consequence, relative to control families, families in the nurse-visited group tended to be spared the occurrence of antecedents such as abuse, neglect, and academic deficiencies that lead to a greater, more expensive, cascading set of problems as children grow older.

Parent Training Is a Bargain

Among the most reasonable candidates for a prevention program, the RAND group concluded that parent training with young offenders (i.e., adolescents) was a relatively inexpensive and a highly effective preventive intervention for serious crime. Although their conclusion was well supported, several important qualifications are in order. First, it appears that the *earlier* parent training is applied, the more successful the outcome. For example, in an archival sample comprising all families who completed assessments before and after time-unlimited parent training in our clinic during the 1970s, 63 percent of children under six and one-half years of age versus 54 percent of children over six and one-half years of age evidenced "clinically significant" change following treatment (Dishion and Patterson 1992). Thus, not only is there a trend for child antisocial behaviors to be more difficult to change the longer the behaviors have been exhibited, but the behaviors of many children (up to 40 to 60 percent) may not change *significantly* despite time-unlimited family-focused treatment. When young offender adolescents are targeted by a program, the likelihood of many of the children having long histories of antisocial behaviors is high, and thus, treatment would be expected to be difficult.

Second, given the difficulty in treating adolescents exhibiting antisocial behavior problems, *more* time and resources will probably need to be expended than Greenwood et al. estimated. For example, in a study of chronically offending delinquents at our center (Bank, Marlowe, Reid, Patterson, and Weinrott 1991), participants in the parent training intervention received an average of twenty-two hours of face-to-face therapy and twenty-four hours of telephone contact. Further, approximately 50 percent of the families requested further treatment (i.e., "booster shot" therapy sessions) for an average of six hours of face-to-face contact in the year following treatment termination and an average of four hours the second year. Thus, although ten to twenty hours of treatment time might be adequate for children who are just beginning to demonstrate antisocial behavior problems, at least forty hours of time is probably a more realistic estimate for children who are farther along the antisocial behavior continuum. Doubling the original cost estimate would be more in the ballpark and would still put parent training as quite an economical "prevention" intervention option relative to the other alternatives.

Third, the likelihood of treatment dropout increases as child antisocial behavior problems become more chronic and severe (Kazdin and Mazurick 1994; Kazdin, Mazurick, and Bass 1993), and the prevalence of more problematic cases increases the older the target population. For example, 86 percent of the families who dropped out of treatment in the analyses by Dishion and Patterson (1992) had children in the "older" age group. When severe parenting problems coexist with child antisocial behavior, such as physical abuse, treatment dropout in nonmandated programs may be as high as 80 percent (Wolfe, Aragona, Kaufman, and Sandler 1980).

Treatment dropout occurs frequently enough that more accurate cost-benefit estimates would be obtained if cost estimates were adjusted by the number of anticipated dropouts. In the case of parent training programs, a number of "at-risk" families will refuse the program outright, and a sizeable number will drop out early in treatment. For example, in a randomized clinical trail of a multimodal elementary school-based prevention program we conducted (Reid, Eddy, Bank, and Fetrow 1994), only 57 percent of "at-risk" families attended four or more of the six group parent training sessions that were a central part of the program. To get this level of attendance, we offered group sessions on multiple days and multiple times and provided free child care. Despite these conveniences, a full 35 percent of families attended two or fewer group sessions. Given that such attendance difficulties are commonplace, if the initial size of a prevention program's infrastructure (e.g., space needs, number of staff members) is based not on the size of the population at risk, but on the percentage of that population who will most likely participate in the prevention program, initial program costs could be decreased significantly. As the program becomes established in the community and techniques are found for increasing participation, the program staff, space, and so on can be adjusted accordingly. The "build it and they will come" mentality might work for baseball diamonds in Iowa cornfields, but for various reasons probably won't work in bringing in a sizable proportion of parents of children with antisocial behavior problems.

Fourth, the older the child, the greater number of potential risk factors may be present, and the more complicated treatment becomes. Prior to entry into elementary school, most children spend most of their time in one or two key settings (i.e., home/neighborhood, day care). Parent training for young children and families focuses on working with the primary adult care givers in these settings and helping them learn how to encourage prosocial child behaviors and discourage antisocial child behaviors. As a child enters elementary school, a new setting is added. Parent training for elementary-school-aged children must now consider and work with adults in this new setting as well as home/neighborhood and day care settings. At some point during elementary school, yet another setting becomes prominent: peers. Once the peer setting includes a significant amount of contact outside the purview of responsible adults, parent training (as well as any intervention meant to change the trajectory of a child behaving in antisocial ways) becomes much more difficult.

The interaction between the deviant peer group, spending time in adult-unsupervised settings (behaviors our colleagues have dubbed "wandering"), and committing antisocial acts is succinctly summarized in Figure 3.2. (Stoolmiller and Eddy 1994). The figure is based on data from the Oregon Youth Study, a longitudinal study of 206 boys drawn from randomly selected "at-risk" schools. The boys and their families have been studied since the boys were in fourth grade in 1983–1984. As time in the deviant peer group and time spent wandering increases, the number of times an adolescent is detained by police increases dramatically. Since less than 5 percent of juvenile crimes are accounted for in detainment records (Dunford and Elliot 1982), this figure may actually "visually" underestimate the strength of the relationship between these three variables. We liken the conical picture these variables create to the volcanoes that pepper the landscape in our home, the Pacific Northwest. Like volcanoes, juvenile crime is something one does not want to be near when it explodes.

Despite the problems with treating child antisocial behavior problems via parent training as children get older, there is evidence that parent training can be effective even with chronically offending delinquents. For example, in the Bank et al. (1991) study, families with delinquents were randomly assigned to parent training or to "services as usual" via the juvenile court and community services. At one year following the termina-

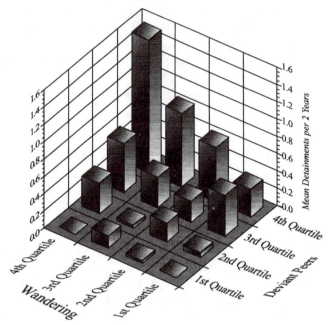

FIGURE 3.2   The Relationship Between Deviant Peer Association, Wandering, and Detainment by Police of At-Risk Boys Across Ages 10 to 16 Years

tion of treatment, adolescents in the parent training group showed greater reductions in juvenile court records of serious crimes than adolescents in the community services group. Further, by three years following treatment termination, on average, adolescents assigned to the parent training condition had cost state government 53 percent less in incarceration costs than those assigned to community services (see Figure 3.3). Even with such successes, Bank et al. (1991) conclude: "It is . . . clear the more powerful or intensive intervention work in this area should focus on intervention strategies beginning earlier in the delinquency process. Without question, prevention efforts that begin early will be more effective, in terms of both cost and desirable outcomes, for these high-risk children and their families."

Programs That Keep Adolescents in School Are Powerful Tools for the Prevention of Serious Crime

Data presented by Greenwood and colleagues indicate that incentive programs designed to keep adolescents in school are not only feasible, but they are effective preventive interventions for crime. Relative to the

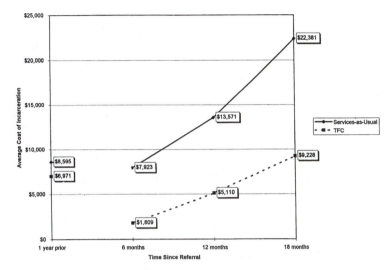

FIGURE 3.3   Average Cumulative Cost of Incarceration (in 1980 U.S. Dollars) for Juvenile Offenders Randomly Assigned to the Parent Training and Services-as-Usual Conditions

amount of crime prevented, the programs are inexpensive. Such programs target at least two powerful antecedents of adolescent crime. First the opportunity for daily and unsupervised association among at risk adolescents (see Figure 3.2) is reduced simply by having them in the classroom each day. Second, opportunities for the continued accumulation of social and work skills are increased. An additional advantage is that youngsters who finish school are more likely to be employed and to get better-paying jobs than those who do not. Overall, such incentive programs should become a universal component of integrated attempts to prevent crime. They do not require expensive professional skills for implementation, their preventive effects on crime are reasonably fast, and they should increase the odds that youngsters will make positive contributions to their communities.

Programs That Bring Delinquent Youth Together for Treatment May Actually Result in Increases in Juvenile Crime

One of the prevention programs proposed by Greenwood et al. is day treatment programs for young adolescent delinquents. Such programs usually pool together children who are exhibiting varying levels of anti-social behaviors from all areas of a community. Although such programs are appealing in terms of cost (i.e., overall, it seems less expensive to treat children in groups rather than individually), day treatment programs and other types of group treatments may actually serve to increase a child's antisocial behaviors, rather than decrease them. As noted previously, deviant peer association is a strong predictor of child antisocial behavior, particularly when peers congregate in adult-unsupervised settings. Since day treatment programs and outpatient groups do not operate twenty-four hours a day, and since by definition, such programs increase deviant peer association, what happens at the end of a treatment day when the adults go home and the adolescents go out to play might not be quite what the program designers envisioned.

Unfortunately, researchers at our center learned this lesson the hard way. For example, in a recent study of adolescents "at risk" for substance use/abuse and other problem behaviors, Dishion and Andrews (1995) contrasted the effectiveness of a group parent training intervention, a peer-group only intervention, and a combined parent training/peer-group intervention. After treatment, adolescents who received the peer-group only intervention used *more* tobacco and were rated by teachers as having *more* behavior problems than children who received no intervention. This phenomenon of increasing problem behaviors due to peer-group only interventions has been found in other types of treatment programs as well (e.g., school dropout prevention [Catterall 1987]).

An alternative to programs that use the contemporary "aggregate and conquer" strategy for child antisocial behavior problems is to use the age-old "divide and conquer" strategy. At our center, Chamberlain and her colleagues have developed a program called Treatment Foster Care (TFC) that places one delinquent youth with two specially trained foster parents for four to twelve months (Chamberlain 1994). During treatment, both the adolescent and his or her biological/step/adoptive parents receive ongoing psychological interventions. A case manager supervises the entire intervention program. In an ongoing study that contrasts juvenile offenders randomly placed in either TFC or in a services-as-usual group-care program (Chamberlain and Frima n.d.), by twelve months after initial referral, adolescents placed in TFC had cost the state approximately 70 percent of their one year prereferral incarceration costs, but group-care participants had racked up costs that exceeded 150 percent of their one year prereferral costs (see Figures 3.4 and 3.5). Neither program managed to terminate the criminal activities of all the adolescents who participated, but TFC had a much greater *suppression* effect than standard group care. By 18 months, adolescents placed in TFC had cost state government an average 143 percent less in incarceration costs than those assigned to group care. Further (not shown in Figure 3.4), two years after program termination, police detainment rates for adolescents in TFC were 50 percent less

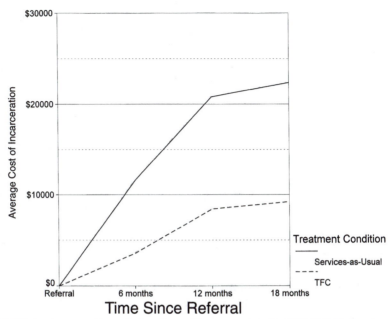

FIGURE 3.4   Average Cumulative Cost of Incarceration (in 1990 U.S. Dollars)
for Juvenile Offenders Randomly Assigned to the Treatment Foster Care and
Services-as-Usual Conditions

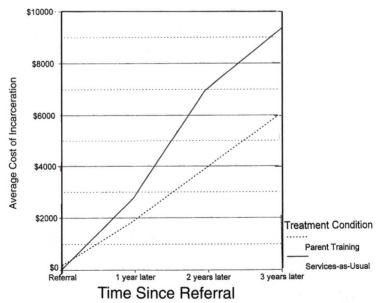

FIGURE 3.5   Average Cumulative Cost of Incarceration (in 1990 U.S. Dollars)
for Juvenile Offenders Randomly Assigned to the Parent Training and Services-
as-Usual Conditions

than those in group care. Interestingly, the current total cost of six months of TFC per adolescent is about the same as the cost of one year of Greenwood and colleagues' hypothetical day treatment and home monitoring program: $10,808. This value includes the additional cost of training foster parents in behavioral management techniques.

Conclusion

Peter Greenwood and colleagues' work in "Diverting Children from a Life of Crime: Measuring Costs and Benefits" offers a straightforward, logical way to plan crime policy in a fiscally responsible way. Their analysis compares the costs and benefits of various approaches to crime prevention and intervention, and in the process, it points out a variety of important factors that policymakers need to consider as they budget for the future. Five key points that the RAND group's chapter highlighted for us are:

1. Prevention is a long-term investment.
2. Early preventive interventions do not have to break the bank.
3. Parent training is a bargain, especially if applied to families with children who are just beginning to display antisocial behaviors.
4. Providing incentives for high school graduation has quick and multiple payoffs.
5. Programs that bring delinquent youth together for treatment may actually result in increases in juvenile crime; treating delinquent youth *separately* appears to be a more effective long-term strategy.

In contrast to incarceration, the early childhood interventions hold a great deal of promise for a society that wants to *reduce* violence because they focus on many of the factors that are ultimately related to violence. By addressing such factors at the beginning of a process that may lead to criminal behavior (as well as other negative individual and societal outcomes), not only may problems in the current generation be averted, but problems in later generations as well.

References

Bank, L., J.H. Marlowe, J.B. Reid, G.R. Patterson, and M.R. Weinrott. 1991. A comparative evaluation of parent-training interventions for families of chronic delinquents. *Journal of Abnormal Child Psychology* 19:15–33.

Bell, G.B., and W.J. Bennett, eds. 1996. *The state of violent crime in America: First report of the Council on Crime in America.* New Citizenship Project publication.

Cairns, R.B., and B.D. Cairns. 1994. *Lifelines and risks: Pathways of youth in our times.*

Catterall, J.S. 1987. An intensive group counseling dropout prevention intervention: Some cautions on isolating at-risk adolescents within high schools. *American Education Research Journal* 24:521–540.

Chamberlain, P. 1994. *Family connections: A treatment foster care model for adolescents with delinquency.*

Chamberlain, P., and P.C. Friman. n.d. "Residential programs for antisocial children and adolescents." In *Handbook of Antisocial Behavior*, edited by D. M. Stoff, J. Breiling, and J. D. Maser. In press.

Dishion, T.J., and D.W. Andrews. 1995. Prevention of escalation in problem behaviors with high-risk adolescents: Immediate and 1-year outcome. *Journal of Consulting and Clinical Psychology* 63:538–548.

Dishion, T.J., and G.R. Patterson. 1992. Age effects in parent training outcome. *Behavior Therapy* 23:719–729.

Dunford, F.W., and D.S. Elliot. 1982. *Identifying career offenders with self-report data.* National Institute of Mental Health publication, Grant No. MH27552.

Fingerhut, L.A., and J.C. Kleinman. 1990. International and interstate comparisons of homicides among young males. *Journal of the American Medical Association* 263: 3292–3295.

Greenwood, Peter W. 1995. "The cost-effectiveness of early intervention as a strategy for reducing violent crime." Paper presented to the University of California Policy Seminar Crime Project.

Greenwood, Peter W., C. Peter Rydell, Allan F. Abrahamse, Jonathan P. Caulkins, James Chiesa, Karyn E. Model, and Stephen P. Klein. 1994. *Three strikes and you're out: Estimated benefits and costs of California's new mandatory sentencing law.* RAND publication, MR–509-RC.

Greenwood, Peter W., C. Peter Rydell, and James Chiesa. 1996. Diverting Children from a Life of Crime. RAND publication, Santa Monica, CA.

Kazdin, A.E., and J.L. Mazurick. 1994. Dropping out of child psychotherapy: Distinguishing early and late dropouts over the course of treatment. *Journal of Consulting and Clinical Psychology* 62:1069–1074.

Kazdin, A.E., J.L. Mazurick, and D. Bass. 1993. Risk for attrition in treatment of antisocial children and families. *Journal of Clinical Child Psychology* 22:2–16.

Olds, David L., Charles R. Henderson, Robert Chamberlin, and Robert Tatelbaum. 1986. Preventing child abuse and neglect: A randomized trial of nurse home visitation. *Pediatrics* 78:65–78.

Olds, David L., Charles R. Henderson, and H. Kitzman. 1994. Does prenatal and infancy nurse home visitation have enduring effects on qualities of parental caregiving and child health at 25 to 50 months of life? *Pediatrics* 93:89–98.

Olds, David L., Charles R. Henderson, C. Phelps, H. Kitzman, and C. Hanks. 1993. Effects of prenatal and infancy nurse home visitation on government spending. *Medical Care* 3:1–20.

Olds, David L., Charles R. Henderson, Robert Tatelbaum, and Robert Chamberlin. 1986. Improving the delivery of prenatal care and outcomes of pregnancy: A randomized trial of nurse home visitation. *Pediatrics* 77:16–28.

Patterson, G.R., T. J. Dishion, and P. Chamberlain. 1993. "Outcomes and methodological issues relating to treatment of antisocial children." In *Handbook of Effective Psychotherapy*, edited by T. R. Giles, 43–88.

Reid, J.B., J.M. Eddy, L. Bank, and R. Fetrow. 1994. "Some preliminary findings from a universal prevention program for Conduct Disorder." Paper presented at the Fourth National Institute of Mental Health National Conference on Prevention Research.

Stoolmiller, M., and J.M. Eddy. November 1994. "The role of unsupervised wandering and delinquent peers in male adolescent delinquent behavior." Paper presented at the Fourth National Institute of Mental Health National Conference on Prevention Research.

Wolfe, D.A., J. Aragona, K. Kaufman, and J. Sandler. 1980. The importance of adjudication in the treatment of child abusers: Some preliminary findings. *Child Abuse and Neglect* 4:127–135.

World Health Organization. 1992. *Annual report on homicide.*

4

Alternative Sanctions

Diverting Nonviolent Prisoners to Intermediate Sanctions: The Impact on Prison Admissions and Corrections Costs

JOAN PETERSILIA

Californians recently passed the toughest "Three Strikes and You're Out" sentencing law in the nation, mandating that persons found guilty of a third felony—whether minor or serious—be imprisoned for twenty-five years to life following prior conviction for two serious felonies. This measure, along with the currently proposed "One Strike" mandatory sentencing law for sexual offenders signals that Californians are in a particularly get tough mood with criminals.

Against this political backdrop, one might reasonably ask: Why bother with a study of *community-based* intermediate sanctions, which often equates in the public's mind with being "soft on crime?" Community-based sanctions—the array of programs that allow the offender to serve his or her criminal sentence while remaining in the community—would seem hopelessly out of touch with the public and political mood. In fact, some would argue that it is the widespread use of probation and parole itself that is to blame for high crime rates. But understanding more about community corrections—its programs, capacity, and potential—is absolutely necessary to the state's ability to control crime through imprisonment, because community corrections and prisons are intricately linked. Policies on probation revocation for instance dramatically affect prison intake. Similarly, crowded prisons can cause a backup in jail populations, which in turn affects probation sentencing practices. Parole policies can drive up or down the number of violators being returned as a result of technical violations. The level of services and treatment provided to parolees and probationers certainly affects their recidivism and return to prison rates. As the prison population expands either as a result of a three-strikes initiative or other mandatory sentencing schemes, persons who are not serving mandatory amounts of time can be released in order to make room for incoming mandated cases.

Government experts and academic scholars agree that the state will be unable to pay for the incarceration of everyone sentenced to prison in years to come, unless something drastic is done. Even before the passage of the Jones Three Strikes Law, California was having to make painful cuts in needed social programs to fund an expanding prison budget. Mandatory sentences, a rise in violent crime, and tough-on-crime judicial attitudes have all combined to push prison populations to the highest level ever—nearly 134,000 adult inmates by January 1995.

At an average annual cost of nearly $22,000 per inmate, the California Department of Corrections budget was over $2.6 billion in 1994, an increase of nearly 10 percent over the previous year. In just the last decade, spending for corrections grew from about 3 percent of total state spending to 7 percent. And, with the passage of Three Strikes, corrections is predicted to be 18 percent of total state budget by the year 2000! The Legislative Analyst's Office estimates that by the year 2000, the California prison population will reach 211,000 adults, and the General Fund costs for the CDC would be about $5 billion—an increase of nearly 60 percent in five years (Legislative Analyst's Office 1995). RAND analysts agree, predicting that implementing the Three Strikes Law in California will cost the state about $5.5 billion per year, which is an additional 100 to 150 percent of what the state currently spends (Greenwood et al. 1994).

The increased dollars must come from somewhere, and the most logical target is the states' higher education budget. Given that spending for K–12 education is locked into the state constitution and mandated spending for health and welfare continues to increase, little is left for all other state services, such as higher education, environmental protection, libraries, and parks—unless taxes are increased, an unlikely event. So, funding the state prisons has created serious conflicts among budget priorities, and implementing Three Strikes is predicted to dramatically change education in California—a social good that many believe is tied to long-term reductions in crime.

And if judges continue to sentence offenders to prison and the state doesn't find the money to expand prisons, the courts will most certainly intervene and judge the system to be in violation of the Eighth Amendment, which protects inmates against confinement in crowded facilities (i.e., ones in which each inmate has less than sixty square feet of floor space). James Gomez, director of the California Department of Corrections has raised this prospect—a realistic one, most believe—that if more criminals are jammed into the prisons by increasingly tough sentences, the state court will eventually rule, as it has in thirteen other states, that prisoners must be released because of overcrowding. As the Little Hoover Commission recently concluded: "The result could be a rushed, wholesale release of offenders, rather than a reasoned, judicious choice arrived at through careful analysis of who belongs in prison and who can safely be handled in the community" (1994, 9).

In sum, California is at a major crossroads in corrections policy. We must either continue to make cuts in vital education and social programs to fund expanded prison space, raise taxes to provide more funds for both, or take a hard look at who is currently in prison and decide whether some of them could be punished in less expensive but tough, community-based alternatives. Other states are using intermediate sanctions, which are sentences that exist somewhere between incarceration and probation on the continuum of criminal penalties. Intermediate sanctions include intensive community supervision, home confinement, electronic monitoring, and boot camps. In some instances, intermediate punishments have helped solve prison crowding problems, and one has to question whether such options would prove helpful here.

A recent poll in California found that three-fourths of Californians feel that the state should find ways of punishing offenders that are less expensive than prison (Irwin and Austin 1994). The public doesn't necessarily want prison, they want public safety. But, if we decide that some prison-bound offenders could be handled in the community, we then face the difficult task of identifying appropriate programs, assessing their costs and benefits, and determining how to implement such programs in California's beleaguered probation and parole system.

To help provide information on what will clearly be a central debate in California during the coming years, the author sought to answer the following questions:

1. Are there persons who are currently being sentenced to prison who could be safely handled in the community? Or have all prison-bound offenders committed crimes that are so serious that the public would not stand for them being placed in the community (retribution), or have such a high probability of reoffending that we can't allow them to be placed in the communities (incapacitation)?
2. If there are prisoners who could be candidates for intermediate sanctions, what kinds of programs would need to be developed to control and supervise their behavior? At what cost? Are such programs punitive enough?
3. What would be the net cost savings of investing in quality intermediate sanctions over what we currently spend to house such offenders in prison?

These questions cannot be fully answered at this time due to the un-availability of necessary data. Cutbacks in the research and data gathering activities of the California Department of Corrections means that only minimal background data is now collected on each incoming inmate (e.g., age, race, conviction crime, length of term to be served). More detailed information, such as an inmates' substance abuse history, juvenile criminal record, or prior participation in treatment programs is no longer collected, making detailed analysis of the costs and benefits of different punishment options impossible. As such, this is but a preliminary attempt to address these issues using existing information.

The problem of how to manage and pay for the state's growing prison population is not new to California, and this is not the first attempt to study it. In 1990, Governor George Deukmejian appointed the Blue Ribbon Commission on Inmate Population Management, a bipartisan panel whose charter was to assess the prison situation and make recommendations on better managing the overcrowded system. That commission, along with the four other recent studies of the problem have all highlighted the same problem and made similar recommendations (California Blue Ribbon Commission 1990; Little Hoover Commission 1994; Petersilia 1993; Zimring and Hawkins 1992; Davies 1993). It has been repeatedly noted that California relies too heavily on prison sentencing and lacks so-called intermediate sanctions that other states have developed. If a more credible system of community-based punishments existed in California, then lower-risk prisoners could be released to them, thus reserving expensive prison beds for the more violent. As the Little Hoover Commission recently concluded: "Alternatives that punish creatively need to be developed and implemented so that offenders who are not a safety risk to the public do not take up needed beds in state prison" (1994, 62).

In the words of the Blue Ribbon Commission, California's sentencing system is "hopelessly out of balance" between prison and community-based sanctions. But if we are to develop a more "balanced" system, we need to first think through the details concerning who might be released, what intermediate sanctions would need to be developed, and how the programs would be paid for.

Who Is in California Prisons?

Are Inmates so Serious That
They Cannot Be Handled Safely in the Community?

If one wishes to consider alternative sentencing strategies, the first question to answer is: How serious are those now going to prison, or alternatively, are there persons who are now being incarcerated who could safely be handled in the community? On the surface, this question seems straightforward. To answer it, however, is exceedingly complex.

Prisons currently serve two major purposes, retribution and incapacitation. In practical terms, this means that we wish to imprison persons whose: (1) crimes are so serious that the public would not allow persons convicted of them to be placed in the community (just deserts or retribution) or (2) risk of recidivism is so high that we can't allow them to return to their communities for fear of the crimes they are predicted to commit (incapacitation).

But although these general notions are well understood, identifying persons who meet such criteria is difficult. For instance, which crimes are "serious" enough to deserve imprisonment, and how "high" a recidivism risk are we willing to take, since any nonincarceration sentence involves some public safety risk? Reasonable persons will disagree on the thresholds, but those questions provide a practical starting point to understanding who is now going to prison.

There has been much debate recently about the relative seriousness of the U.S. prison population. According to Lawrence Greenfeld (1992) of the U.S. Bureau of Justice Statistics, 94 percent of all state prisoners have either been convicted of a violent crime or been previously sentenced to probation or incarceration as a juvenile or adult. Piehl and DiIulio (1995, 22) argue that if one accepts that fact, along with the knowledge that most prisoners have plea bargained away crimes they have committed, and committed dozens of undetected crimes before their incarceration, the myth that prisoners are "petty, first time, or mere drug offenders with few prior arrests" is not only wrong but "downright dangerous."

But Michael Tonry says that using the numbers this way to portray the prison population as particularly violent and dangerous is patently false. He finds that "well over half of state prisoners have been convicted of crimes not involving violence, and two-fifths had never been sentenced to jail or prison." (1995, 25). Moreover, he cites studies showing that nationally about a third of prisoners are committed to prison not for new crimes but rather for violations of the technical conditions of their probation or parole.

Whether prison populations comprise mostly dangerous repeat offenders or minor criminals who have violated technical conditions is critical to the debate over alternative sentencing. Public opinion polls have shown that Americans are quite receptive to alternative sentencing for property and other minor offenders and very much against it for violent recidivists (Doble 1987).

This debate about "who is in prison" is similar to so many others being waged in criminal justice: It just depends on what sample you choose to analyze and how the data is aggregated. The prison population will look less serious if you use an incoming (admissions) sample rather than an in-prison cohort, since more serious offenders tend to receive longer sentences (and therefore to accumulate in prison). For instance, persons convicted of murder were less than 3 percent of those admitted to California prisons in 1992, but they were about 10 percent of all those in prison on June 30 of that year. Similarly, violent offenders were about 25 percent of those admitted to prison in 1992 but 42 percent of the in-prison population on June 30 of that year.

Prisoners will also look less serious if one only considers their adult and not juvenile criminal histories, or chooses to report as repeaters only those who have been previously imprisoned (e.g., leaving out those who have served probation or jail terms). And descriptions of prison admission cohorts often include only offenders being admitted by the courts for a new criminal convictions, ignoring inmates returned to prison for technical parole or probation violations. But since technical violators are often a third to a half of all incoming inmates and will generally be admitted for less serious crimes than the new convictees, eliminating them from the calculation is misleading and makes incoming prisoner cohorts appear more serious.

For these and other reasons then, answering the question "Who goes to prison?" is not straightforward, and the data is often selectively analyzed and presented depending on the purpose to be served. Liberals tend to report data portraying the prison population as less serious, thereby eliciting support for alternatives; conservatives portray most prisoners as violent, repeat offenders, thereby supporting greater imprisonment.

For our purposes, we want to answer as comprehensively and objectively as possible the question: Who goes to prison in California? It makes most sense therefore to describe a prison admissions cohort (not an in-prison cohort), include all persons admitted to prison (including technical violators), and describe the criminal backgrounds in as much detail as possible.

Another subtle but important point deserves mention. Researchers have often singled out "parole violators" who are returned to prison by parole boards rather than the courts as a group who is less serious and a prime target for prison diversion. Several scholars have noted that parole violators account for nearly half of all persons admitted to California prisons each year, a much higher figure than exists anywhere else in the nation. Further, they argue, this particularly high revocation rate is one of the prime reasons for the growth in prison populations and that this group is a prime target for prison diversion due to their troublesome but not necessarily criminal conduct (California Blue Ribbon Commission 1990; Petersilia 1993; Davies 1993; Zimring and Hawkins 1992; Messinger et al. 1988).

But the California Department of Corrections has countered by saying that although this group may technically be "parole violators," they are *not* being returned to prison for *technical violations* but rather are being returned as a result of new *criminal* conduct. They say that although it is true some parole violators are returned through "administrative" channels, it is erroneous to assume that these offenders are simply violating their technical probation or parole conditions. The parole board is responsible for returning to prison persons who have violated their "conditions of parole," including *not violating any laws*. Thus, when offenders are returned by the parole board, rather than the courts, it does not necessarily mean that they have not committed new, sometimes serious, crimes. The parole board may simply choose to administratively revoke the person, rather than go through the time and expense of prosecuting a new offense. The parole board revokes on the basis of an administrative review and a "preponderance of evidence" finding (a weaker standard than the "beyond a reasonable doubt" standard needed to convict on a criminal offense). To get an accurate picture of the seriousness of this group, we must go further in detail than simply learning whether they are "administrative" or "new court" commitments to identify those who, although revoked by parole boards, have committed new criminal offenses.

The Crime Characteristics of Persons
Admitted to California Prisons

Using data supplied by the California Department of Corrections (Data Analysis Unit, 1991) and the Legislative Analyst's Office (Legislative Analyst's Office 1994), Table 4.1, "Prisoners Admitted to California Prisons, 1991" was compiled (1991 is the most recent year for which such data is readily available). Table 4.1 also shows the percent of prison population by commitment offense, average (median) prison months served by offense,[1] and the average corrections cost incurred in carrying out each prison sentence.

Table 4.1 shows that in 1991, there were 84,197 adults admitted to the California Department of Corrections (CDC). Forty-five percent were "Felons, New Court Admissions," meaning they were sentenced by the court for a criminal conviction, whereas the remainder were "Parole Violators," having either been sentenced by the courts to additional terms of imprisonment (Parole Violators with a New Term, 19 percent) or being returned to prison by the Board of Prison Terms (i.e., the parole board) for having violated one or more conditions of parole (Parole Violators Returned to Prison, 36 percent). These two "parole violator" categories equal 55 percent, and this is the figure frequently cited to argue that more than half of all persons admitted to California prisons have not been con-

TABLE 4.1   Persons Admitted to California Prisons, 1991, by Commitment Offense, Average Prison Term Served, and Average Cost per Prison Sentence Served

	No. of Persons	% of Total Admissions	Avg. Months Served[a]	Avg. Cost per Prison Sentence[b]
Felons, New Court Admissions	38,240	45.41%		
Violent offenses	10,616	12.61%	19.0	
Homicide	1,840	2.19%	33.2	$60,357
Robbery	3,701	4.40%	17.7	$32,178
Assault	2,881	3.42%	16.2	$29,451
Sex crimes	1,936	2.30%	33.2	$60,357
Kidnap	258	0.31%	34.6	$62,902
Property offenses	10,537	12.51%	11.0	
Burglary, 1st	2,547	3.02%	20.5	$37,269
Burglary, 2nd	2,154	2.56%	9.9	$17,998
Grand theft	1,174	1.39%	10.0	$18,180
Petty theft w/pri.	1,520	1.81%	8.8	$15,998
Rec. stolen prop.	1,003	1.19%	8.9	$16,180
Auto theft	1,384	1.64%	11.5	$20,907
Forgery, fraud	755	0.90%	9.9	$17,998
Drug offenses	12,459	14.80%	11.8	
Possession	3,943	4.68%	7.7	$13,998
Poss. for sale	4,173	4.96%	12.9	$23,452
Drug sale	3,052	3.62%	17.4	$31,633
Drug mfg.	376	0.45%	21.5	$39,087
Marijuana	915	1.09%	10.4	$18,907
Other offenses	4,628	5.50%	8.9	
Driv. under infl. (DUI)	2,911	3.46%	8.3	$15,089
Weapons poss.	604	0.72%	10.6	$19,270
Escape	68	0.08%	8.4	$15,271
Arson	138	0.16%	13.6	$24,724
Misc.	907	1.08%	9.1	$16,543
Parole Violators with New Term (PV-WNT)[c]	16,010	19.01%		
Violent offenses	2,705	3.21%		
Homicide	136	0.16%	33.2	$60,357
Robbery	1,553	1.84%	17.7	$32,178
Assault	751	0.89%	16.2	$29,451
Sex crimes	233	0.28%	33.2	$60,357
Kidnap	32	0.04%	34.6	$62,902
Property offenses	7,156	8.50%	11.0	
Burglary, 1st	1,106	1.31%	20.5	$37,269
Burglary, 2nd	1,776	2.11%	9.9	$17,998

(*continues*)

TABLE 4.1 (*continued*)

	No. of Persons	% of Total Admissions	Avg. Months Served[a]	Avg. Cost per Prison Sentence[b]
Parole Violators with New Term				
(PV-WNT)[c]	16,010	19.01%		
Grand theft	516	0.,61%	10.0	$18,180
Petty theft w/pri.	1,905	2.26%	8.8	$15,998
Rec. stolen prop.	701	0.83%	8.9	$16,180
Auto theft	853	1.01%	11.5	$20,907
Forgery, fraud	299	0.36%	9.9	$17,998
Drug offenses	4,627	5.49%	11.8	
Possession	2,205	2.62%	7.7	$13,998
Poss. for sale	1,036	1.23%	12.9	$23,452
Sale	890	1.06%	17.4	$31,633
Mfg.	172	0.20%	21.5	$39,087
Other offenses	1,522	1.81%	8.9	
Driving under inf. (DUI)	479	0.57%	8.3	$15,089
Weapons	672	0.80%	10.6	$19,270
Escape	34	0.04%	8.4	$15,271
Arson	19	0.02%	13.6	$24,724
Other	318	0.38%	9.1	$16,543
Parole Violators Returned to Prison				
(PV-RTP)[d]	29,944	35.56%		
Admin., noncriminal (technical violations)	3,116	3.70%	4.0	$7,272
Admin., criminal	26,828	31.86%	7.0	
Type 1	8,382	9.95%	4.0	
Drug use	3,035	3.60%	4.0	$7,272
Drug poss.	2,427	2.88%	5.0	$9,090
Misc., minor	2,920	3.47%	5.0	$9,090
Type 2	12,010	14.26%	8.0	
Sex offenses	535	0.64%	6.0	$10,908
Assault	1,431	1.70%	8.0	$14,544
Burglary	880	1.05%	9.0	$16,362
Theft	3,714	4.41%	8.0	$14,544
Drug sales	1,449	1.72%	10.0	$18,180
Weapons	380	0.45%	8.0	$14,544
Driving viol.	1,334	1.58%	8.0	$14,544
Misc. nonviolent	2,287	2.72%	6.0	$10,908
Type 3	6,436	7.65%	12.0	
Homicide	119	0.14%	12.0	$21,816
Robbery	1,168	1.39%	12.0	$21,816
Rape/assault	353	0.42%	12.0	$21,816

(*continues*)

TABLE 4.1 (*continued*)

	No. of Persons	% of Total Admissions	Avg. Months Served[a]	Avg. Cost per Prison Sentence[b]
Parole Violators Returned to Prison				
(PV-RTP)[d]	29,944	35.56%		
Battery	2,394	2.84%	12.0	$21,816
Burglary	704	0.84%	10.0	$18,180
Drug-major	253	0.30%	10.0	$18,180
Weapons	1,093	1.30%	12.0	$21,816
Driving viol.	171	0.21%	10.0	$18,180
Misc.	181	0.21%	12.0	$21,816
Total Admissions	84,197		11.83	$21,502[e]

Note: It is important to note that the median time served in CDC institutions does not count time served in local jail prior to CDC transfer. It is calculated as the months served prior to first release to parole for first time and parole violators returned with a new term by the courts and paroled for the first time following the new offense. It is also true that the median time served is less than the mean time served by about 15 percent.

[a]The average months reported is the median. This column reflects the actual time in CDC custody and is determined by subtracting prior jail time and CDC work credits. The admissions and time served data in this table is drawn from *California Prisoners and Parolees 1991*, 1993.

[b]The annual operational cost per sentence of California prisons is estimated to be $21,816, which is taken from *Crime State Rankings 1994*, 1994.

[c]Parole Violator with a New Term (PV-WNT) is a parolee who has received a court sentence for a new crime and been returned to prison.

[d]Parole Violator Returned to Prison (PV-RTP) is a parolee who has violated the conditions of parole and been ordered by the Board of Prison Terms (i.e., parole board) to return to prison. Persons who were revoked by the parole board in 1991 but "continued on parole" (8,700 persons) were not included in this table nor were those with missing offense data (2,690 persons).

[e]This is the average of the total operational CDC costs incurred in carrying out the prison portion of the court-imposed sentence.

victed of new crimes but rather are returned for violating the technical conditions of their probation or parole, for example, not reporting to parole officers at specified intervals.

Table 4.1 also provides the more detailed information concerning violators who are returned by the parole board (see Parole Violators Returned to Prison [PV-RTP]). The table supports what CDC has been saying: that few parole violators are being returned for strictly technical violations. In Table 4.1, true technical violators are contained in the category "Admin., noncriminal." This group equals 3,116 offenders or 4 per-

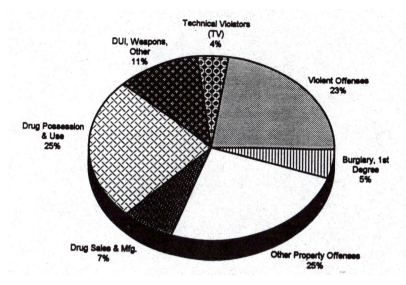

FIGURE 4.1   California Prison Admissions by Crime Type, 1991

cent of all admissions. These offenders serve, on average about 4 months in prison at a cost of about $7200 per inmate. *The bottom line is that true technical violators do not currently represent a large portion of incoming inmates and they do not serve very long prison terms. Hence, diverting them to intermediate sanctions may be entirely justified but will have little effect on prison crowding or corrections costs.*

For our purpose, it is less important how they got to prison (BPT or new court admission) than what their conviction crime was. It is their underlying crime that is related to the incapacitative and retributive benefits of prison, and hence the public's willingness to consider alternative sentencing. Figure 4.1 shows prison admissions, by crime type (new court commitments and the two categories of parole violators combined).

Simulating the Cost Savings of Eliminating Prison Sentences for Selected Nonviolent Offenses

Using the information in Table 4.1, we are able to estimate the impact of a number of alternative sentencing proposals on the prison population and associated CDC operational (not construction) costs.[2] In this manner, we can discuss the costs and benefits of diverting from prison different offender groups. Table 4.2 contains the policy options considered, the percent of offenders affected, and the percent of total CDC operating costs saved by eliminating prison sentences for the specified category.[3]

TABLE 4.2 Impact on Prison Admissions and Corrections Cost by Eliminating Prison for Selected Nonviolent Offenders

Eliminate Prison for:	Number of Admissions	% of Admissions	Avg. Months Served	Total CDC $ Spent on Group ($millions)	% CDC $ Spent on Group
Technical Violators	3,116	4%	4.0	$23	1%
TV, Minor Property	13,160	16%	6.7	$167	9%
TV, Minor Prop., Minor Drug Possession	21,542	26%	6.1	$238	13%
Drug Use and Possession	20,978	25%	7.9	$302	17%
All Drugs (Use, Poss., ßSale, Mfg.)	27,170	32%	9.7	$479	26%
TV, Minor Prop., All Drug	38,881	46%	8.8	$620	34%
Less Serious Property	20,921	25%	9.0	$343	19%
Persons Serving 6 months or less	14,320	17%	4.8	$124	7%
Persons Serving 9 months or less	36,828	44%	6.9	$459	25%
All Except Violent Crimes	64,873	77%	9.8	$1,151	64%

Options 1 through 8 have been recommended by either the Blue Ribbon Commission (1990), the Little Hoover Commission (1994), Petersilia (1993), the Legislative Analyst's Office (1993), or Zimring and Hawkins (1992) as potential means to reduce prison crowding. The policies either divert from prison those who have been convicted of less serious crimes or those who are predicted to serve only a few months in prison (generally, these are the same groups). *We consider no policy options that divert any violent offenders (including robbery) from prison.* The following options were considered, and their cost implications are estimated in Table 4.2:

Eliminate Prison Sentences for:

Option 1: Administrative, noncriminal (true technical violators)

Option 2: Administrative, noncriminal, and less serious property (e.g., grand theft, rec. stolen property, petty theft w/prior, forgery, fraud)

Option 3: Administrative, noncriminal, less serious property, and minor drug (use and possession)

Option 4: Minor drug (use and possession)

Option 5: All drug (use, possession, sale, manufacturing)

Option 6: Administrative, noncriminal, less serious property, and all drug (use, possession, sale, manufacturing)

Option 7: Less serious property

Option 8: Persons serving 6 months or less

Option 9: Persons serving 9 months or less

Option 10: All persons, but those convicted of violent crimes

Let's begin with the impact of the least controversial option, Option 1. It estimates that if we eliminated prison terms for "true technical violators," we would affect about 3,100 admissions each year. But since they serve, on average, just four months in prison each, completely eliminating prison terms for this group saves about $22 million, which is but 1 percent of the total (operational) dollars spent by CDC on the total admissions cohort. Certainly this amount is not trivial, but diverting this group will not have the major impact on prisons that many have suggested.

Let's look at Option 2, which might be considered the next least controversial. It estimates the impact of diverting from prison offenders who are either "true" technical violators, or returned by the parole board for less serious property offenses (e.g., theft, receiving stolen property). This group comprises 16 percent of all admissions and serves an average prison term of nearly seven months. By eliminating prison for this group, we would save about $167 million or 9 percent of the operational dollars expended by CDC. *It should be noted that even if we eliminate prison sentences for a sizable portion of admissions, the overall effect on the prison budget may be much less than anticipated, because the cost savings reflect a combina-*

tion of the number of offenders diverted and the average length of prison term they would have served—a point often missed in current policy debates.

Options 4 and 5 estimate the impact of eliminating prison for different categories of drug offenders. Option 4 eliminates prison for only those convicted of drug use and possession; Option 5 eliminates prison for all drug offenders, including sales and manufacturing. Sending drug offenders to prison has impacted prison populations more so than any other category, and as shown in Figure 4.1, 32 percent—nearly a third—of all California prison admissions are a result of drug offenses. Option 4, persons sentenced for drug use or possession, are currently 25 percent of incoming inmates, they serve an average of nearly eight months in prison, and eliminating prison for them would save an estimated 17 percent of CDC costs. Option 5, diverting all drug offenders from prison, would divert 32 percent of incoming inmates, for a cost savings of about $480 million or 26 percent of total corrections costs.

This analysis shows that significant savings are incurred by diverting drug offenders from prison since they account for a larger portion of incoming inmates and they serve relatively longer prison terms. Public opinion polls have shown that Americans are receptive to alternative sentencing for drug use and possession but less so for drug sales or manufacturing (Mande 1993).

Options 8 and 9 simulate the impact of diverting from prison persons who would serve six months or less, or nine months or less, respectively. Several experts, including those who operate the prisons, have noted the waste incurred by sending offenders with very short sentences to prison. Such offenders have very few, if any, opportunities to participate in prison programs, although the state nevertheless incurs all transactional costs of admitting them to prison. Since it generally takes between three and four months to complete the intake process for new felons, most of these individuals never leave the reception center. It has also been noted that short-term commitments create security and administrative burdens on staff, and such policies are also not cost effective, since prison beds (with their added security and programming costs) are more expensive than jail beds. The Blue Ribbon Commission wrote that it "questions the appropriateness of sending new commitments to state prison with less than six months to serve of a sentence" (1990, 106). They recommended that such short-term stay inmates be redirected into intermediate sanctions.

It should not be interpreted that inmates serve a *total* sentence of less than this amount, only that they spend less than this amount in state prisons. When inmates are admitted to prison, they are credited with preconfinement time served in local jails and this determines the length of remaining prison sentence to be served. In 1992, inmates were credited with nearly eight months of preconfinement (or jail) credits.

Our analysis of Option 8 shows that about 17 percent of incoming inmates serve six months or less in prison, and if they were diverted, the prison system would save about $124 million or 7 percent of the operating dollars spent on incarcerating this admissions cohort. Option 9, diverting those serving less than nine months, affects 44 percent of incoming prisoners, and diverting them would save a quarter of all corrections costs.

If the data were richer, other sentencing options could be simulated as well. Ideally, we would want to create categories for this simulation exercise that considered both prior criminal record and current crime. For example, we might want to consider the impacts of diverting only first time burglars, but not repeaters, or those possessing *only* drug use or possession convictions and no other crime. Unfortunately, details of an inmate's prior criminal record is not routinely entered into the California Department of Corrections (CDC) data files, making this finer distinction impossible. CDC used to be able to collect such vital information (along with other demographic data), but budget cuts have resulted in most data collection activities being stopped—ironically, just at a time when such data is most needed. The author urges that CDC initiate or permit a research project collecting more detailed prior record, substance abuse, and current offense data on a sample of prison admissions so that more sophisticated analysis of the costs and benefits of alternative sentencing options can be undertaken. This information is critical if the legislature is to understand the population impacts and cost implications of a number of proposals for controlling prison populations. This study should also follow-up the admissions cohort once released, collecting detailed recidivism information. Such data would permit a better understanding of the public safety risks of releasing different offender groupings to the community.

The bottom line from this simulation exercise is that there are perhaps as many as a quarter of incoming inmates who might be judged as appropriate candidates for diversion to community-based programs. These inmates have been sent to prison as a result of technical violations, minor drug use, or nonviolent property offenses. Such offenders currently serve about four to eight months in prison. Diverting such offenders would save the CDC about $300 million to $500 million, or 17 percent to 20 percent of the operating dollars it expended on this admissions cohort. If we wish to save more sizable dollar amounts, we must be willing to divert the larger category of drug offenders (possibly including drug sales), or more serious property offenders (including burglary). These later categories are likely to evoke strong public resistance—but they are the categories that produce significant cost savings due to their high number of offenders and associated longer lengths of prison stay.

There is no one "right" answer in terms of who should be diverted from prison. Rather, these prison-or-not choices reflect the public's notions of punishment, historical patterns of sentencing, and resource constraints. But some of the costs and benefits of different sanctions can be empirically illustrated, and we need to begin debating these important questions on empirical rather than solely political grounds.

We have spent much time in recent years discussing technical violators, and many have urged that they be diverted from prison to help solve the prison crowding problem. This analysis shows that although such a policy might indeed be appropriate (and the author believes it is), it is not going to do much to reduce prison populations or associated costs. We need to begin to debate the feasibility of diverting other offender categories—which have higher predicted cost savings—from prison. If it is decided that such offenders cannot be diverted from prison for public safety, political, or other considerations, then policymakers must focus on building more prisons.

Where Would Prisoners Go if Released?: Creating a System of Safe, Punitive Intermediate Sanctions

In considering prison alternatives, we often fail to answer the other half of the question: If not prison, then what? Can we assure public safety if offenders are in the community? And, considering the cost of the community-based alternatives, what net criminal justice savings really results?

The offenders we have considered in the options above cannot simply be released outright with no supervision, and it is also not appropriate to sentence them to routine probation supervision. In large urban California counties, "routine" supervision often equates with minimal contact between offender and officer, infrequent drug tests, and perhaps referrals to local substance abuse or employment programs. Such a sentence seems too lenient for felons and has been shown to be ineffective in forestalling recidivism in California (Petersilia et al. 1985; Petersilia and Turner 1993).

Other states have addressed this problem by developing "intermediate sanction" programs. Intermediate or middle-range sanctions are designed for offenders who are too serious to be supervised on routine probation but not so serious as to require a prison bed. The programs are tougher than traditional probation and parole but less stringent and expensive than prison. And perhaps most importantly, they are designed to provide "partial incapacitation" benefits either by reducing the time available to commit crime or contacts with tempting targets or victims.

Prisons are so popular because of their simplicity: Criminals behind bars cannot get at the rest of us. As William Spelman recently explained:

No doubt there is something especially reassuring about the notion of 24-hour per day protection. On the other hand, incapacitation works, not by changing the motivations of offenders, but by separating them from opportunities to commit crime. In theory, less-drastic means could be used to separate offenders from opportunities: They may be required to spend their free time in locations that are secure (halfway houses) or that have few potential victims (house arrest); they may be restrained from staying out late, or from seeing former colleagues, former victims, or others who might tempt them to commit further crimes. Such methods will probably not prevent all the crimes in which these offenders would otherwise have taken part, but—depending upon how much they cost—they may prevent enough of these crimes to be worth the trouble for some offenders (1994, 304).

Intermediate sanctions are designed to provide "partial incapacitation" benefits without the expense of prisons. Intensive supervision probation, home confinement, and the like are all designed around these aims. They are considerably cheaper to operate than prison because they do not require the state to provide secure structures, guards, food, utilities, or the other round-the-clock expenses of prison. And because the offenders remain on the street, they may continue to hold down jobs, support their families, and pay taxes or supervision fees.

Intermediate sanctions were initially developed in the mid-1970s in the southern United States (primarily Georgia), the region with the highest rate of incarceration and the earliest prison crowding problems. But as prison crowding became commonplace across the nation, so did the search for alternatives, and during the past decade nearly every state has implemented intermediate sanctions. The most popular of these programs are intensive supervision, house arrest, electronic monitoring, substance abuse treatment, and boot camps. Although the dimensions, degree of formality, and other specifics differ from jurisdiction to jurisdiction, all intermediate sanctions are designed to be safe, punitive, and less expensive than prison.

California, for the most part, has chosen not to experiment with intermediate sanctions to the extent that other states have. In fact, since the passage of Proposition 13, which restricted local revenues used for community punishments, California's community corrections system has suffered terribly. The California Legislative Analysts Office recently concluded: "California currently does relatively little in the area of community corrections" (1991, 217).

Two reasons seem to explain this. First, California's motivation to consider prison alternatives was not great until recently, since the state's growing economy was able to support the growth in prison populations. Second, our political leadership (and public opinion) has not been receptive to prison alternatives, believing that we have already tried such programs, they didn't work, and they are "soft on crime." But the experience of other states has shown that, if properly designed, *intermediate sanctions can reduce prison commitments, keep communities safe, foster offender rehabilitation, and gain public support. Experience has also shown that such effects are neither easy to obtain nor inexpensive.* Moreover, success depends in large measure on targeting the right offenders to the right kind of program.

Three reviews of intermediate sanctions have recently been written, so there is no need to reproduce them here. The interested reader is referred to Byrne, Lurigio, and Petersilia (1992), Clear and Braga (1995), and Tonry and Lynch (1995) for more details. Here we briefly summarize what the evaluations have shown and what lessons they suggest for California.

Intensive Supervision, Probation, and Parole

Intensive supervision, probation/parole (ISP) is a form of release into the community that emphasizes close monitoring of convicted offenders and imposes rigorous conditions on that release. Most ISPs call for weekly contacts with a supervising officer, random drug testing, and a requirement to participate in relevant treatment, hold a job, and perhaps perform community service.

Between 1980 and 1995, every state developed and implemented ISP programs. Several of the ISPs were solidly evaluated, so we now have a rather complete understanding of the effects of ISP programs on offender recidivism, public safety, and costs.

Most ISP programs were designed foremost to save prison dollars—identical to our purpose here. Programs were designed, and ISP candidates were generally drawn from two offender pools: lower-risk prison bound (diversion ISPs) or the higher risk probationers (enhancement ISPs). Enhancement-ISP programs were by far the easiest to implement (in fact, only a handful of true ISP prison diversions were successfully implemented). Most ISP programs allowed judges and other local officials to control intake, and given the potential risks and political backlash of placing a prison-bound offender on ISP, most participants were drawn from the population of persons already on probation. As such, ISP served to "enhance" routine probation rather than divert offenders from prison.

In 1986, three California counties—Ventura, Los Angeles, and Contra Costa—participated in a Department of Justice-funded national ISP demonstration, which ran from 1986–1989 and was evaluated by Petersilia and Turner (1993). Officials in those counties identified (either from existing case files or new probation grants) probationers who were high-risk and placed them on smaller caseloads, where intensive surveillance was possible. ISP offenders were required to report to officers more frequently, submit to weekly drug tests, perform community service, be employed or in school, and seek alcohol and drug treatment if appropriate. In Los Angeles, selected offenders were required to wear electronic monitoring bracelets and adhere to a nighttime and weekend curfew.

The result after one year of ISP participation in the ISP program (across the three sites) was that the ISP programs did not reduce offender recidivism. ISP resulted in more technical violations, court appearances, revocations, and incarcerations, resulting in costs up to twice as high as the costs for routine probation and parole supervision. Annual ISP program costs averaged $7,300 per offender compared with about $4,700 per year for routine supervision. (These figures include judicial system costs and so are higher than those commonly reported for routine probation or parole supervision.) Although ISP offenders had higher rates of technical violations—mostly for failing drug tests—there were no differences in their new crime arrests. About one-third of both groups had new arrests during the one-year follow-up.

But there were some positive findings as well: *Offenders in all the California sites who received drug counseling, held jobs, paid restitution, and did community service were arrested at rates 10 to 20 percent lower than others.* These components of the ISPs had little effect on overall crime rates because only a small proportion of the probationers participated in the programs. California probation officers reported that there were not enough slots in drug treatment programs for all who wanted them.

Outcomes might have been better if a greater proportion of the sample had participated in treatment. Evaluations have suggested that programs that have a high "doses" of *both* treatment and surveillance are necessary for assuring public safety and reducing recidivism. Participation in drug treatment, particularly, might have a high payoff. Across all sites, about half the offenders were judged "drug-dependent" by their probation or parole officers. Many of the rest probably had some drug involvement. Yet ISP staff often reported difficulties obtaining drug treatment for those people. It comes as no surprise, therefore, that about one-third of new arrests were drug related. In Los Angeles, for example, 41 percent of offenders were judged to be in "high need" of drug treatment, but only 15 percent of ISP (and 2 percent of routine probationers) participated in *any* drug or alcohol treatment during the one-year follow-up.

Although none of the ISP programs in California chose to divert prison-bound offenders to ISP, several other sites have, and the lessons are instructive. Programs where judges control the intake have had difficulties identifying enough offenders to make the programs viable. In two sites that allowed judges to identify (from a pool of prison-bound offenders) those who were appropriate candidates for release back to the community under ISP, few participants were identified. In Marion County, Oregon, for example, during the eighteen-month study period, 160 offenders were judged eligible for ISP based on initial screening criteria, but the local judge reduced that to just 28. Judges said they were unwilling to take the chance and political backlash of placing prison-bound offenders back in the community. This experience has now been repeated elsewhere with similar results: If judges or other local officials control the placement into ISP, few prison-bound cases will be diverted. Tonry and Lynch have suggested that we should "shift control over program placement from judges to corrections officials wherever possible. . . . The alternative is to structure judges' decisions about intermediate sanctions by use of sentencing guidelines." (1995, 42).

There are a couple model programs of this type. A long-running and highly regarded ISP program has operated in New Jersey since 1983. The program is based on the premise that certain prisoners can be released to the community with minimal public risk if placed in a highly structured environment. Only inmates who are currently serving a prison term are eligible to participate—judges are not permitted to sentence directly to ISP. The program was developed to reduce prison crowding, and the state has set up procedures to ensure that only persons who would otherwise be occupying a prison bed are ISP participants.

ISP participants must be serving prison sentences for nonviolent crimes. Inmates can apply for admission to the ISP after they have served at least thirty but not more than sixty days in prison. Each offender who applied for the program must develop a personal plan to govern his activities upon release. This information, along with relevant criminal history data, is then reviewed by an ISP screening board, composed of representatives from corrections and the public. If the inmate is deemed eligible, the board forwards his application to a three-judge resentencing panel for a final decision. If the panel approves the application, the offender returns to the community and reports to the ISP program. Offenders must participate in ISP for one year. The ISP caseloads involve extensive client contact, surveillance that includes the use of electronic monitoring, a restrictive curfew, urine monitoring for alcohol and drugs, treatment, and education. The program is widely regarded as a success in terms of saving prison beds and fostering long-term offender rehabilitation.

Home Confinement with or Without Electronic Monitoring

Home confinement (also called house arrest), where offenders are ordered to remain confined in their residences for certain specified hours, can be ordered as a sanction in its own right or as a condition of ISP. Most affected offenders, however, do not remain in their homes but instead are authorized to work or participate in treatment, education, or training programs. House arrest, with or without electronic surveillance, can be used as an independent sanction, requiring no supervision beyond that necessary to ensure house arrest.

The results for house arrest programs are identical to those for ISP. Basically, the programs' potential to save dollars depends heavily on whether participants derive from probation caseloads or prison-bound offenders. If placement is not controlled by corrections officials, intake is difficult and usually results in "net widening," when they are controlled by corrections officials or a composite board, they can achieve prison diversion impacts.

House arrest (with or without electronic monitoring) is oriented more toward surveillance than treatment (more so than ISP programs). Without much of a treatment emphasis, offenders (particularly drug offenders) have more of their violations uncovered by officials and, if taken seriously by the courts, are more often revoked to custody—thereby driving up prisons costs and eliminating any cost savings. But again there is an example of a successful house arrest program, which seems to have rehabilitation and cost savings impact.

Florida operates the largest house arrest program in the nation, and has done so rather successfully since 1987. Recent data shows that Florida currently has about 14,000 offenders on house arrest (called Community Control), and on any one day, about 2,000 are being monitored electronically. The state argues that the program is saving prison beds, but researchers question whether that it true. Most of Community Control participants are offenders who are "predicted" to go to prison, but haven't actually been sentenced to go to prison. As such, it is impossible to know whether the program is truly diverting prison-bound offenders. However, officials say that regardless, Community Control offenders have very low rates of recidivism and cost much less than incarcerated offenders, and the programs are accepted by the public as a punitive sentence and offer some prospects for offender rehabilitation. Again, officials caution the key to success is threefold: identify the right offenders, offer them doses of both surveillance and treatment, and quickly remove failures from the program to gain public confidence.

Electronic monitoring has grown dramatically in recent years, and it is estimated that there are over 50,000 persons being "electronically" supervised in the United States today. But the evaluation evidence is extremely weak. There are no large-scale evaluations, except for a series of studies done in Indianapolis. But on recidivism, Renzema notes that most of the research is uninterpretable because of shoddy or weak research designs. Braumer and Mendelson stress that the "incapacitation and public safety potential of this sanction have probably been considerably overstated "because the technology cannot control offenders' movements."(1992, 66) They predict that house arrest will continue primarily to be used for low-risk offenders and will play a small role as a custody alternative. Again, the lesson is: Pay attention to which offenders are being assigned to the program.

Boot Camps or Shock Incarceration

Boot camps, also called shock incarceration, have a great deal of popular appeal and are one of the hallmarks of the new Federal Crime Bill. Begun in 1986 in New Orleans, they quickly spread, and by April 1993, according to an NIJ report (MacKenzie 1993), thirty states and the U.S. Bureau of Prisons were operating boot camps. Evaluations have suggested that boot camps do appear to reduce overall corrections costs by releasing prisoners earlier, but participants generally show little improvement in recidivism.

Boot camps are the one program that the California Legislature has shown interest in for diverting prison inmates, although in 1992, California had only forty-eight prison boot camp participants, whereas New York had 1,500 participants. The 1993 legislature approved about $4 million to expand boot camps, called Alternative Sentencing Program (ASP). The program was designed to place bout 200 nonviolent offenders, in a short-term "shock incarceration program, followed by intensive supervision of the offenders on parole." The ASP is intended to be more cost effective than regular incarceration. The ASP provides a short period of confinement (120) days in prison during which less serious, nonviolent offenders, who have never served a sentence in a state or federal prison, are placed in an intensive military-style drill and ceremony, physical exercise and labor, along with structured counseling and education. The program will only accept offenders from six Bay Area counties.

First-time nonviolent felons who had at least one year and not more than two years to serve at the time of admission to state prison were eligible. Upon successful completion of the period of incarceration, a forty-four-member platoon of offenders are placed on intensive parole supervision in the community for 180 days. During the first sixty days, ASP parolees live together at a work furlough facility in Oakland and work with the parole staff to locate employment and housing to ensure that parolees successfully transition back into their communities. During the final 120 days, the parolees are required to meet frequently with their parole agents and in platoon meetings and are subject to drug testing. Parolees who can successfully complete the intensive parole supervision phase may be fully discharged. CDC is planning to track inmates to assess the program's effects on recidivism.

California's boot camp incorporates many program components that should be associated with success. Previous boot camp evaluations have shown that participation in boot camps has no discernible effect on subsequent offending and increase costs and crowding (MacKenzie and Parent 1992). Back end programs to which imprisoned offenders are transferred by corrections officials for service of a 90- or 180-day boot camp sentence in lieu of a longer conventional sentence do apparently save money and prison space, although they too often experience high failure rates and higher than normal technical violation and revocations rates (Tonry and Lynch 1995).

But again there are positive effects associated with specific boot camp programs, specifically those that provide treatment services and aftercare. Researchers have found evidence in Illinois, New York, and Louisiana of "lower recidivism on some measures" that they associated with strong rehabilitative emphases in those states' boot camps (MacKenzie 1990, 16). An earlier article describes a "somewhat more positive finding" that graduates under intensive supervision after release "appear to be involved in more positive social activities (e.g., work, attending drug treatment) than similar offenders on parole or probation" (MacKenzie and Shaw 1990, 465). New York already operates boot camps that draw their clientele from state prisons and that result in much shorter terms of confinement for those who complete the program. Program planners have cautioned that boot camps must provide both treatment and tough regiments and provide transitional services to offenders upon release. California's program incorporates such elements, but its impacts have yet to be evaluated. The legislature does report problems in case flow, however. Case flow has been too little and the restrictions too many (mostly very short-term offenders—less than eight months to serve on their CDC sentence), so cost savings are relatively minimal to date.

Drug and Alcohol Abuse Treatment Programs

The programs described above are principally surveillance-oriented, rather than service-oriented programs, meaning that their primary mission is monitoring the court-ordered conditions, identifying failures, and returning to court (and possibly, incarceration) the failures. Most do not emphasize treatment and they do not have the resources to provide it. Yet, the evidence of all these intermediate sanctions—and criminal sentencing more generally—shows that without treatment components, most programs simply end up identifying and reprocessing the failures.

California inmates are heavily drug and alcohol involved. According to the CDC's Offender Information Services Branch, which examined a small random sample of new admissions in 1990 for drug and alcohol indicators, 72 percent of new admissions had a history of drug use, including 30 percent having used cocaine as their most serious drug, 16 percent heroin, and 7 percent amphetamines. Recorded use was higher among women than men. For men, rates were highest among Hispanics; for the women, among the African-Americans. The survey found that 14 percent reported being under the influence of alcohol at the time of the offense, and nearly twice as many indicated heavy use of alcohol. Most of the drug abusing sample had no prior prison sentence, although most admittees had been sentenced to county jail for prior convictions. Many had local juvenile commitments (Holtby et al. 1993, 68).

Most agree that criminal recidivism is not likely to be reduced without an affective means to address the substance abuse problems of inmates. But, what works? Most of the public is supportive of treatment generally, but there is skepticism about whether we know how to design and deliver such programs.

Researchers in California recently conducted an assessment of treatment programs and identified those that were successful, concluding that it can now be "documented that treatment and recovery programs are a good investment." (Gerstein et al. 1994). The researchers studied a sample of 1,900 treatment participants, followed them up for as much as two years of treatment, and studied participants from all four major treatment modalities, including therapeutic communities, social model, outpatient drug free, and methadone maintenance. Gerstein et al. (1994, 33) conclude:

> treatment was very cost beneficial: for every dollar spent on drug and alcohol treatment, the State of California saved $7 in reductions in crime and health care costs. The study found that each day of treatment *paid for itself on the day treatment was received*, primarily through an avoidance of crime. . . .

> the level of criminal activity declined by two-thirds from before treatment to after treatment. The greater the length of time spent in treatment, the greater the reduction in crime. Reported criminal activity declined before and after treatment as follows: mean number of times sold or helped sell drugs (–75 percent), mean number of times used weapon/physical force (–93 percent), percent committing any illegal activity (–72 percent), and mean months involved in criminal activity (–80 percent).

Regardless of type of treatment modality, reduction in crime was substantial and significant (although participants in the social model recovery programs had the biggest reduction). Social Model Recovery Houses are a particular type of residential program that focus on recovering alcoholics, stressing peer support and communal sober living.

Gerstein and his colleagues suggest treatment participation seems to reduce criminal activity in at least two ways. It directly provided new ref-

TABLE 4.3   Annual Cost of Intermediate Sanction and Treatment Option

State prison	$21,816
County jail	$19,710
Boot camps (121 days prison, plus 244 days ISP)	$11,652
House arrest with electronic monitoring	$3,500–8,500
Intensive supervision probation/parole	$4,000–8,000
Routine supervision probation/parole	$200–2,000
Substance abuse treatment programs	
Residential	$22,436
Social model (drug-free home)	$12,559
Outpatient	$2,872
Methadone maintenance	$2,478

erence groups and new moral and ethical standards to substitute for reference groups and standards that helped to support past criminal activities, or it indirectly affected criminal activity by reducing the economic motivations for crime (Gerstein et al. 1994, 24).

Costs of Community-Based Intermediate Sanctions

The previous review suggests that it is possible to develop effective community-based sanctions programs but that they are not inexpensive. In essence, you get what you pay for, and if you don't pay for some treatment services, the programs end up costing more simply because of the reprocessing and reincarceration costs incurred by the failures.

Let's now return to the option categories we considered earlier (in Table 4.2) for prison diversion and compare the costs of intermediate sanctions programs with those we currently spend on prison. In the past, discussions of the costs of prison versus intermediate sanctions has been overly simplistic. We often hear that intermediate sanctions cost substantially less than prison, because such sanctions costs about $5,000 per year, whereas prison averages $20,000 per year. But good intermediate sanctions—combining treatment and surveillance—do not cost as little as $5,000, and low-risk prisoners who get targeted for these sanctions do not serve a full $20,000-year in prison. Both sides of the equation are thus misleading.

Table 4.3 shows the annual cost of some of the more popular treatment and sanction options.

Table 4.4 contains estimates of the dollar amounts we could afford to spend on the different target groups if we wished to divert these offenders to intermediate sanctions and spend no more than we are currently spending to house such offenders in prison. This table computes the cost savings or cost increases incurred in sentencing the different target

TABLE 4.4   Net Savings or Loss by Diverting Prisoners to Intermediate Sanctions (cell entries in millions)

Eliminate Prison for:	Sanction Costs: $5,000 per year	Sanction Costs: $10,000 per year	Sanction Costs: $20,000 per year	Equivalent CDC $ for Intermediate Sanctions (Thousands)
Technical Violators	$7.1	($8.5)	($39.7)	$7,272
TV, Minor Property	$101.5	$35.7	($95.9)	$12,712
TV, Minor Prop., Minor Drug	$130.3	$22.5	($192.9)	$11,047
Minor Drugs (use and Drug Poss)	$197.4	$92.5	($117.2)	$14,412
All Drugs (Use, Poss., Sale, Mfg.)	$343.5	$207.7	($64.0)	$17,644
TV, Minor Prop., All Drug	$425.9	$231.5	($157.3)	$15,955
Minor Property	$238.3	$133.7	($75.5)	$16,391
Persons Serving 6 Mon. or Less	$52.5	($19.0)	($162.2)	$8,667
Those Serving 9 Mon. or Less	$275.3	$91.1	($277.1)	$12,475
All Except Violent Crimes	$826.8	$502.5	$146.3	$17,745

groups to intermediate sanctions, using three annual costs for intermediate sanctions ($5,000, $10,000, and $20,000). The last column is perhaps the most interesting. It reveals the amount "available" for community-based sanctions if we want to spend no more than we are currently spending to house them in prison, that is, the break-even point between intermediate sanctions and prison costs.

Note that figures appearing in parentheses represent an *increase* in costs over current incarceration policies. For example, if we eliminated prison for Option 1 Technical Violators, and sentenced them instead to an intermediate community-based sanction that costs $10,000 per year, per offender, a net loss of about $8.5M in corrections costs would be experienced. On the other hand, if the Option 1 offenders were diverted to a program costing $5,000 per year, a $7.0M cost savings would result. The analysis suggests that if we wish to divert Option 1 prisoners to intermediate sanctions, the community-level program must cost less than $7,272 per year, per offender (last column) to break even with dollars currently spent on imprisonment. In essence, the last column shows the dollars available for intermediate sanctions, if we wish to not spend more than we currently are.

An important finding is that we have available $14,000 to $17,500 per year, per offender, to alternatively treat drug offenders—and the review above suggests the effective treatment programs can be delivered for that amount. If we could divert such offenders to treatment programs and realize true reductions in recidivism, then funds spent on intermediate sanctions could be viewed as an investment not a cost.

As in the previous analysis, these numbers are intended to provide an illustration of the types of preliminary analyses we should be providing the California Legislature. But it needs to be expanded considerably. The "option groups" considered should be further refined to include prior criminal record, and perhaps substance abuse. And, more significantly, the true costs and benefits of prison versus community alternatives is more complicated than simply comparing the annual costs of the relative sanctions.

The "costs" of prison include not only operating costs but also the amortized start-up and construction expenses for the cell. Prisons costs might also be increased for the social welfare system's support of prisoners' dependents. In addition, people living in the neighborhood of prisons bear costs (fear and reduced property values), as do prisoners and their families (current and future economic loss and emotional suffering).

The "costs" of community sanctions are equally complicated, particularly when one tries to monetarize the costs of any new crimes the offender might commit while in the community. First, there is the problem of knowing how to estimate the number of crimes offenders commit while in the community, since most remain unknown to officials. The most thorough work along these lines was conducted by a special panel of the National Research Council, the research arm of the National Academy of Sciences. The panel's 1986 report estimated that the rate of these incidents would be in the range of two to four violent crimes per year for active violent offenders and five to ten property crimes per year for active property offenders (Blumstein et al. 1986).

Analysts then take this average number of crimes committed while free and multiply by a figure representing the dollar costs of each crime. There is, as yet, however no commonly accepted framework for estimating such costs. Suggested figures range from several hundred dollars to over $50,000 per crime. The disparities are due, at least in part, to the type of crime being committed, how the costs of the criminal justice system are allocated, and how and whether the costs of mental pain and suffering are handled. Accurately weighing all of these cost items has been amply described by Piehl and DiIulio as an "analytical migraine" (1995, 22).

Researchers have argued that, while difficult to quantify, the pain and suffering caused by recidivists are real and their associated costs must be added when considering the cost benefits of community sentencing. Crime victims incur out-of-pocket expenses, such as costs of medical expenses, lost income, or the value of stolen or damaged property. They also incur pain and suffering, such as psychological impairment and fear.[4] The "social costs" of crime have been estimated to be from $6,000 to $300,000 per crime, depending on the crime type.

Because the major parameters of more complicated models of prison versus alternatives are unknown (and mostly unknowable), some studies show that prison can sometimes be more cost effective and socially beneficial than probation or parole, although in other cases, the reverse may be the case. The primary factors are the differences in the estimated costs of crime and predicted offender recidivism rates.

For our purposes, the current estimates are not particularly useful, since we are considering alternative sentencing for the lower-risk prisoners (and therefore, the *average* number of crimes the average inmate is predicted to commit if free is an overestimate), and more importantly, we are proposing diverting such offenders to more effective community-based alternatives, where recidivism is reduced (hence the average recidivism rate for probationers and parolees overall in the United States is an overestimate and inappropriate). In truth, we don't currently have valid estimates to do a more detailed cost/benefit analysis. Developing these more accurate cost/benefit models should certainly be a priority for California researchers.

Are Intermediate Sanctions Punitive Enough?

A major obstacle to diverting prison-bound offenders to alternatives is the public perception that community sanctions are not punitive enough. Morris and Tonry argue that we overuse prison in the United States simply because "Americans tend to equate criminal punishment with prison. To the public, to the public official, even to the judge, sentencing is often seen as a choice between prison and nearly nothing. Probation is often seen as a 'letting off,' which, when one consider the sizes of probation caseloads in our metropolitan courts, it often is" (1990, 39).

But things have changed. Intermediate sanctions have changed the face of probation, making it more harsh and punitive, while at the same time, prison has lost some of its punitive sting. In fact, recent surveys of offenders in Minnesota, Arizona, New Jersey, Oregon, and Texas reveal that when offenders are asked to equate criminal sentences, they judge certain types of community punishments as *more* severe than prison.

One of the more striking examples comes from Marion County, Oregon. Selected nonviolent offenders were given the choice of serving a prison term or returning to the community to participate in Intensive Supervision Probation (ISP) program, which imposed drug testing, mandatory community service, and frequent visits with the probation officer. About a third of the offenders given the option between ISP or prison, chose prison (Petersilia 1990). Minnesota inmates (and corrections staff), for example, rated three years of ISP as equivalent in punitiveness to one year in prison (Petersilia and Deschenes 1994).

What accounts for this seeming aberration? Why should anyone prefer imprisonment to remaining in the community—no matter what the conditions? Some have suggested that prison has lost some of its punitive sting, and hence its ability to scare and deter. For one thing, possessing a prison record is not as stigmatizing as it was in the past, because so many of the offenders' peers (and family members) also have "done time." A recent survey shows that 40 percent of youths in state training schools have parents who have been incarcerated. Further, about a quarter of all U.S. black males will be incarcerated during their lives, so the stigma attached to having a prison record is not as great as it was when it was relatively uncommon. And the pains associated with prison—social isolation, fear of victimization—seem less likely with repeat offenders, where offenders have learned how to do time.

In fact, far from stigmatizing, prison evidently confers status in some neighborhoods. California's Task Force on Gangs and Drugs reported that during public testimony, gang members themselves "repeatedly stated that incarceration was not a threat because they knew their sentences would be minimal"(1992, 29). Further, some gang members considered the short period of detention as a "badge of courage," something to brag about when they returned to the streets." Jerome Skolnick (1990) of UC–Berkeley found that for drug dealers in California, imprisonment confers a certain elevated "home boy" status, especially for gang members for whom prison and prison gangs can be an alternative site of loyalty. And according to the California Youth Authority, inmates steal state-issued prison clothing for the same reason. Wearing it when they return to the community lets everyone know they have done "hard time."

Some also have argued that for poor people, prison may be preferred, but few scholars take such discussions seriously. It is undoubtedly true, however, that the quality of a person's lifestyle when free certainly has some bearing on the extent to which imprisonment is considered undesirable. The grim fact—and national shame—is that for most people who go to prison, the conditions inside are not all that different from the conditions outside. The prison environment may be far below the ordinary standards of society, but so is the environment they come from. As the quality of life that people can expect when free declines, the relative deprivation suffered while in prison declines.

The length of time an offender can be expected to serve in prison has also decreased in California—from 2.4 years in 1984 to 1.7 years in 1994. But more to the point, for marginal offenders (those targeted for prison alternatives), the expected time served can be much less (as illustrated in Table 4.1). Offenders on the street seem to be aware of this, even more so with the extensive media coverage such issues are receiving.

For convicted felons, freedom of course is preferable to prison. But, "intermediate sanctions" do not represent freedom. In fact, as suggested previously, such community-based programs may have more punitive bite than prison. Consider a comparison between Contra Costa County's

Intensive Supervision Program (ISP) for drug offenders, which was discontinued in 1990 due to a shortage of funds, with what drug offenders would face if imprisoned:

ISP. Offenders are required to serve at least one year on ISP. During ISP, offenders are supervised by probation officers who are responsible for no more than forty adult offenders. In addition to twice weekly face-to-face contacts, the ISP program included a random drug testing hotline, Saturday home visits, weekly Narcotics Anonymous meetings, special assistance from local police to expedite existing bench warrants, a liaison with the State Employment Development Department. To remain on ISP, offenders had to be employed or participating in relevant treatment or training, perform community service, pay victim restitution (if required by the court), and remain crime and drug-free.

OR

Prison. A sentence of twelve months will require that the offenders serve about half of that. During his term, he is not required to work, and he will not be required to participate in any training or treatment but may do so if he wishes. Once released, he will probably be placed on routine parole supervision, where he might see his officer once a month.

Offenders interviewed in Contra Costa judged the ISP program as punitive, and they believed probation officers would identify and revoke them to prison if court violations were uncovered (Byrne, Lurigio, and Baird 1989). As Morris and Tonry observed about the punitiveness of intermediate sanctions: "We started by worrying whether these intermediate punishments could provide sufficient control of the offender; we end in anxiety that they may prove excessive" (1990, 218).

These results are important particularly for policymakers, who say that they are imprisoning such a large number of offenders because of the public's desire to get tough with crime. Such officials might be convinced that there are other means besides prison to extract punishment. These results confirm what many have suggested: It is no longer necessary to equate criminal punishment solely with prison. The balance of sanctions between probation and prison appears to have shifted, and at some level of intensity and length, intermediate punishments are the more dreaded penalty.

Summary and Conclusions

No one doubts that the unprecedented growth in prison populations will continue beyond the year 2000 and that the gigantic new expense will create new conflicts, chief among them the competition for dollars between higher education and prisons. And, it is likely that education will lose, because voters fear criminals more than they fear the consequences of an uneducated or undereducated mass of young adults. Walter Massey, the UC vice president for academic affairs says, "If additional funding is not forthcoming, we face choices about enrollment that have important implications for California. Some students who want to get higher education may not have the opportunity to do so."

Shifting money away from higher education to fund prisons has dramatic effects, both on the state's overall economy and crime. California's jobs are increasingly high-technology, and these jobs have displaced jobs previously performed by lower-skilled workers. The inability of the lower class to obtain the needed new skills is one of the primary reasons cited for the widening income and wage gap that has occurred in California and across the nation during the past decade. Persons who fail to become educated in these new fields are being squeezed out and unable to compete in a more competitive market, facing higher unemployment rates and downward mobility, which is in turn associated with poverty, substance abuse, female-headed households, homelessness—all factors associated with increased crime. RAND demographer Lynn Karoly concludes: "Education is the single most important factor in increasing the chances of upward transitions and in reducing the likelihood of downward movement"(1992, 69).

The United States has often tolerated a higher level of inequality than other industrialized countries because there is presumed to be a reasonable opportunity for upward movement through higher education that is available to all. By limiting access to publicly funded higher education, we restrict the major avenue that many populations have for gaining the skills needed to compete in a competitive and changing employment market. Our short-term need to fund prisons at the expense of higher education may well backfire, and ensure that the next generation cannot find legitimate employment, thus ensuring that the built prison cells will remain filled.

It does not have to be an either-or choice between prisons and education. Violent offenders must be imprisoned and serve lengthy terms. But this analysis has shown that the majority of prison admissions (76 percent) have not been convicted of a violent crime, and depending on the thresholds one wishes to adopt, perhaps a quarter of prison admissions might be suitable candidates for diversion to intermediate sanctions.

The least objectionable group is the technical violators, and the analysis has shown that diverting them saves only 4 percent of admissions, and 1 percent of total dollars. If we were to divert less-serious property offenders or those convicted of drug use or possession, we could eliminate about a quarter of the prison admissions and save perhaps 200–300 million correctional dollars. And further analysis shows that we could spend $11,000 to $12,000 per offender on an intermediate sanction program and have a net cost savings over what we are now spending to imprison. And the evaluation evidence suggests that safe, punitive, and effective intermediate sanctions can be delivered for that dollar amount. Moreover, intermediate sanctions that combine both surveillance and treatment services have shown to have more long-lasting, rehabilitation effects.

There is much room for strenuous argument about all of this and much more empirical analyses that needs to be done. Such arguments should be going on in the California Legislature now. For the last few years, sentencing and corrections policy has been driven by media and political hype, rather than by considered analysis and debate. Very little solid data exists to project the costs and benefits of prison versus alternative sentencing policies or the impact of expanding community corrections on crime, offender rehabilitation, or criminal justice costs. We have no accurate portrait of what characterizes "community corrections" in California or the kinds of offenders being subjected to it or the prison system. And, unbelievably, we have no follow-up studies of offenders sentenced to prison, jail, or community punishments. We must change that, particularly in California where the situation seems most perilous.

Having said that, we can't wait until all of the data is in. Policymakers might wish to begin cautiously by implementing an experiment to test whether the program successes of other states can be replicated here. Electronically monitored house arrest, intensive supervision, and boot camp prisons, if designed properly, have all enjoyed some success at reducing prisons costs while keeping communities safe.

Moreover, in the end, many of the choices we make affecting prison populations are not empirical but normative questions, reflecting our value system. After all, much of the prison bulge has been caused by our decision as a society to imprison offenders convicted of drug use and possession, something other countries don't do, and the United States didn't do frequently until the 1980s (Lynch 1995). So in the end, our decisions about who to imprison are not totally empirical matters, but policymakers should at least be guided by empirical data of the costs and benefits of alternative policies.

The author recommends that the state appoint a nonpartisan Blue Ribbon Commission on Community Based Punishments, similar to that appointed in 1990 to study prison crowding. This commission would work with the Department of Corrections and the California Probation, Parole, and Corrections Association (CPPCA) to:

- collect detailed background information on a sample of persons being admitted to prison for the purpose of being able to further delineate the seriousness of persons who on the basis of their conviction crime category alone appear potential candidates for intermediate sanctions;
- design an intermediate sanction experiment, where the least risky (based on well-known recidivism prediction models) of the target population are released to participate in a model intermediate sanction program. The experiment would be evaluated to determine the costs and benefits of such a diversionary program; and
- collect information on the capacity of community corrections agencies in California, what services offenders are receiving, and how prison crowding impacts probation and parole effectiveness.

Until such information is collected and debated, we are unlikely to change the course of corrections policy in California, which seems guaranteed to consign every available dollar to funding prisons. The result will be yet again, no money for treatment, no money for children, and no money for education—programs we know help prevent criminal activity in the first place and enable offenders to make changes in their lives. With such information at hand, we might be able to agree upon reasonable intermediate sanctions for nonviolent offenders, not out of misguided sympathy for criminals but rather for the sake of citizens who deserve protection from violent criminals and more effective, less-bankrupting penalties for the rest.

References

Blumstein, Alfred, Jacqueline Cohen, Jeffrey A. Roth, and Christy A. Visher, eds. 1986. *Criminal Careers and "Career Criminals."* National Research Council, National Academy of Sciences, vol. 2.

Braumer, Terry L. and Robert I. Mendelsohn. 1992. "Electronically Monitored Home Confinement: Does It Work?" In James Byrne, Arthur Lurigio, and Joan Petersilia, *Smart Sentencing: The Emergence of Intermediate Sanctions.*

Byrne, James, Arthur Lurigio, and Christopher Baird. 1989. Effectiveness of the New Intensive Supervision Programs. *Research in Corrections* 2(1):1.

Byrne, James, Arthur Lurigio, and Joan Petersilia. 1992. *Smart Sentencing: The Emergence of Intermediate Sanctions.*

California Blue Ribbon Commission on Inmate Population Management. 1990. Final Report.

Cavanaugh, David. 1990. *Cost Benefit Analysis of Prison Cell Construction and Alternative Sanctions.* BOTEC Corporation publication.

Clear, Todd, and Anthony A. Braga. 1995. "Community Corrections." In *Crime,* edited by James Q. Wilson and Joan Petersilia.

Crime State Rankings 1994. 1994. Morgan Quitno Corporation publication.

Data Analysis Unit. 1991. *California Prisoners and Parolees 1991*. California Department of Corrections publication.

Davies, Malcolm. 1993. *Punishing Community-Based Intermediate Sanctions*.

Doble, John. 1987. *Crime and Punishment: The Public's View*.

Gerstein, Dean, et al. 1994. *Evaluating Recovery Services: The California Drug and Alcohol Treatment Assessment (CALDATA)*. California Department of Alcohol and Drug Programs publication.

Greenfeld, Lawrence A. 1992. *Survey of State Prison Inmates, 1991*. U.S. Department of Justice, Bureau of Justice Statistics publication.

Greenwood, Peter W., C. Peter Rydell, Allan F. Abrahamse, Jonathan P. Caulkins, James Chiesa, Karyn E. Model, and Stephen P. Klein 1994. *Three Strikes and You're Out: Estimated Benefits and Costs of California's New Mandatory-Sentencing Law*. RAND publication, MR–509-RC.

Holtby, Sue, et al. 1993. *Data Set Summary: Alcohol and Drug Use in California*. UCLA School of Public Health publication.

Irwin and Austin. 1994. *It's About Time: America's Imprisonment Binge*.

Karoly, Lynn Al. 1992. "The Widening Income and Wage Gap Between Rich and Poor: Trends, Causes, and Policy Options." In *Urban America: Policy Options for Los Angeles and the Nation*. RAND publication.

Legislative Analyst's Office. 1991. *Community Corrections*. State of California publication.

_____. 1993. *Judiciary and Criminal Justice*. State of California publication.

_____. 1994. *Crime in California*. State of California publication.

_____. 1995. *The "Three Strikes and You're Out" Law—A Preliminary Assessment*. State of California publication.

Little Hoover Commission. January 1994. *Putting Violence Behind Bars: Redefining the Role of California's Prisons*.

Lynch, James P. 1995. "Crime in International Perspective." In *Crime*, edited by James Q. Wilson and Joan Petersilia.

MacKenzie, Doris. 1993. Boot Camp Prisons: Components, Evaluations, and Empirical Issues. *Federal Probation*, 54(3):44–52.

MacKenzie, Doris, and Dale Parent. 1992. "Boot Camp Prisons for Young Offenders." In *Smart Sentencing: The Emergence of Intermediate Sanctions*, edited by J. Byrne, A. Lurigio, and J. Petersilia.

MacKenzie, Doris, and J. W. Shaw. 1990. "Inmate Adjustment and Change During Shock Incarceration: The Impact of Correctional Boot Camp Programs." *Justice Quarterly* 7(1):125.

Mande, Mary. 1993. *Opinions on Sentencing in Washington: The Results of Four Focus Groups*. Washington State Sentencing Guidelines Commission publication.

Messinger, Sheldon L., et al. 1988. *Parolees Returned to Prison and the California Prison Population*. BCS Collaborative Report, California Attorney General's Office.

Morris, Norval, and Michael Tonry. 1990. *Between Prison and Probation: Intermediate Sanctions in a Rational Sentencing System*.

Petersilia, Joan. 1990. Crime and Punishment in California: Full Cells, Empty Pockets and Questionable Benefits. RAND Corp., Santa Monica, CA.

Petersilia, Joan. 1993. "Crime and Punishment in California: Full Cells, Empty Pockets, and Questionable Benefit." Paper prepared for California Policy Seminar, Berkeley.

Petersilia, Joan, and Elizabeth Piper Deschenes. 1994. "Perception of Punishment: Inmates and Staff Rank the Severity of Prison Versus Intermediate Punishments." *The Prison Journal* 74 (September).

Petersilia, Joan, and Susan Turner. 1993. "Intensive Probation and Parole." In *Crime and Justice*. Vol. 17:281.

Petersilia, Joan, Susan Turner, James Kahan, and Joyce Peterson. 1985. *Granting Felons Probation: Public Risks and Alternatives*. RAND publication.

Piehl, Anne, and John J. DiIulio. 1995. "Does Prison Pay? Revisited." *Brookings Review* 13(1): 21–25.

Skolnick, Jerome. 1990. Gangs and Crime Old as Time, But Drugs Change Gang Culture. In Bureau of Criminal Statistics, California 1980–1989. Sacramento, CA.

Spelman, William. 1994. *Criminal Incapacitation*.

Task Force on Gangs and Drugs. 1992. California Association of Counties. California County Fact Book, Sacramento, CA.

Tonry, Michael. 1995. *Malign Neglect: Race, Crime, and Punishment in America*.

Tonry, Michael, and Mary Lynch. 1995. "Intermediate Sanctions." In *Crime and Justice*. Vol. 19.

Zimring, Franklin E., and Gordon Hawkins. 1992. "Prison Population and Criminal Justice Policy in California." Paper prepared for California Policy Seminar, Berkeley.

_____. 1995. *Incapacitation: Penal Confinement and Restraint of Crime*.

Comment: Net Repairing: Rethinking Incarceration and Intermediate Sanctions

JOHN J. DIIULIO JR.

No one who has followed her work will be surprised to learn that Joan Petersilia has done it again. Her chapter, "Diverting Nonviolent Prisoners to Intermediate Sanctions: The Impact on Prison Admissions and Corrections Costs," represents an outstanding contribution to our knowledge about California's prison population and the social costs and benefits of incarceration as well as various types of intermediate sanctions programs. Characteristically for Petersilia, she makes every effort to let the data speak for itself, weighs competing findings and moral claims, and strives to speak truth to power.

California has enacted one of the country's most expansive three strikes laws. Many states are pushing ahead with truth-in-sentencing legislation. A few jurisdictions are inching toward blanket no-parole policies. Petersilia's chapter should be of interest to all who seek an open-minded, empirically grounded perspective on the future of sentencing policy in California and nationally. I want to focus on four issues raised by her fine chapter: (1) who really goes to prison in California and nationally; (2) the case for investing more in intermediate sanctions; (3) the politics of "get-tough" sentencing policy; and (4) the possibility of a new intellectual consensus on crime policy.

Who Really Goes to Prison?

Like most citizens, if not like most criminologists, I have long believed that almost all state prisoners in California and nationally are violent or repeat offenders, that incarcerating them contributes in a significant way to public safety, and that the social benefits of imprisonment, even if measured solely in terms of its incapacitation value (i.e., the number of serious crimes averted by keeping convicted criminals behind bars), far exceed the social costs.

Based on data representing 711,000 state prisoners in 1991, Lawrence Greenfield of the U.S. Bureau of Justice Statistics (BJS) has found that fully 94 percent of state prisoners have been convicted of a violent crime or served a previous sentence to probation or incarceration (Bureau of Justice Statistics 1993, 11). Performing the same analysis on BJS data sets on state prisoners in 1974, 1979, and 1986 yields virtually the same results: Over 90 percent of state prisoners have been, and continue to be, violent or repeat offenders. In 1991, 61 percent of federal prisoners were serving a sentence for a violent crime or were either on probation or incarcerated in the past (Bureau of Justice Statistics 1994a, 6).

Based on two of the largest surveys in state prison systems (Wisconsin in 1990, New Jersey in 1993) ever conducted, Harvard economist Anne Morrison Piehl and I have found that state prisoners commit a median of twelve nondrug felonies in the year prior to their imprisonment (DiIulio and Piehl 1991; Piehl and DiIulio 1995). Other recent studies offer higher estimates. For example, National Bureau of Economic Research economist Steven D. Levitt has found that "(i)ncarcerating one additional prisoner reduces the number of crimes by approximately 13 per year, a number in close accordance with the level of criminal activity reported by the median prisoner in surveys"(1995, 25). Likewise, economists Thomas B. Marvell and Carlisle E. Moody Jr. of William and Mary College have estimated that "in the 1970s and 1980s each additional state prisoner averted at least 17 index crimes. . . . For several reasons, the real impact may be somewhat greater, and for recent years a better estimate may be 21 crimes averted per additional prisoner"(1994, 136).

Without exception, widely cited studies that suggest that most prisoners are not serious criminals have been found to be based on shallow data and inferior methods (Logan 1991). No self-respecting policy analyst can shrink either from ongoing econometric and other research on the public's investment in incarceration, or from the growing body of empirical findings about who really goes to prison and how many crimes they commit when free (DiIulio 1995).

Still, I have also always harbored at least two sets of doubts about who really goes to prison and whether there exists either a sufficient public safety rationale or a sufficient public retribution rationale, or both, for incarcerating them.

The first set of doubts concerns drug law violators. Of the 241,709 new court commitments to thirty-five states' prison systems in 1991, 72,423 (30 percent) were drug law violators, 16,632 (6.8 percent of the total) of them for possession, the remaining 55,791 (23.2 percent of the total) for drug trafficking and other drug crimes (Bureau of Justice Statistics 1994b, 626). Of the 36,648 new court commitments to federal prisons in 1991, 14,564 (42 percent) were drug law violators, 703 (2 percent of the total) for possession, the remaining 13,861 (40 percent of the total) for drug trafficking and other drug crimes (Bureau of Justice Statistics 1994b, 633). Most imprisoned drug traffickers are hardly low-level dealers. For example, the average quantity of drugs involved in federal cocaine trafficking cases was 183 pounds, whereas the average for marijuana traffickers was 3.5 tons (Bureau of Justice Statistics 1994a, 13).

The fact remains, however, that some small but as yet undetermined fraction of imprisoned state and federal drug law violators are neither major drug traffickers nor persons who have committed lots of serious nondrug felonies. At present, it is impossible to know how many low-level "drug-only" offenders—first-time or repeat criminals whose only crimes, or most serious crimes, have been low-level drug crimes or mere possession—are behind bars in America today. One recent survey of state prisoners suggests that the figure could be as high as 15 percent (Piehl and DiIulio 1995, 25).

From most of the empirical research on the subject, there would appear to be little public safety (incapacitation) argument for keeping drug-only offenders behind bars: A low-level drug offender sent away is replaced by a new one.

Is there any public retribution argument for incarcerating drug-only offenders? Joan Petersilia asserts that the "public doesn't necessarily want prison, they want public safety!" Amen, but the same undoubtedly goes double for intermediate sanctions and prevention programs. As I will discuss in more detail, the national public consensus in favor of locking up violent and repeat criminals is not only 3,000 miles wide but many layers of justifiable outrage at revolving-door justice deep. The public most definitely wants hardened criminals (and not just violent ones) to do long, hard time. Whether there is, in fact, a measurable public retribution argument for incarcerating any given category of convicted criminals, from mass murderers to drug-only offenders, from high-rate property thieves to high school graffiti vandals, can be known only after more extensive and refined public opinion research on sentencing policy has been completed.[5]

My second set of doubts about who really goes to prison and whether they need to be incarcerated centers on parole violators. In 1990 I attended a conference at Berkeley on California's blue-ribbon report on inmate population management. Almost every speaker at that conference took the line that the growth in the state's prison population was being fueled by the return to prison of mere technical parole violators. Since then, other high-level reports on the growth in California's prison population have taken the same line. Likewise, as Petersilia notes in her paper, respected criminologists have argued that nationally about a third of prisoners are committed to prison not for new crimes but rather for violations of the technical conditions of their probation or parole.

But Petersilia reveals that the picture of the mere technical parole violator is *not* the true picture of who really goes to prison in California; diverting these quick-in, quick-out convicts would save little money and free up little prison space. She finds that in 1991 some 45,954 (55 percent) of the 84,194 persons admitted to California prisons were indeed "parole violators." But only 3,116 of them (3.7 percent of total admissions, 6.7 percent of parole violator admissions) were "true, technical violators." The other 42,834 parole violator admissions (51 percent of total admissions, 96 percent of parole violator admissions) were responsible for thousands and thousands of new crimes, including 255 who were convicted of murders. This finding on parole violators is not terribly surprising. After all, based on national data gathered and analyzed by BJS, we have long known that about a third of all violent crime arrestees are on probation (16 percent), parole (7 percent), or pretrial release (12 percent) at the time of their arrest. Data on particular jurisdictions mirror that persistent national finding. For example, over a fifty-eight-month period between January 1987 and October 1991, Florida parolees alone committed over 15,000 violent and property crimes, including 346 murders (Statistical Analysis Center 1993, 3). Likewise, from 1990 to 1993, Virginia convicted 1,411 persons of murder, 474 (33.5 percent) of whom had an active legal status at the time they did the crime, 156 (11 percent) on probation, 91 (6.4 percent) on parole, and 227 (16 percent) on pretrial release, unsupervised community release, or with suspended sentences.[6]

Beefing up Probation and Parole

What are the policy implications of such findings on the crime toll exacted by parole violators and other convicted community-based felons? Like most Americans, my main answer is to keep dangerous convicted criminals behind bars where they belong rather than letting them slip and slide in and out of custody. But I also agree with Petersilia that part of the answer is to invest more in intermediate sanctions. More generally, I believe that we need to stop worrying about net-widening and start doing some serious net-repairing.

Over five years ago I argued that we needed to begin "punishing smarter"(DiIulio 1989). There was, I maintained, absolutely no escape from the need to build more prisons and jails while investing more in well-managed community-based corrections programs (DiIulio 1991a). After predicting that prison, jail, probation, and parole populations would soar in the 1990s, I argued that some "community-based programs work, but most of them do not. And those that do work, like the institutional practices that are successful, have in common that they are highly structured, intensively managed, and embody an unblinking recognition of the fact that their clients are people who, if left to their own devices, might well break the law."(1991a, 84) I further argued that "conventional probation and parole programs are a farce"(1991a, 99). "Our choice," I concluded, "is not between more incarceration and more use of alternatives"(1991a, 102). Rather, "the future of American corrections must involve *both* aggressive efforts to build and staff more prisons and jails *and* careful efforts to expand the use of ISPs and kindred alternative programs, ending the insanity of alternatives that permit offenders to do what they please and find new victims at will"(1991a, 102). (Emphases in original.)

Over the last five years, the intellectual and political case for more incarceration has only grown stronger and stronger. But the case for intermediate sanctions has faltered, not only because too many violent and high-risk offenders have been placed on probation and parole, but also because too many community-based corrections programs have continued to be poorly designed, poorly funded and poorly administered—still "a farce."

For starters, about 90 percent of all probationers are part of the very graduated system of punishment called for by advocates of intermediate sanctions—substance abuse counseling, house arrest, community service, and so on. But about half of all probationers simply do not comply with the terms of their probation, and only a fifth of the violators ever go to jail for their noncompliance. "Intermediate sanctions are not rigorously enforced"(Langan 1994, 791). Likewise, in her own coauthored work on intensive supervision programs for high-risk California probationers, Petersilia concluded that these programs "are not effective" and are "more expensive than routine probation and apparently provide no greater guarantees for public safety"(Petersilia and Turner 1990, 98). And in her coauthored study of high-risk Texas parolees, she concluded that the "results were the opposite of what was intended," as the programs produced neither fewer crimes nor lower costs than routine parole (Turner and Petersilia 1992).

But in her chapter for this volume, Petersilia offers an excellent overview of the evidence on ISPs, substance abuse programs, and other intermediate sanctions that, *if* properly designed, funded, and administered, may reduce recidivism among community-based felons.

As I have been saying for over a half decade now, intermediate sanctions can and must be used more fully and more sensibly. In 1987 I wrote the report on corrections for New Jersey's State and Local Expenditure Revenue Policy Commission. In 1990 I cochaired Governor Jim Florio's task force on corrections. And in 1993 I served as chief consultant to the New Jersey Sentencing Policy Study Commission. New Jersey has been inching down the road to reinvesting in certain types of intermediate sanctions—community service ("labor assistance") programs in lieu of jail terms, enforcement court dispositions rather than ongoing probation for unpaid fines and restitution, and more (Governor's Management

Review Commission 1990; Sentencing Policy Study Commission 1993). These experiences have reinforced my sense that reinvesting in some species of intermediate sanctions programs makes sense and is politically doable. But make no mistake: In New Jersey, California, and other states, intermediate sanctions will have no political and fiscal future—and will deserve none—unless certain conditions are met, and met soon.

First, if they wish to be taken seriously as something other than mere anti-incarceration ideologues or elite penal reformers, then advocates of intermediate sanctions must freely and openly admit that prison is now and has long been the alternative sentence of choice, even for violent crime convictions. According to the latest BJS data, 72 percent of all persons under correctional supervision at any given moment in this country are *not* incarcerated. As Table 4.5 shows, nearly a quarter of convicted violent state felons with three or more felony conviction offenses are *not* sentenced to prison.

TABLE 4.5   Convicted Violent Felons Not Sentenced to Prison, by Number of Conviction Offenses, 1992

Most serious conviction offence	*Percent of convicted felons not sentenced to prison for 1, 2, or 3 conviction offenses*		
	One	*Two*	*Three or More*
All Violent Offenses	47%	31%	23%
Murder	9%	5%	3%
Rape	39%	23%	20%
Robbery	30%	21%	38%
Assault	61%	45%	38%
Other	65%	51%	36%

Note: This chart reflects prison non-sentencing rates for felons based on their most serious offenses. For example, if a felon a convicted for murdern, larceny, and drug possession, and not sentenced to prison, he would be represented in this table under murder (the most serious offense) with three or more conviction offenses. "Assault" means aggravated assault; "other" includes offenses such as negligent manslaughter, sexual assault, and kidnapping.

Source: Adapted from *Felony Sentences in State Courts* (Bureau of Justice Statistics 1995, 6).

Such data on felony sentencing help to explain a rather striking finding reported in another recent paper by Petersilia, namely, that in 1991 "there were approximately 372,500 offenders convicted of violent crime **IN** prison, and approximately 590,000 **OUTSIDE** in the community on probation and parole! Overall, we can conclude that nearly three times as many violent offenders (1.02 million) were residing in the community as were incarcerated in prison (372,000)"(Petersilia 1995, 8). (Capitals in original.)

I have absolutely no doubt that most citizens, if presented with (a) the complete criminal histories of the violent and repeat offenders out on probation and parole; (b) the true facts about how little supervision of any kind most such offenders actually receive; and (c) the total picture of the fiscal and other opportunity costs of incarcerating these criminals for all or most of their terms would vote to imprison half or more of them forthwith. But I am equally certain that they would also vote to increase substantially public spending on community corrections and to demand that probation and parole agencies develop the administrative muscle needed to do their work in a way that enhances rather than chances public safety.

As Petersilia argues, there is a clear and compelling crime control rationale for reinvesting in community corrections, for "a failure to provide adequate funding for community corrections invariably places the public at risk"(Petersilia 1995, 8). But in her paper, she weakens her budding case for beefing up probation and parole in three ways.

First, she asserts that community-based programs can have "more punitive bite than prison." As Douglas C. McDonald was among the first to show by means of first-rate empirical research, for some types of low-level offenders under some types of community-based programs, punishment without walls is experienced as more punitive than secure confinement (1987). And having once studied California's prison system, I need no persuading either that the state's prisoners can do pretty much what they please behind bars, including consort with fellow gang members, or that California's incarcerated convicts are not starved for amenities and services.

But if you were to ask a large random sample of California prisoners whether they would rather remain incarcerated or do time on an ISP or community-based substance abuse program, I would be surprised if you turned up only a few volunteers.

Also, dare to consider the criminologically incorrect possibility that America's prisons need to be more "punitive" (more restrictions on inmate movement and association, few inmate amenities and services), both in absolute terms and relative to community-based sanctions. In a survey of Wisconsin prisoners, over 75 percent of the inmates reported that being in prison was about what they thought it would be like or better than they thought it would be like (DiIulio 1990, 20). Today, few state prisons are country clubs, but even fewer are real hell holes. No one advocates a return to slave-of-the-state-style prisons. But average citizens are entirely justified in asking "Must our prisons be resorts?"(BiDinotto 1994). As I have argued for nearly a decade now, prisons, including "overcrowded" prisons without lots of inmate "treatment" program, can and should be governed in a more administratively disciplined, humane, and cost-effective fashion (DiIulio 1987; DiIulio 1991a; Gaes 1994; Logan and Gaes 1993).

Second, Petersilia attempts to embroider her case for diverting non-violent offenders to intermediate sanctions with various opportunity cost arguments. She pits budget-busting state prisons against the struggling UC system, intoning that "education will lose, because voters fear criminals more than they fear the consequences of an uneducated or undereducated mass of young adults." She frets about the consequences for America's global economic competitiveness. She even quotes a UC vice president for academic affairs who warns of impending fiscal doom and has visions of knowledge-thirsty students forced to go dry.

Isn't that a bit much? After all, every spending decision under the California sun imposes opportunity costs. A dollar spent on prisons is a dollar not spent on schools—and a dollar spent on a UC criminologist's salary is a dollar not spent on an environmental protection agent, a public hospital nurse, a biomedical researcher, or a tax cut.

By the same token, although it is certainly true that the extra dollars spent on implementing the Jones three-strikes law will not solve California's crime problem, it is equally true that the trillions of dollars spent over the last three decades in California and the rest of the country on anti-poverty and social welfare programs have not eradicated poverty, not anymore than the tens of billions of dollars poured into environmental regulation have removed the last traces of pollution (or, for that matter, cleaned up even a quarter of known hazardous waste sites nationally). In truth, it is hard to know whether the returns on the taxpayers' investment in incarcerating the nth thrice-convicted California criminal is greater than, less than, or equal to the returns on hiring the nth UC criminology professor or removing the nth particle of pollution from a California stream. At a minimum, however, we know that opportunity costs fly in all directions and that no increment of public spending solves any of the problems (crime, pollution, poverty, ignorance) that concern us. In each case, progress is made only at the margins, and estimating the marginal social costs and benefits is no easy task.

Third, Petersilia insists that a significant amount of money can be saved by sorting offenders more rationally as between prisons and intermediate sanctions. I simply do not find the limited evidence that she musters in support of this point to be persuasive. Where the fiscal facts about intermediate sanctions are concerned, we must not let the wish be father to the thought. Doing intermediate sanctions right for the big criminal populations that Petersilia has in mind is bound to be expensive—very expensive, I would predict. Remember, too, that even the best people-processing agencies rarely reap fiscal economies of scale, least of all in cases where their clients are dangerous, disorderly, or dysfunctional people. Finally, I see no reason to assume, as Petersilia apparently does, that any money saved on prisons will be used to finance or improve other parts of the justice system. Neither politics nor public finance economics work that way, not even in sunny California.

But if it is truly corrections savings that we are after, then let us look toward spending less than we now do on the biggest of the big-ticket items—prison construction and operations. New modes of prison construction continue to shrink the cost of building high-quality, low-maintenance secure facilities. I remain philosophically opposed to private prison administration, but the post-1985 record clearly supports the privatizers' contention that they can often build high-quality prisons faster and cheaper than the public sector can (not to mention manage low-custody facilities for less).

Moreover, California is one of at least twenty states that now spends less than half of every prison dollar on custody or security (Bureau of Justice Statistics 1994b, 14). Most of the money for prisons goes to staffing and facilities for inmate treatment programs (many of which are ineffective), inmate health care (which includes such things as sex offender therapy), and other inmate amenities and services. In Texas, for example, since 1980 federal court orders have led to an inflation-adjusted ten-fold increase in spending while the inmate population has barely doubled. Much frivolous spending on prisoner amenities and services is court-induced. Pending federal legislation may help to reverse this court-mandated budgetary tide (U.S. House of Representatives 1995).

But with or without legislative relief, let no one suppose that California must spend as much on prisons as it presently does. And let no one estimate the costs of implementing three strikes laws in California or other states without first including an estimate of how many more violent or repeat convicted criminals could be incarcerated "for free" by reducing present levels of per prisoner spending.

Voters Are Not Fools

Petersilia's preliminary findings on who really goes to prison, her case for beefing up probation and parole, and her arguments in favor of drug treatment and several other intermediate sanctions programs are compelling. But the political analysis that surfaces now and again in her chapter is arguably misguided and potentially self-defeating.

At the core of her political analysis is an image of an American mass electorate incapable of figuring out its own interests and ideals in relation to politics, unwilling to make tradeoffs via the policy process, and incorrigible when it comes to heeding the advice and warnings of ostensibly neutral, objective, policy scientists. Like most leading criminologists, she seems settled in the view that public policies in general and crime policies in particular are made by weak-willed politicians who react in knee-jerk fashion to the demands of ill-informed, ill-advised voters. The ballot box, she implies, is stuffed with irrational opinion while the criminology and law journals are teeming with expert knowledge.

But this image of the American voter and domestic politics in the United States bears absolutely no resemblance to the last three decades' worth of empirical findings on public opinion, electoral behavior, and policymaking (Bartels 1993; Fiorina 1981; Kelley 1983; Key 1966; Lodge et al. 1994; Nie et al. 1976; Page and Shapiro 1992; Stokes and DiIulio 1993; Zaller 1992). As the point was famously stated by the father of this empirical literature, the late Harvard political scientist V. O. Key, "Voters are not fools."(Key 1966) As all the research shows, voters know lots about issues that really matter to them. They may have hazy, erroneous, or incomplete information about the details of this or that electoral or policy choice, but they generally have a very good idea as to whether unemployment is up or down, prices at the supermarket are stable or rising, or crime is a problem in their neighborhood.[7] They are remarkably savvy in processing competing information about the short- and long-term consequences of given policy choices. They "consider the source" and discount or filter information from individuals and organizations that they code as ideological, partisan, or materially self-interested. And on some issues— such as abortion, race relations, and punishment for crime—they tend to have strong principles and moral views and outlooks that they want politicians to obey almost without regard to tangible or pecuniary costs.

Likewise, there is overwhelming evidence to suggest that, far from mirroring the public majority's views on crime and other issues, representative institutions routinely and successfully work to mediate them, often resulting in policies that are quite at odds with mass public preferences. Indeed, the American political landscape is marked by many wide gaps between majority preferences and public policies (Forum 1994). Crime policies are no exception to the rule of what political scientists call opinion-policy incongruence. If you doubt it for a moment, just put to a vote the laws and policies that grant pretrial release to half of the defendants with one or more prior felony convictions, sentence nearly half of convicted felons with one violent offense to probation, or keep about seven of every ten persons under correctional supervision on probation and parole.

But although the American political system is designed to frustrate temporary public majorities, it is also designed to *empower persistent public majorities* where "persistent" may be defined as lasting over a period of many staggered legislative and executive elections and across several levels of government. Pressures for direct democracy are normally siphoned off into representative institutions that not only register but refine the persistent demands of mass opinion. But when representative institutions do not respond in ways that narrow the opinion-policy gap in

accordance with persistent majority preferences, then citizens are constitutionally, politically, and legally free to take back their government via
established institutions and procedures. They do so either by wholesale
electoral changes (e.g., voting out incumbents), or, where they are available, by such instruments of direct democracy as the referendum, or
both.

The pot of direct democracy is boiling over on crime policy now because the public feels duped by lawmakers who have talked thought but
have yet to heed public demands for an end to revolving-door justice and
betrayed by experts and policy elites who falsely claim a scientific war-
rant for trashing or trivializing persistent public preferences. On November 8, 1994, conservative Republicans won, won big, and won just about
everywhere, federal, state, and local. For the first time voters for whom
crime was a major issue in deciding how to vote split their votes almost
evenly between Republicans (51 percent) and Democrats (49 percent).
Why? Because for the first time candidates of both parties delivered virtually identical—and identically get-tough—messages on crime and
punishment.

Thus, on the politics of three-strikes laws and the rest, my message for
Petersilia and other superb, progressive-minded criminologists is "Wake
up!" and "Get real!" You have got to learn the political difference between a ripple in a lake and a tidal wave. And you must stop substituting
weak reeds of evidence (for example, the Public Agenda Foundation's reports on how much people, once duly "enlightened," really love alternatives to incarceration after all)[8] for real survey research and the political
realities that are everywhere one turns.

In his methodologically first-rate and comprehensive review of all relevant survey and polling data on crime and punishment published between 1965 and 1990, political scientist William G. Mayer found "clear,
strong evidence that American public opinion" has become "substantially more conservative in its assessment of how to deal with
crime"(1992, 20). Solid majorities of whites and blacks favor the death
penalty; doubt that violent criminals can be rehabilitated; demand that
juveniles who commit violent crimes be treated the same as adults; support making parole more restrictive; want to impose more severe prison
sentences on repeat offenders; and the list goes on (Bureau of Justice Statistics 1994b, section 2).

Of course, as is true on almost every social policy issue, there are all
manner of cracks and crevices in the get-tough consensus on crime policy. For example, one survey found that 91 percent of Americans favor
"tougher parole boards"(Gaubatz 1995, 6). But 79 percent of Americans
also agreed that "in most cases society would be better served if nonviolent criminals were not jailed but were put to work and made to repay

their victims"(Gaubatz 1995, 7). As political scientist Kathryn Taylor Gaubatz observes in her recent and fascinating probe into crime in the public mind, "To say that there is a public consensus about harshness does not mean that Americans across the board hold *thoroughly* harsh views about criminal justice" (1995, 7) (*emphasis in the original*).

Still, Petersilia and most other criminologists are much too quick to seize upon actual or perceived divisions within the get-tough consensus as if they held some potential political importance or could be exploited successfully by raising fears about the real or imagined fiscal stresses created by incarcerating ever more violent or repeat criminals for ever longer terms.

There are always two sides to public opinion on social policy, just as there are always two boxers who climb into the ring for a prize fight. But when one side repeatedly knocks out the other, and does so over a period of decades, then it's time for the persistent loser to acknowledge the superior punching powers of the consistent winner.

Like them or not, the hard facts of political history must be acknowledged. From 1935 to 1975 every state and the federal system had a criminal code based on indeterminate sentencing. As Lawrence Friedman has argued in his brilliant single-volume study of crime and punishment in American history, indeterminate sentencing reflected the political power of and intellectual ascendancy of progressive-minded elites and professionals. But for good or ill (I'd say it's both), the days of expert-led crime policy are dead and gone, and no amount of expert huffing and puffing about opportunity costs, saving money via intermediate sanctions, and the like is going to bring them back.

A New Intellectual Consensus?

In my view, the public has been wiser than the experts on prisons and crime policy all along. But no experts (not even me!) can get to the right of where the public is now heading on crime policy. The only chance policy-oriented crime scholars have of remaining something other than a nuisance to conservative lawmakers and a source of malcontent commentary for liberal journalists is to pool their strength and frame a new intellectual consensus that maybe, just maybe, can help mediate the mass political consensus on crime policy.

In my view, Petersilia's paper advances this cause. The core challenge for policy-oriented criminologists is to identify the general conditions, if any, under which government policies and programs can enhance public safety at a reasonable human and financial cost. If "the future of criminal policy" is one in which we continue to debate incarceration and intermediate sanctions without first identifying the common ground on which we stand, then we will send forth precisely the wrong message at precisely the wrong time, *whatever* that message is—longer sentences, or shorter ones; end "three strikes," or make it two; you'll go bankrupt if you don't expand intermediate sanctions, or you'll suffer lots more crime by repeat offenders if you do.

Instead, I believe that unless the community of interested scholars can recast in common its approach to conceptualizing, analyzing, and articulating crime policies for America, then it will become even more crashingly irrelevant to major federal, state, and local justice decisions than it already is, and deservedly so.

As a beginning, I would suggest that criminologists think in terms of crime and social capital. By social capital I mean socializing forces, civilizing institutions, or cooperative mechanisms for achieving collective social purposes (for example, families, schools, churches, civic associations, community organizations) and the prosocial, community-oriented, public-regarding norms, values, virtues, and behaviors that they foster, facilitate, and enforce. To think in terms of crime and social capital is to stand at the intersection of traditional liberal beliefs about "root causes" and traditional conservative beliefs about the primacy of private institutions. To analyze the nation's crime problem in relation to its stock of social capital is to ask what, if anything, government can do to enrich or preserve rather than deplete the capacity of citizens to check community-sapping disorders and victimizations. And to tie the debate over sentencing policy to the post of social capital is to give plenty of running room to competing perspectives while constraining anyone from straying too near the view that any particular set of sanctioning options is the be all and end all of crime policy.

Conceptually, social capital is a useful way of leveraging what I sense to be our fundamental agreement that crime is mainly a function of demographic and other factors over which no government (certainly no free, limited government) can or should exercise much direct control; that violent crime has become concentrated among America's most truly disadvantaged citizens; that community-oriented solutions to the crime problem are the only ones that can reap real dividends; and, last but not least, that no amount of incarceration, no mix of intermediate sanctions, and no menu of prevention programs can bend crime trends in the absence of an overriding commitment by government to target resources on at-risk children and sinking neighborhoods.

For now, we will all watch and witness what happens with California's expansive three-strikes law and kindred crime policy changes throughout the country. My guess is that these measures will prove to be neither strike outs nor home runs. In the end, the voters will live with and evaluate the consequences, and, in due course, the voters will decide whether to roll back, modify, or end the policy. In the meantime, a new intellectual consensus on crime policy, if one can be fashioned and articulated broadly, may help to persuade the voters and elected leaders to change their preferences. But let us never forget that in a free democratic society the people are sovereign. They have the right to be wrong.

References

Bartels, Larry M. 1993. Messages Received: The Political Impact of Media Exposure. *American Political Science Review* 87:267–285.

BiDinotto, Robert. 1994. Must Our Prisons Be Resorts? *Reader's Digest* (November): 65–71.

Bureau of Justice Statistics. 1993. *Survey of State Prison Inmates, 1991.* U.S. Department of Justice publication.

_____. 1994a. *Comparing State and Federal Prison Inmates, 1991.* U.S. Department of Justice publication.

_____. 1994b. *Sourcebook of Criminal Justice Statistics, 1993.* U.S. Department of Justice publication.

_____. 1995. *Felony Sentences in State Courts.* U.S. Department of Justice publication.

John J. DiIulio Jr. 1987. *Governing Prisons.*

_____. 1989. Punishing Smarter: Penal Reforms for the 1990s. *The Brookings Review* 7(3), 3–12.

_____. 1990. *Crime and Punishment in Wisconsin.* Wisconsin Policy Research Institute publication (December).

_____. 1991a. *No Escape: The Future of American Corrections.*

_____. 1991b. Understanding Prisons: The New Old Penology. *Journal of Law and Social Inquiry* (Winter): 65–99.

_____. 1995. Help Wanted: Economists, Crime and Public Policy. *Journal of Economic Perspectives* 10(1): 3–24.

DiIulio, John J. Jr., and Anne Morrison Piehl. 1991. Does Prison Pay? *The Brookings Review* 9(4): 28–35.

Fiorina, Morris P. 1981. *Retrospective Voting in American National Elections.*

Forum: Public Opinion, Institutions, and Policy Making. 1994. *P.S.: Political Science and Politics* (March).

Friedman, Lawrence. 1993. *Crime and Punishment in American History.*

Gaes, Gerald G. 1994. Prison Crowding Research Examined. *The Prison Journal* 74(3): 329–363.

Gaubatz, Kathlyn Taylor. 1995. *Crime in the Public Mind.*

Governor's Management Review Commission. 1990. *Corrections in New Jersey: Choosing the Future?* State of New Jersey publication.

Kelley, Stanley. 1983. *Interpreting Elections.*

Key, V.O. Jr. 1966. *The Responsible Electorate.*

Langan, Patrick. May 1994. Between Prison and Probation: Intermediate Sanctions. *Science* (264): 791.

Levitt, Steven D. February 1995. *The Effect of Prison Population Size on Crime Rates: Evidence from Prison Overcrowding Litigation.* National Bureau of Economic Research publication, 25.

Lodge, Milton, M. R. Steenbergen, and S. Blau. 1994. The Responsive Voter: Campaign Information and the Dynamics of Candidate Evaluation. *American Political Science Review* 89:309–326.

Logan, Charles H. Who Really Goes to Prison? 1991. *Federal Prisons Journal* (Summer):57–59.

Logan, Charles H., and Gerald G. Gaes. 1993. Meta-Analysis and the Rehabilitation of Punishment. *Justice Quarterly* 10(2):245–263.

McDonald, Douglas C. 1987. *Punishment Without Walls.*

Marvel, Thomas B., and Carlisle E. Moody Jr. 1994. Prison Population Growth and Crime Reduction. *Journal of Quantitative Criminology* 10(2): 136.

Mayer, William G. 1992. *The Changing American Mind,* 20.

Nie, Norman H., Sidney Verba, and John R. Petrocik. 1976. *The Changing American Voter.*

Page, Benjamin I., and Robert Y. Shapiro. 1992. *The Rational Public: Fifty Years of Trends in Americans' Policy Preferences.*

Petersilia, Joan. April 1995. A Crime Control Rationale for Reinvesting in Community Corrections. Paper prepared for the American Society of Criminology Task Force on Community Corrections.

Petersilia, Joan, and Susan Turner. 1990. *Intensive Supervision for High-Risk Probationers.* RAND publication.

Piehl, Anne Morrison, and John J. DiIulio Jr. 1995. Does Prison Pay? Revisited. *The Brookings Review* 13(1): 21–25.

Sentencing Policy Study Commission. 1993. *Final Report of the New Jersey Sentencing Policy Study Commission.* New Jersey State publication.

Statistical Analysis Center. 1993. *SAC Notes: Study Examines Inmate Recidivism.* Florida Department of Corrections publication.

Stokes, Donald E., and John J. DiIulio Jr. 1993. "The Setting: Valence Politics in Modern Elections." In *The 1992 Elections,* edited by Michael Nelson.

Turner, Susan, and Joan Petersilia. 1992. Focusing on High-Risk Parolees. *Journal of Research in Crime and Delinquency* 29 (February): 34.

U.S. House of Representatives. *Report on Title III, "Violent Criminal Incarceration Act of 1995,"* H.R. 667, February 6, 1995.

Zaller, John. 1992. *The Nature and Origins of Mass Opinion.*

Comment: Intermediate Punishments

NORVAL MORRIS

Joan Petersilia's chapter maintains the excellent standard we have come to expect of her; but the result is disappointing. Disappointing not in the sense that my preference for intermediate punishments over imprisonment for the nonviolent is only hesitantly indulged, but disappointing in the sense that even when one of our very best researchers takes on what look like three fairly simple questions, she cannot give definitive answers.

So, I lead my hobbyhorse from its stable in the cupboard and ride off, colors flying, against the mindless attitudes that make up current public policy about crime and its treatment.

Insofar as knowledge of the efficacy of our interventions in the lives of criminals is concerned, we stand about where medicine stood in relation to illness and injury in 1914. The doctors then knew quite a lot about the prevention of some disease. They knew about clean water, about the disposal of sewage, about sepsis; they knew something of the relief of pain and of anaesthetics. We know quite a lot about poverty, about broken homes, about unemployment, and about the relationships between age and crime. They knew how to minimize disease; we know how to minimize crime—though our means are less swift and far less certain than theirs. But they were very unsure what were the best interventions once disease or illness was present; it was quite clear that they helped some sick people but equally clear that they further injured others. They could not desist from trying to help any more than we can desist from punishing and treating convicted offenders; but the results remained inscrutable. No, not inscrutable, rather *inscruted*—to coin an admirable word.

The year 1914 was significant. There followed the greatest human carnage the world had then seen, with injury and disease so rampant, so extensive, that more and more the consequences of the actions of the field hospitals and the casualty clearing stations became starkly manifest. And, after the war, medicine moved slowly but steadily from case studies and war stories to critical methodological evaluation of competing treatments for more and more precisely defined conditions. We have yet to do so.

Lacking clinical trials we rely on unreliable, retrospective statistical matching techniques and evaluations by partisans (conscious or self-deceptive) of the outcome of the study. And recently we have been collecting these unreliable studies into what we pretentiously call megastudies, multiplying error into confusion. This is by no means one-sided; mega-studies can establish that "deterrence works" as well as that "treatment works;" the trick lies in the spurious belief that adding together a steady flow of faulted studies rectifies their defects. And, in any event, all these outcomes are related to definitions of the group to be treated so wide as to defy useful outcome analysis.

I lead this hobbyhorse from its stable because it is a sad day indeed that the Petersilia chapter has to reveal that what used to be regarded as the best statistical data on crime and criminals in the country, that of California, cannot now provide her with the basic data on offenders necessary to answer the three basic questions she sought to answer. It is not that knowledge is lacking on how to gather the necessary data on crime and criminals to bring our discipline into the twentieth century (let alone the twenty-first); we know what needs to be done. And we know how to run clinical, prospective studies of the consequences of our interventions. But prejudice and ignorance have their attractions to which we cling.

When I gallop along in this ill-mannered way before an audience, I find myself looking out at them and telling them that if medicine had adhered to the fact-finding processes to which we adhere, a large number of them would not be in the audience—they would be dead. This does not seem to move them. I then point out that, by and large, we seem willing to wait for years while the Food and Drug Administration insists that pharmaceutical companies rigorously test the drugs they claim would save lives and inhibit diseases before they may sell them. Nor does this move anyone to rousing cheers; it is seen as just more unreal, pie-in-the-sky, academic dreaming.

Even the ambitious "roots of crime" project, financed jointly by the National Institute of Justice and the MacArthur Foundation, has as one of its leading original purposes the testing of alternative interventions for some sections of the cohorts there being studied; but this has been dropped from the project.

At some point I am challenged by a critic of my wooden, equestrian adventure who suggests that controlled clinical trials would, in the response to the convicted offender, be unethical. We must, the critic avers, do our best to protect the community and lead the criminal to lawfulness; we cannot use him as an experimental artifact. We can use the injured and ill in this way, but not the criminal. I still do not understand this. Provided there is genuine doubt of the outcome of alternative punishments/treatments for a precisely defined category of offense/offender, it baffles me that some see their random allocation and equal follow-up as an unethical exercise.

Of course, it is expensive, as are clinical trials in medicine. So, the argument opposing my view must be that it is better to leave crime rates as they are and to waste lives than to spend substantial resources to learn how to minimize these losses. Or is it even worse than that: Being "tough on crime" is required of the politician; it is too much to expect that they could be "tough on crime" *and* tough on the causes of crime *and* toughly insist that our response to crime must become as effective and humane as it can be.

By way of confession and avoidance of the thrust of the critic's argument, I sometimes relate the difficulties that beset one of the two clinical trials that I have been associated with. It aimed to test the consequences of a defined program of imprisonment on a defined group of violent offenders, as contrasted with the then existing imprisonment program to which they were subject. The prison program in the federal prison at Butner, North Carolina, was to be compared with the program existing in the other federal prisons for the same group of offenders. The group having been defined, prisoners in that group were randomly placed between the two programs (though there were arrangements to preserve the comparisons while allowing some to remove themselves from Butner back to the prison from which they had been sent). Two important differences in the Butner program were that release dates were fixed (subject to good behavior), which was not so for the control group, and all treatment programs, other than work, were voluntary in Butner though not elsewhere. The comparison broke down. Observation of Butner by wardens of other prisons led swiftly to an adoption of voluntary programming in their institutions (since more enrolled and completed such programs when they were voluntary). And the then powerful parole board independently came to rely on its parole prediction data to fix release dates reasonably firmly early in the prisoner's sentence, thus removing the other element from the comparison. It was too ambitious a project; it bit off more than we could properly chew; but important lessons were learned and acted upon that would not have been learned absent such an effort. And it was expensive.

The punishment scene is at the moment crowded with questions that could be answered by clinical trials. Let me indulge myself in just one. Are drug treatment programs in prison a sensible expenditure of effort and funds? Would it not be better to run brief preparatory programs in prison and discharge those needing such treatment to community-based residential or nonresidential intensive drug programs, properly monitored? A clinical trial of that question could and should be pursued. No series of studies of in-prison programs, no mega-analysis of their results, will answer that question, nor will similar studies of community-based programs. It is probable that for some offenders one program will do better than the other, and for other offenders it will have the contrary effect. But for which? How to know? It is a sin against the light to continue to deny ourselves

growing knowledge of that categorization. It is the posture of the threatened ostrich to assume that a growing punishment/treatment taxonomy is
beyond our capacity.

Let me lead my tired horse back to its stable and return briefly to intermediate punishments and Joan Petersilia's excellent chapter.

The arguments usually advanced for a great expansion of intermediate
punishments and a consequent reduction of incarcerative punishments
are: Intermediate punishments will save money, will reduce prison
crowding, and will reduce crime. Critical evaluations of these claims suggest that all three are, in the present state of our knowledge, unsubstanti-
ated. In the short run, certainly, IPs do not better protect the fisc, and
even in the long run it is unlikely that the savings would be other than
slight. Likewise, the increase of prison populations progresses relentlessly in today's punitive environment and is only very slightly influenced by the existence of IPs, which, unless they are very carefully protected, tend to draw more from those otherwise sentenced to probation
than those otherwise sentenced to prison. And, finally, we have been unable with any confidence to demonstrate a crime-reductive effect with
the introduction of IPs into a punishment system.

The Petersilia chapter advances discussion on these issues by examining the possible pools of prisoners for whom IPs may be the more appropriate punishments and the cost consequences of alternative community-
based punishments for various categories of prisoners. She helps to
exorcize the misleading mantra of commentators like William Barr and
John DiIulio, uttered with hypnotic frequency, that the fact that the overwhelming proportion of prisoners are "violent or repeat offenders" es-
tablishes something about the appropriateness of their incarceration.

Nevertheless, that mindless mantra still seems to seduce policymakers
who, one would have thought, would quickly see its quality of disinfor-
mation since it is really quite hard to attract a prison term unless either
you commit a crime of violence or have a criminal record. The first category, the violent, form a relatively small group, unless violence is most
widely defined, and the second category, repeat offenders, form a very
large group indeed once all offenses in adulthood or youth and all revocations of probation and parole are included. Many of the latter would,
one would think, be appropriate subjects of IPs; but at the present state of
knowledge there is no firm utilitarian data to buttress such a statement or
to undermine it. On the question of crime reduction, consider Petersilia's
cri de coeur late in her paper, "unbelievably, we have no follow-up studies of offenders sentenced to prison, jail, or community punishments."

So, Petersilia is on rock-hard ground indeed in advocating "an intermediate sanction experiment, where the least risky . . . of the target population are released to participate in a model intermediate sanction pro-

gram. The experiment would be evaluated to determine the costs and benefits of such a diversionary program." This should be done whether or not her other recommendation for the appointment of a Blue Ribbon Commission on Community Based Punishments is acted on. To fail to acquire knowledge, which could so readily be obtained, is to emulate the posture of the threatened ostrich.

In the interim, in our present 1914 gloom, what can be said about expanding IPs? One has to turn from the utilitarian to larger values, values of fairness and decency—to deontological values. And then the answer seems to me fairly obvious. We don't know with any precision what impact IPs have on prison populations, on costs, or on recidivism. We do know that fair and parsimonious punishment requires a graduated range of severity of punishment in which degrees of separation from the community define the degrees of severity. The case for expansion of IPs is thus strong and becomes compelling when there is added serious evaluations of their social consequences.

Notes

1. It is important to note that the median time served in CDC institutions does not count time served in local jail prior to CDC transfer. It is calculated as the months served prior to first release to parole for first time and parole violators returned with a new term by the courts and paroled for the first time following the new offense. It is also true that the median time served is less than the mean time served by about 15 percent.

2. Operational costs cover the care and feeding of inmates but exclude the costs for the cells they occupy. It has been estimated that operational costs are less than a quarter of total costs incurred through imprisonment.

3. The percent of CDC budget saved is not over one year (annualized), since some of the prison terms served were greater than one year. Rather the calculation is based on summing the total operational dollars expended in carrying out the prison sentence for all of those admitted in 1991 (which equaled about $1.8 billion) and computing a percent of the total accounted for by that offense category.

4. Two excellent attempts to identify and monetarize the costs associated with alternative sanctions can be found in Cavanaugh (1990) and Zimring and Hawkins (1995).

5. I am in the early stages of conducting such research.

6. These data are from my ongoing national study of the legal status of convicted murderers, 1980 to 1995.

7. One might expect criminologists to know as much with respect to crime: All the survey data show that Americans' fears of being victimized by crime in their neighborhood vary directly with the objective chances that they will be victimized; hence inner-city minority children are the most worried, followed by central city blacks, and all the way down to affluent and elderly Americans.

8. I have criticized these reports before: For example, see (DiIulio 1991a). Years ago in the course of a meeting at the Edna McConell Clark Foundation, I offered anyone who cites these reports a deal. I will do my best to find the funds to redo the "surveys" exactly as the Public Agenda Foundation did them, but substitute facts and figures about the horrors of revolving-door justice for the anti-incarceration propaganda used in the Public Agenda Foundation's "surveys." You agree to cite the results of my "surveys" as many times, as prominently, as favorably, and as uncritically as you have cited the Public Agenda Foundation's. The offer still stands.

5

Drug Policy

Drug Enforcement, Violent Crime, and the Minimization of Harm

JEROME SKOLNICK

Any discussion of crime policy in the United States necessarily confronts the issue of drugs; in fact, drugs are an important subtheme in all the other principal chapters in this volume. But the way that drugs interact with other issues is neither simple nor obvious. In addition, as Edward Rubin observes in the introduction to this volume, public policy recommendations must mediate between the optimal, as discerned by experts in crime policy, and the politically possible, as determined by real-world decisionmakers and, ultimately, the general public. This adds a further complexity, for nowhere is the gap between the two as wide as in the area of drugs. Crime policy analysts generally agree that imprisonment for drug use, or even drug sale, is an ineffective strategy, but the public seems to demand increasingly severe sanctions for these behaviors.

In this chapter, I will begin by identifying the issues that the other chapters in this volume raise about drug policy. I will then consider the different approaches to this subject: that taking drugs is private behavior which cannot be prohibited by the government; that it is undesirable behavior that the government may prohibit, but need not do so; and that it is reprehensible behavior that the government is obligated to prohibit and combat. The United States has obviously adopted the third policy, dramatically, or melodramatically christened the "War on Drugs." In the third section, the problems associated with this policy are considered; these include the difficulties of enforcing the prohibition; the failure to consider the underlying social and economic causes of drug use; and the deleterious effects of this policy on the nation's character. I will then proceed to a consideration of possible solutions. The fourth section discusses legalization, and suggests that legalization has a number of intrinsic problems, but, in any case, is not a viable policy recommendation because it is entirely unacceptable to the American people. The last section considers ways of modifying, rather than reversing, the War on Drugs approach that are politically feasible and concludes that a drug policy that retains existing prohibitions but focuses more directly on harm minimization would be substantially more effective than the existing approach. This policy of harm minimization is related to the recommendations advanced by the other chapters in this volume. The central point is that drug abuse does indeed underlie many aspects of the crime problem and that an effective, politically acceptable crime policy must incorporate an effective, politically acceptable policy regarding drugs.

Crime Policy and Drugs

Franklin Zimring and Gordon Hawkins argue that the broad category of "crime" is not what Americans fear most. Rather, it is violent crime that they find odious—assault, rape, robbery, and, of course, homicide. Americans do not lie awake worrying about securities fraud, nor are they terrified at the loss of a TV set or a stereo. Moreover, what is most troubling about a burglary is not the economic loss, which is often covered by insurance. Rather, it is the loss of personal security, the invasion of privacy, the apprehension that one might be assaulted by a burglar, even though, as Zimring and Hawkins point out, such assaults are relatively rare.

There are several aspects of the relationship between drugs and crimes that are illuminated by this observation. On the one hand, the possession of drugs, the use of drugs, and the sale of drugs to an adult belong in a category of crimes that is usually categorized as "vice," and that category also includes gambling and prostitution. These crimes are sometimes called "victimless" because they are consensual, involving the sale of an unlawful substance or service to a willing buyer. Dictionaries define "vice" as evil or wicked conduct, but that cannot be right. Homicide and beatings of innocent victims are also "evil." The difference, of course, is that the willing buyers of vice are gratification seekers, whether through drugs, sex, or gambling. Consequently the concept of "vice" connotes more than wickedness, although it surely may connote that—it suggests both wickedness and *pleasure* (Skolnick 1988). Clearly, these are not the sorts of crimes that people fear, according to Zimring and Hawkins. Just as very few people lie awake at night worrying about securities fraud, few people lie awake worrying that other adults will buy drugs or engage in gambling.

On the other hand, drugs clearly play a major role in many of the crimes that people fear most. Because drugs are illegal, their prices are unusually high, and many addicts must resort to crime, including violent crime such as robbery, to obtain the money that they need to support their habits. In addition, drug dealers regularly resort to violence to enforce agreements, first because criminal organizations are the natural sellers of an illegal product, and second because these organizations do not have access to legal enforcement mechanisms such as the courts. Finally, people who are taking drugs may commit violent offenses because of the disinhibiting character of these drugs. Between the two categories of pure vice crime and truly violent crime lies the sale of drugs to a minor; this is something that people fear, generally on behalf of their own children, but it does not seem to produce the same sense of dread that violence does.

Joan Petersilia's chapter is also about distinctions among crimes and criminals, as a chapter on intermediate sanctions must be. As she points out, 32 percent of the inmates of California's prisons have been convicted of "drug-only" offenses—use, possession, or sale, and most of those, some 78 percent, or 25 percent of the total prison population, have been convicted only of use or possession. This means that we are making extensive use of prisons to incapacitate people who harm only themselves, or who at most facilitate those who are harming only themselves. Petersilia's suggestion is that we can place such people in less restrictive settings without creating significant risk of harm and that we can use some of the funds we save for treatment programs, which have a demonstrably higher success rate than prison in ending drug use. Again, there are complexities. Many of those who are incarcerated on drug-only charges have in fact committed more serious crimes as part of their "criminal career." Many of those incarcerated for violent offenses, on the other hand, have committed their offense as a result of drug addiction and might be as well served by treatment programs as the less serious offenders.

With respect to Peter Greenwood's chapter, it seems clear that a large part of preventing crime involves the prevention of drug use. At the simplest level, the reason is that drug possession, use, and sale constitute a large and growing proportion of the crimes committed in this country. But it is also because the drug culture is a criminogenic culture, and that prevention, when it is successful, frequently involves changing people's social patterns so that they are not exposed to continual inducement to commit crimes of any sort. Greenwood's chapter leaves open the question of whether treatment programs that are specifically focused on drug use would be effective. The findings he summarizes, however, strongly suggest that there are some general prevention programs that will produce significant, beneficial effects on the level of drug use.

Differing Approaches to Drug Policy

There are a wide range of attitudes about drug use. For present purposes, three major views can be identified: first, that drug use is private conduct; second, that drug use is undesirable, even deviant behavior that the state can treat as *mala prohibitum*; and third, that drug use is morally repugnant, and that the state is obligated to criminalize it as *mala in se*.

The belief that drug use is a private matter is most closely associated with John Stuart Mill's theory of individual liberty. Mill feared the tyranny of the majority, which he described as "the tyranny of the prevailing opinion and feeling." He did not deny that collective opinion had a legitimate need to interfere with individual independence. But he believed that unless society found the proper limit and maintained it against encroachment, the result would be a form of political despotism. This limit is widely known among philosophers as the "harm principle." "The only purpose for which power can be rightfully exercised over any member of a civilized community, against his will," Mill says "is to prevent harm to others" (Mill, 1982, 68). Mill did not oppose persuading, entreating, or remonstrating with people who engage in admittedly self-destructive conduct. But he believed that the criminal law, the coercive power of government, should not be used to deter and to punish individuals in that part of conduct that "merely concerns himself."

At the time Mill was writing *On Liberty*, Maine had recently passed a nineteenth century alcohol prohibition statute. The "Maine Law" figures prominently in Mill's discussion of liberty. He recognized that those who sold alcoholic beverages—"strong drink" as he called it—had an interest in promoting sales that might be harmful to the common good. Contrary to popular assumptions about Mill, and his commitment to freedom of speech, he was not opposed to regulating such sales and their advertising. On the contrary, he saw intemperance as a "real evil," justifying state restrictions.

Given that recognition, Mill uses the example of drunkenness to illustrate the boundaries of the harm principle. Whether someone becomes drunk or not is their business. But when, under the influence of alcohol, the drunken person commits an act of violence against another, it becomes the government's business. The key distinction for those who stand by the harm principle is between private and public space. Individuals should be free to gamble in their own homes or private clubs, but public gambling should not at all be permitted. A Millian liberal distinguishes between being in a state of intoxication in the privacy of one's home, thereby doing whatever harm intoxication does to oneself; and driving on public roads under the influence of drugs or alcohol. And a Millian liberal opposes, on principle, as "legal paternalism," any form of coercive legislation that seeks to protect individuals from self-inflicted harm.

A second view regards drug use as at worst undesirable or deviant, but not necessarily so socially harmful as to demand its characterization as a "crime." How we should deal with it is less a matter of the principled relationship between the government and the individual than a weighing of the costs and benefits of one policy over another. In this view, drug use should be regulated as *mala prohibitum*, not because it is a serious "evil," but because drug use threatens individual health and welfare and entails external costs that society must bear. This position is—dare we say post-Millian—in that it calculates the interests of society as against individual freedom. It balances the costs and benefits of proposed policies. Thus, the Millian vision is broadened to include a plurality of other considerations, including costs to community and public safety. This vision, I suggest, infuses most of the chapters in this volume.

The third approach to drugs is based on the premise that drug dealing and use is something morally repugnant in and of itself; the solutions that flow from this premise treat people's involvement in drugs as major crimes that must be punished severely. From the perspective of the *mala in se* theorist, the social structural causes of crime and drug use are largely irrelevant, as if they were invisible. Since individual moral failure, the failure of will, activates the drug problem, environmental or medical causes—poverty, unemployment, family breakdown, addiction—need not be given high priority. Punishment rather than treatment or prevention becomes the primary and preferred response. This vision has, of course, serious implications for the workings of our criminal justice system at every level—for the police, the courts, and the prisons.

When, in September 1989, the Bush administration published its first *National Drug Control Strategy*, that document set a tone and direction that continued throughout the Bush and, until recently, the Clinton presidency. (Another Bush presidential *Strategy* was published in January 1992, with only a slightly different ordering of priorities.) The original strategy, as formulated by William Bennett, opted strongly for the *mala in se* approach; it declared that the use of any drug, in whatever quantity, was attributable to the deficient moral character of individuals, a weakness of will. Drug use was said to "degrade human character" and a good society "ignores its people's character at its peril" (Office of National Drug Control Policy 1989).

The high priority accorded repressive law enforcement seemed to flow naturally from the moralistic attitudes expressed toward drug use and the role of government in the 1989 strategy. Adopting "The War on Drugs" as its overriding metaphor, the *1989 Strategy* fulfilled the metaphor's promise by advocating a vast expansion of the apparatus of social control, particularly of law enforcement and prisons. When he introduced the *1989 Strategy* on national television, President Bush proposed that the federal government increase spending to combat drugs by $1.5 billion for enforcement and $1.5 billion for interdiction but only by $321 million for treatment and $250 million for education. The *Strategy* advocated that billions more be spent by the states, particularly to expand the criminal justice system. And it has indeed been expanded.

The Dilemmas of the "War on Drugs" Approach

A natural question is whether the current federal policy, based on the *mala in se* approach, has been effective in achieving that policy's stated purpose, which is to abolish drug use in the United States. One would think that the heightened penalties and huge resources we have devoted to drug enforcement at the state and national levels would long ago have dried up the drug trade. That never really happened. As Reuter and MacCoun recently concluded: "Even among its supporters, the American drug control strategy provides few grounds for enthusiasm. Despite many indications that the prevalence of drug use has declined over the past decade, in many ways the severity of the drug problem has remained fairly constant" (1995).

The "get tough" approach is based on a theory of deterrence that is superficially persuasive. If we raise the cost of selling and using drugs by increasing penalties, it is assumed, we will drive out dealers and sellers. In the abstract, the theory seems to make sense. In practice, when we delve more deeply into its operation, we can understand how and why it doesn't work and may even worsen the drug problem.

The drug problem has two facets: one is abuse and addiction, whether of legal or illegal drugs; the second is the crime and violence connected to illegal drug use and sale. The War on Drugs approach has had little impact on either of these problems, except to worsen street violence, because it underestimated the difficulties faced by law enforcement agencies in controlling the distribution and use of drugs; was insensitive to the social and economic aspects of drug marketing and use in the United States; and was oblivious to the implications of a "war" on drugs for the character of the nation.

The Difficulties of Law Enforcement

One reason why the War on Drugs is inefficient is that there are specific impediments to law enforcement that do not seem soluble, no matter what level of resources is devoted to the effort. In 1990, I spent four days reviewing the border situation in California with the assistance of the California State Narcotics Agency. The agency assigned a Mexican-American agent to me in Los Angeles, to help me understand the drug scene in southern California. Through his assistance, I was able to observe DEA operations and to interview local and federal police. As with most narcotics police, they seemed to be intelligent, energetic, and well supplied with equipment. I was told that 60 percent of the narcotics entering the United States passed through California. However, the Mexican border posed a major and virtually insolvable problem. The Mexican-American state narcotics agent who was my guide, and who had been raised in a Los Angeles gang neighborhood, took me to a Mexican restaurant for lunch and told me about his childhood and his entry into the police. He looked at me earnestly and said with some exasperation: "Look professor, four-hundred thousand of my people cross the border illegally every year. How can you stop a much smaller number who carry a kilo or two of cocaine on their back?" (Skolnick et al. 1988). A 1993 study funded by the White House Office of National Drug Control Policy reported that about 70 percent of all cocaine smuggled into the United States comes across the Mexican border. The study, conducted by the Advanced Systems Integration Department of the Sandia National Laboratory at Albuquerque, New Mexico, said that past experience has shown that no single measure such as one fence, one patrol road, one set of lights will prevent illegal crossings. "The illegal aliens," the report states, "have shown that they will destroy or bypass any measure placed in their path" (*San Diego Union-Tribune* 1995, B4).

"As we have expanded our interdiction efforts," the *1989 Strategy* stated, "we have seized increasing amounts of illegal drugs. Stepped up interdiction has also forced drug traffickers to make significant operational changes. . . . Every time we disrupt or close a particular trafficking route, we have found that traffickers resort to other smuggling tactics that are even more difficult to detect" (Office of National Drug Control Policy 1989, 73). This is undoubtedly true, but it argues against—rather than for—stepped up interdiction.

More recently, the *1992 Strategy* took pride in record drug seizures. I ran a LEXIS search on September 30, 1995, for "record w/5 seizures" under the "News" library and the file "curnews," that is, the past two years. The search brought up an astonishing 3,116 stories. The first story reported that British Customs officials were "celebrating" a record seizure of 906 kilograms of heroin in Britain in 1994–1995, "more than 300 kg more than the previous record." But should record seizures—in Britain or the United States—be considered an accomplishment or a concern? If we interpret the record seizures as a cutoff of the drug supply, they are a triumph. But if we believe, as most observers of the drug trade do, that authorities interdict around 10 percent to at most 15 percent of the shipments of drugs, record seizures suggest the enormity of the drug supply and the relatively efficient organization of the suppliers. Data reported in the 1996 strategy report underscores the point. The *Strategy* (National Drug Control Policy 1996, 48) reports that between 1988 and 1993, cocaine amounts available for U.S. consumption remained at a fairly constant level. "However, cocaine availability appears to have increased in recent years." This, of course, despite the record seizures.

Given this failure to reduce the volume of drugs, what is the justification for enormous expenditures for interdiction? The *1989 Strategy* claims that interdiction "has major symbolic and practical value"(National Drug Control Policy 1989, 74). The symbolic value is gained from showing foreign governments and trafficking organizations our commitment to combating the drug trade. Although symbolism may seem an odd, even fanciful, reason for policy, much of the current strategy is grounded on symbolic themes and on the appearance of determination, rather than on a careful assessment of its costs and benefits.

The practical value of these expenditures is just as elusive. Interdiction is supposed to reduce street sales by increasing smuggling costs—in effect, taxing smuggling—and thus raising the street price. This assumes that smuggling costs constitute a significant percentage of street price. But that simply is not true. It is relatively cheap to produce and refine a kilo of cocaine, perhaps around $1,000 for a kilo that might eventually retail for $250,000 when broken down into quarter- or even eight-gram units. Smuggling costs amount to a slight percentage of retail price, less than 10 percent (Reuter 1988, 56). In other words, all our interdiction efforts can only produce a minor effect on the drug market.

Another law enforcement problem is that even the apparent successes can have unexpected and counterproductive effects. Our national drug policy has made the incarceration of "drug kingpins" a focus of the drug war. But when we succeed in incarcerating kingpins, we face what I have elsewhere called The Felix Mitchell Dilemma, named in honor of the West Coast's formerly most infamous drug distributor. In the mid-1980s, a federal strike force, with considerable assistance and dogged investigation by an Oakland Police vice squad, succeeded in convicting and imprisoning the East Bay's three leading drug dealers. Among these was the legendary Mitchell, who, the prosecution charged, was largely responsible for Oakland's becoming a major drug dispensary. A federal district court sentenced him to life without possibility of parole for his drug-related convictions (Covino 1985). Mitchell was murdered in federal prison and commanded the largest public funeral in the history of Oakland. Deterrence theory would predict that confining three leading drug dealers, and the killing of one of them, would reduce the violence and other crimes related to narcotics. On the contrary. Oakland then experienced a continued increase in narcotics crimes and the absence of any indication that the Oakland residents perceived the community to be safer (Center for the Study of Law and Society 1988).

The post–Felix Mitchell drug-related homicide rate proved especially vexing. Gangs competing for the Mitchell territory accounted for multiple murders, high-speed chases, daytime assassinations, four assaults on police officers, and scores of other shootings. Drug sales continued unabated. With Mitchell's monopolistic pricing eliminated, competition reduced the price of crack cocaine. Thus, the main effect of Mitchell's imprisonment was to destabilize the market, lowering drug prices and increasing violence as rival gang members challenged each other for market share. By indirection, effective law enforcement, followed by incapacitation, had stimulated serious violence.

This pattern is endlessly repeated. On January 3, 1994, the *San Francisco Chronicle* reported the successful arrest and prosecution of some of Mr. Mitchell's successors, Timothy Bluitt and Marvin Johnson. The *Chronicle* also reported that other gangsters are already vying for control of the Bay Area drug market. "When a guy like Bluitt goes down, someone takes his place and gets an even bigger slice of the pie," the *Chronicle* reported an anonymous federal agent as having said. "The whole process is about consolidating turf and power"(Doyle 1994, A1).

Another counterproductive effect of interdiction is what might be called "the Darwinian Trafficker Dilemma." Interdiction undercuts the marginally efficient drug traffickers and their operations, while the fittest—the best organized, the most corrupting of authorities, the most ruthless and efficient—survive. As Stephen G. Trujillo, a former Army Ranger, Green Beret, and enforcement specialist with the Drug Enforcement Administration's Operation Snowcap wrote of his experiences in Peru: "Paradoxically, the destruction of dozens of cocaine labs by U.S. and Peruvian forces has only encouraged the coca processors to be more efficient. Smaller, more decentralized labs are processing purer cocaine in the impenetrable jungles" (Trujillo 1992).

If purer cocaine is being produced, so is purer opium, which likely accounts for record seizures. Michael Specter recently reported in the *New York Times* (1995, A1) that Central Asia—especially Kyrgyzstan, Tajikistan, and Afghanistan—has become a drug runner's paradise, lacking effective borders, effective police forces, and alternative sources of hard currency.

As more efficient producers exercise greater control over markets, they may exercise monopolistic control to raise prices. Law enforcement officials may mistakenly assume that rises in the street price of drugs are a result of efficient interdiction strategies. In actuality, higher prices may bring greater profits to efficient suppliers without producing a significance decrease in demand.

The Social and Economic Aspects of Drug Marketing

Although the current policy of interdiction does not appear to be particularly effective, it also seems unlikely that any other "War on Drugs" or crime-control strategy would represent much of an improvement. The reason lies in basic economics. Drug use is a typical "vice" crime in that it is enjoyed by millions, sometimes by the very people who deplore it. Attitudes toward drugs are ambivalent in some cases, and in others, strongly conflictual. According to a recent Gallup poll, almost one-half (45 percent) of Americans say that they, someone they know, or someone in their family has used drugs. Of these, 28 percent report moderate use, and 29 percent describe the drug use as a serious addiction. The *1996 National Drug Control Strategy*, which reports these findings (Office of National Drug Control Policy 1996, 11), goes on to point out that most of these respondents were whites living in households with an income in excess of $35,000.

Thus, the sale of drugs is economically motivated and is responsive to market incentives and disincentives. The question is to how these operate in the context of the drug trade. The 1989 report acknowledged that "[d]espite interdiction's successful disruptions of trafficking patterns, the supply of illegal drugs entering the United States has, by all estimates, continued to grow"(Office of National Drug Control Policy 1989, 73). Why should that have happened? One reason is that demand generates supply for drugs. In 1994, the Drug Enforcement Administration and local police carried out the largest roundup of drug dealers ever conducted in Northern California. Authorities arrested twenty-five suspected gang members, seized twenty kilograms of cocaine and confiscated forty-three weapons and $200,000 in cash. Bob Bender, the special agent in charge with the Drug Enforcement Administration entertained no illusions about the impact of the raid on drug marketing. "We certainly have not stopped the flow of cocaine coming from South America," he said, "and probably won't in the foreseeable future as long as we have a demand"(Lee 1994, A12).

Moreover, in economic terms, much of this demand appears to be relatively inelastic. Addicts have a physical or powerful psychological need for the drug to which they are addicted, and their level of use tends to be driven by their needs rather than the price. Other users may have psychological needs that also make them relatively insensitive to price, as people are with respect to medical care and funeral services. This is not to suggest that prices do not vary, but only that a large part of this large market is insensitive to these variations. Moreover, as Stephen J. Schulhofer recently observed in the *University of Chicago Legal Forum*, if we should succeed in reducing supply and raising prices, what we have done in a market where addict demand is largely inelastic, is to create an "increased need for those who do buy to commit predatory crime to support their purchases"(Schulhofer 1994, 222).

Although the War on Drugs is not likely to alter the demand or the supply of drugs, it can alter the kinds of drugs that are consumed. Although the demand for drugs is relatively inelastic, it may be subject to product substitution. This is not necessarily beneficial.

When the Nixon administration succeeded in reducing the supply of low-potency Mexican marijuana to California in the early 1970s by poisoning Mexican fields, agriculturally skilled drug entrepreneurs developed a high-potency marijuana (sensimilla) industry in Northern California. This example is illustrative of what I have in earlier writings called "The Drug Hardening Paradox"(Skolnick 1990). The more successful law enforcement is at cutting off supply, the more incentive drug dealers have for hardening drugs—that is, developing varieties that are more potent, portable, and dangerous. Thus, the crackdown by state narcotics agents on the California marijuana market has reduced its supply, but the marijuana that is available is far more potent. When I studied drug enforcement thirty years ago, marijuana's active ingredient (THC) was 1 or 2 percent. Hydroponically grown sensamilla measures out at 15–20 percent.

Worse yet, crack cocaine emerged to replace marijuana. My colleagues and I have interviewed Oakland and south central Los Angeles youngsters who have never used marijuana, but who have used crack cocaine, which has been less expensive and more available on California streets (Skolnick et al. 1988) In sum, when law enforcement ignores market forces it may spawn more severe public health problems by generating demand for and production of more potent and dangerous drugs.

Closely related to drug hardening is what I have called "The Demand Substitution Paradox"(Skolnick 1990). Those who are interested in faster living through chemistry often find it possible to substitute one type of drug for another. (Most drug abusers usually ingest more than one drug anyway.) Thus, price rises or lack of availability of one drug may activate consumers to seek out cheaper alternative drugs.

This accounts, in part, for the recent renewed popularity of heroin. Twenty or thirty years ago, heroin was the "problem" drug in American society (Kaplan 1983; Kleiman 1992). In the 1980s it was cocaine. More recently, it has been crack cocaine, which is becoming less popular. By 1992, according to the *National Drug Strategy*, "the price of heroin has dropped, the purity has increased, seizures by law enforcement officials have increased, and there has been an upsurge in heroin emergency room mentions—all, it would seem, indicative of a resurgence in drug use"(Office of National Drug Control Policy 1992, 11). More recent statistics show that the problem has worsened. Deaths from heroin overdose rose 52 percent in San Francisco from 1991 to 1995. In Marin, San Mateo, and San Francisco Counties, heroin deaths more than doubled from 1991 to 1994, and emergency hospital visits due to overdose rose 81 percent (Eranson and Whiting 1996, A1). And since heroin is mostly consumed intravenously, its users are more likely to spread the HIV virus.

Even if we were to succeed in destroying all agricultural drugs through crop destruction efforts, which is virtually inconceivable, we could find an increase in the use of alternate drugs and in the supply of synthetic, designer drugs that are more potent and destructive than anything we have yet seen. These include fentanyl, for example, which is around 100 times as powerful as morphine and twenty times stronger than heroin. Fentanyl may be more widely used than we now know, since it cannot be detected by drug tests (Ziporyn 1986, 3061). Recently, crystal methamphetamine seems to have become more popular in the midwest, and LSD is resuming its popularity. As demand for particular drugs waxes and wanes, new drugs will be demanded by consumers and supplied by innovative entrepreneurs.

Effects on the Nation's Character

Whatever the latest trend in drug use, manufacturers, smugglers, and distributors can operate more efficiently by corrupting public officials. This is something we expect, although it is clearly an impediment to effective interdiction. When we attempt to pressure foreign producers, we necessarily work with authorities in such countries as Colombia, Bolivia, Panama, and Peru, where the bribe is a familiar part of law enforcement. Concerning Columbia, journalist Tina Rosenberg observed (1989, 28):

> In general, the closer an institution gets to the traffickers, the more corrupt it becomes. Cocaine's new income opportunities for judges have been well documented. Prosecutors are less corrupt, but it is a matter of logistics, not morals: it is simply easier to win cases by bribing judges, or the police. . . . Policemen, the infantry in the war on drugs, are usually young men from slum neighborhoods with third grade educations—exactly the profile of a drug dealer, and the line between the two tends to blur on the job.

U.S. drug enforcement agents operating abroad typically find themselves operating in a climate of official corruption. In Peru, police officers bribe their superiors to be transferred to interdiction zones, where illegal landing fees can bring $5,000. Peru's attorney general said in March 1992 "Many policemen, instead of fighting against drug trafficking . . . are involved in it"(Brooke 1992, 4). Indeed, in Peru, according to DEA's

Stephen Trujillo, the corruption is so pervasive and so sinister—the military are also in league with and protective of the drug dealers—as to endanger the safety of American advisors and DEA agents (1992).[1]

But domestic police officers are equally susceptible to the temptations of drug money. Unfortunately, we are all too familiar with the legendary narcotics scandals that have plagued police departments in various cities. Perhaps the most famous have occurred in New York City where the Knapp Commission investigations reached both narcotics and other forms of vice. Patrick V. Murphy, a man with a reputation for reform, was recruited as police commissioner in New York in the wake of the scandal uncovered by the Knapp Commission. In his autobiography, he writes, "[W]e ultimately discovered that the narcotics units under the previous police administration had made major contributions to the city's drug traffic. It was this area of corruption more than anything else which most shocked me"(Murphy and Plate 1997, 245). The situation in New York appears, however, to have worsened since the Knapp Commission days. The Mollen Commission found that drug enforcement has brought about a subculture in which stealing, brutality, and perjury by police are commonplace in the poorest and most drug-infested neighborhoods in the city. And narcotics corruption is not confined to New York City. Deputies in the Los Angeles County Sheriff's Department were involved in what the *Los Angeles Times* called "one of the worst corruption cases" in the department's history. Videotapes revealed one deputy hurriedly taking three $10,000 bundles of $100 bills from a dealer's shoulder bag and putting them into his partner's leather briefcase (*L. A. Times* 1989, B1).

The desire of law enforcement officials to show results in the War on Drugs, specifically by obtaining large fines or large numbers of convictions, has lead to a more subtle form of corruption. A *Boston Globe* investigative team recently found that Massachusetts prisons are increasingly populated by "hundreds of low-level drug offenders, many serving mandatory prison terms averaging 6.5 years" (O'Neill, Lehr, and Butterfield 1995a, 1). By contrast, high-level drug traffickers with money or information to trade rarely do hard mandatory time because their assets have become decisive in plea bargains with district attorneys. Law enforcement officials have grown dependent on drug money seizures to pay for such expenses as out-of-state conferences, police overtime, and office rents that run as high as $75,000 a year. The money is also used to pay for business lunches and summer seminars on Nantucket. The *Globe* team's major finding was that "In the narrow top tier of drug prosecutions where dealers with money were facing long terms, most were able to get their sentences reduced"(O'Neill, Lehr, and Butterfield 1995b, 1) Kennedy School criminologists Mark Kleiman and Mark Moore are both quoted in these articles to the effect that this is a form of corruption. "It amounts to a legal bribe," says Moore, "with the obvious difference being that it doesn't enrich anyone personally."

A second problem that the War on Drugs poses for the national character is that prison has begun to lose any sense of terror for many urban youth. Imprisonment is not necessarily stigmatic, or even worrisome, for those who sell drugs, a point made by Joan Petersilia. My students and I have been interviewing imprisoned drug dealers in California since 1989 and learned that imprisonment may bring a certain elevated "home boy" status, especially for gang youths for whom prison and prison gangs can become an alternative site of loyalty (Skolnick et al. 1988, 13).

Given the rate of imprisonment for inner-city populations, this is hardly surprising. When penalties for sale and use of a vice are comparable to those for rape and robbery—as they have become in California and most states, as well as federally—the impact on criminal justice institutions must be extraordinary. Only a very small percentage of the population are murderers, robbers, and rapists. But millions gamble illegally or patronize prostitutes, and millions use illegal drugs.

As penalties for drug use and sale have escalated, increasing numbers of sellers and users have been incarcerated. As of March 7, 1996, the second anniversary of the passage of California's Three Strikes Law, data released by the California Department of Corrections (CDC) and analyzed by San Francisco's Center on Juvenile and Criminal Justice showed that more persons have been imprisoned under the "three strikes" law for possession (not sale) of drugs than for all violent offences combined (Davis, Estes, and Schiraldi 1996). CDC data show that 3,749 persons have been imprisoned under "three strikes" for simple possession of a controlled substance, compared with 2,342 defendants who have been imprisoned for all violent offense categories. Indeed, the data show that twice as many defendants have been imprisoned under the "three strikes" law for marijuana possession than for murder, rape, and kidnapping combined.

An even larger percentage of federal prisoners—approximately 60 percent—are imprisoned for drug offenses. Consequently, as our crime policies have come to draw a slight distinction between vice crimes, especially drug crimes, and traditional *mala in se* offenses, the number of Americans under the control of the criminal justice system has expanded enormously. According to a recent Bureau of Justice Statistics Report, it reached 5 million by the end of 1994 (Davis, Estes, and Schiraldi 1996). If the trend continues, the number behind bars or on probation or parole will soon approximate the 6 million students who are enrolled full time in American colleges and universities; by 2005, more Americans will be behind bars than New York City's 1995 population of 7.3 million.

This massive incarceration program has had a disproportionate effect on minorities, particularly African Americans. African Americans are being arrested for felonies at 4.7 times the rate of whites, but they are being incarcerated at 7.8 times the rate of whites and are being imprisoned for a third "strike" under the California law at 13.3 times the rate of whites (Davis, Estes, and Schiraldi 1996). By 1990, the Sentencing Project calculated that on any given day one out of every four African American males between the ages of twenty and twenty-nine is in prison, pretrial detention, on probation, or on parole (Mauer and Huling 1990). The same research organization released a report five years later (Mauer and Huling 1995) showing that the ratio of black men under the supervision of the criminal justice system was nearly one in three. The authors of the study attribute the increase to tougher sentencing laws, harsher punishments for drug use and sale, the boom in prison construction, which allows more incarceration to occur, and the deteriorating conditions in the inner cities.

Under these circumstances, prison ceases to be a dreaded punishment and becomes instead an integral part of the dominant culture for urban minorities. Readers of my book *Justice Without Trial* (Skolnick 1993) may recall that I participated in what was then the largest drug bust in the history of Northern California. (The drug was, of course, heroin.) Rather than being contained as a result of such enforcement, illegal drug selling and accompanying violence and neighborhood decay have become a familiar American institution portrayed in movies, books, and documentaries. Youngsters who sell drugs in Oakland, Detroit, Los Angeles, Kansas City, Atlanta, and New York are part of generations who have learned to see drug marketing and associated crime as economic opportunity. Whether because of criminal records, lack of education, or lack of technical skills, inner city youth are increasingly being separated from the world of legal work. And the Mitchells, Bluitts, and Johnsons and the youngsters they hire to do their dirtiest work do not rationally calculate as deterrence theory suggests. Given their alternatives, and because many live in a world already more foreboding than any prison—one which continually threatens street-imposed death penalties—imprisonment is not necessarily a powerful deterrent.

Moreover, imprisonment often reinforces prisoners in their troublesome behavior. Already consigned to the margins of society, prisoners join gangs, use drugs, and make useful connections for buying and selling drugs. Perhaps the penitentiary was once a place for experiencing penance. Today's correctional institutions, however, especially when overcrowded with short-term parole violators who have failed their court-mandated drug tests, often serve purposes similar to those advanced by academic and business conventions—as an opportunity for "networking"(Skolnick et al. 1988).

Legalization as a Solution

Legalization has often been proposed as an alternative to the vast expansion of law enforcement that we witnessed during the Reagan-Bush years. But legalization is no panacea for two different reasons. First, implementation of a legalization program raises many complex questions: What form would legalization take; are all or only some drugs to be legalized; what would be the costs and benefits and to which groups; and can legalization can be reconciled with a positive moral message? Second, and even more seriously, there is no foreseeable possibility that any legalization program would be acceptable to the American public.

Essentially, there are four models for legalization of drugs. Under the least-restrictive, free-market model, every drug, even cocaine and heroin, could be sold as we do aspirin, over the counter. At one stroke, the free market would wipe out smuggling (and allow drugs to be taxed), organized drug syndicates, street sales, and street violence.[2] Scarcely less restrictive is the cigarette paradigm, regulating only the age of the purchaser. Alcohol offers a third, slightly more regulated model, while the most restrictive of the legalization models is the prescription drug paradigm, which is already employed for methadone treatment and for treatment accorded to a vast patient population who use tranquilizers and sleeping pills.

Marijuana offers the most plausible case for legalization. Were we to regulate marijuana no more tightly than we do alcohol, we would end half or more of our current drug arrests without a significant impact on public health. We would expect that more people would use marijuana, but not so many more, given the increasing concern for health and sobriety between the 1960s and the 1990s. To be sure none of this will succeed perfectly. The more controls government imposes, the greater the incentives to develop illegal markets. If we allow the sale and use of low-potency marijuana, we will stimulate illegal markets in high-potency cannabis. If we control sales to youngsters, some will surely buy illegally as they already do with alcohol. Thirty percent of high school seniors reported in 1991 that they had drunk heavily (five or more drinks in a row) at least once in the previous two weeks. Since alcohol is illegal for those under twenty-one, all of this drinking was in violation of the law (Ellickson et al. 1996).

If cocaine HCL (powder cocaine) were to be legalized, we would generate incentives for producing crack cocaine. Since crack cocaine, heroin, and phencyclidine (PCP) remain inner city favorites, the actual and symbolic consequences of legalizing these drugs are worrisome. We would probably not generate a sharp rise in use among the truly disadvantaged, especially among teenagers already inclined to use these drugs, since the drugs are already easily obtainable with slight search costs. The population we're currently protecting is a portion of the middle class, especially college students, who fear purchasing in the illegal market structure, but who might experiment with legal drugs.

The issue is not only whether to legalize a drug but how to influence the message accompanying legalization. Legalization of a vice does not necessarily connote approval or promotion of the activity, although it so often has in the United States. When Prohibition was repealed, the saloon doors were thrown open. We not only legalized distilled spirits but also the cocktail lounge and a culture of recreational drinking. When our state governments have legalized gambling—lotteries, casinos, and off-track betting—they have also promoted gambling, and done so shamelessly. When the British legalized casinos in 1968 their purpose was to control organized crime. They did not permit casinos to advertise at all, not even with matchbooks or advertisements in the telephone directory.

If we eliminated criminal penalties for possession or use of any drugs and strictly regulated their sale, such decriminalization would need to be accompanied by public recognition of a larger moral purpose—to reduce crime and violence, to enhance public health and safety through drug education and treatment, and to invigorate a sense of community. The goal of any move toward reducing criminal penalties would need to be articulated as harm minimization, accompanied by a strong community commitment to appreciating the causes and dynamics of addiction.

These complexities involving the legalization of drugs are serious, but they are not necessarily insoluble. It is possible that optimal solutions, at least in a specific set of circumstances, might be found. Any such solutions, however, would confront a further, and almost certainly fatal, difficulty—the pragmatic problem that legalization is politically unacceptable to the American people. Government officials may have dreamed up the notion of a War on Drugs, but they did not invent the underlying selection of the punitive or *mala in se* approach to drug use. Americans overwhelmingly regard drug use as reprehensible and demand severe punishment for those who sell drugs, possess them, or even simply use them. No politician in a democratic regime can safely ignore such a widespread sentiment, and no politician in such a regime would be justified in doing so.

The origin of this public feeling about drugs is not entirely clear. As previously noted, a large proportion of the American public uses illegal drugs, or knows someone who does; the high levels of support for continued prohibition means that many people favor criminal penalties for conduct that they themselves engage in. Perhaps the very ubiquity of drugs is part of people's concern, particularly that their children or other family members will succumb to addiction. Perhaps the motivation comes from general moral attitudes that people do not connect with people's own individual behavior. Conservatives have generally been in favor of punishing drug use, quite possibly because such use is thought to reflect a general licentiousness and breakdown of values. Liberals have been less adamant, but many turned against the idea of legalization when leaders of the African American community, arguing that drugs were destroying their neighborhoods and their youth, endorsed the punitive approach. Whatever the reason, opposition to the legalization of drugs is now a social fact that no real-world politician or policymaker can ignore.

Drug Policy and Harm Minimization

The ineffectiveness of the "War on Drugs" approach and the political unacceptability of the legalization approach present a familiar divergence between expert and popular opinion. One is presented with two unappealing options; either frame recommendations that rest on valid research but stand no chance of real-world adoption, or abandon the effort to frame rational responses and accept popular opinion as an absolute determinant of public policy. As Mark Kleiman (1992, 388) writes: "The more important the problem, the less adequate a response based on symbols alone. We need policies that express both disapproval and compassion and the debate about what we disapprove of and whom we have compassion for is worth conducting." The question is whether there is any way to mediate between extremes, to frame policy recommendations that would increase the effectiveness of drug policy and yet represent feasible alternatives in the current political environment.

The principle of harm minimization provides a possible solution.[3] In essence, the idea is that the public's real fear, as Zimring and Hawkins note, is violent crime. Drugs are condemned primarily because of their connection to violent crime, and nonviolent drug use is condemned by an association of ideas. As in the case of burglary, drug use is also considered wrongful on its own terms and induces additional condemnation because of people's concern that their children will be affected. Given how extensively drugs are used by all segments of the population, however, it seems unlikely that drug use would be regarded as serious enough to justify the current, draconian approaches without being connected in the public's mind with violence. One possibility for drug policy, therefore, is to identify more effective ways of combating drug-related violent crime—in other words, ways of minimizing harm—that would provide alternatives to current policy. Given that people do consider drug use wrongful on its own terms, it seems unlikely that purely non-punitive approaches, even if they stop short of legalization, would be politically acceptable. However, if less-punitive approaches can demonstrate better results in minimizing harm, these results may counteract at least part of the demand for punishment and create a real possibility that the public will find them acceptable.

Peter Greenwood and Joan Petersilia each suggest approaches to harm minimization that can be applied directly to crime policy. Greenwood argues that there are a variety of prevention programs, operating at the early childhood or teenage levels, that can produce significant reductions in the crime rate and thereby reduce the amount of crime, particularly violent crime. These programs would naturally reduce the level of drug use that has proved to be so criminogenic in inner city populations, although the programs themselves are not specifically directed toward drugs. In addition, there are a variety of other prevention strategies that focus more directly on drug use and show considerable promise in minimizing harm. Perhaps the best known are needle exchange and methadone maintenance.

Programs to increase access to sterile intravenous equipment ("needle exchange") are not directed at violent crime, but they are intended to reduce the obvious harm of HIV (human immunodeficiency virus) infection. Transmission to adolescents and adults occurs either directly from contaminated drug paraphernalia or through sexual contact with an infected partner. Infants may become infected transplacentally or perinatally from mothers who themselves are intravenous drug users, or who become infected by sex with partners who are IV drug users. In an ideal world, treatment and prevention programs would seek to reduce drug use, not HIV infection alone. In the real world, drug users may not enter or remain in treatment or abstain from injecting drugs while in treatment.

Consequently, needle-exchange programs can only reduce the harm of HIV infection. Nevertheless, that is an important public health goal. The spread of AIDS in the United States was once concentrated among men who have sex with men, but it is now shifting dramatically to drug users. A report by a joint panel of the National Research Council and Institute of Medicine found that the proportion of cases involving illegal injection drug use has increased steadily, from 12 percent in 1981 to 28 percent in 1993, while the proportion of new AIDS cases attributed to men who have sex with men has declined from 74 percent to 47 percent during the same time period. Moreover, the rate of HIV infection among people who inject illegal drugs has led to more women and children having the virus. After a review of the evidence, the NRC panel found the programs effective and recommended that the surgeon general of the United States lift the federal ban on funding these programs.

At the same time, because they do not confront the causes and consequences of illicit drug use, needle-exchange programs are controversial.

Some express concern that needle-exchange programs suggest tacit community approval of illegal IV drug use. Others fear that programs that increase access to sterile needles and syringes might actually increase injection drug use by creating an impression of safety. Such evidence as there is suggests that access to clean equipment does not increase drug use. From a public health and overall harm reduction perspective, the benefits of addict access to clean needles and syringes clearly outweigh the costs. Consequently, a harm minimization perspective suggests that such programs should be expanded (Am. Academy of Pediatrics 1994).

A similar argument can be made regarding methadone maintenance, a program that is more directly linked to crime prevention. Methadone is an opioid that was synthesized by German chemists during World War II. When it is administered to previously intractable heroin addicts in an adequate, daily oral dose, methadone blocks acute narcotic effects and ceases the recurrent craving usually associated with long-term abstinence from heroin and other opiate drugs. Methadone does not cure narcotics addiction. Instead, it controls withdrawal symptoms and normalizes the functioning of heroin addicts while the medication is being taken. According to Dr. Vincent Dole, one of the major innovators (with Dr. Marie Nyswander) of methadone maintenance treatment, "It is clear that the treatment has contributed to the survival of thousands of patients who entered the program in New York fifteen or more years ago. A majority of their peers who did not enter treatment are now dead, in prison or vanished"(Dole 1994).

Nevertheless, methadone maintenance treatment has been and continues to be controversial for three reasons: First, methadone is a drug; many people believe that ingesting drugs is simply wrong, that users should be punished, and that the goal of treatment should be total abstinence. By contrast, harm reduction advocates can point to extensive research showing that, as Dr. Marsha Rosenbaum, a leading drug researcher puts it, methadone maintenance has been found to be "expedient," by which she means that it reduces criminality and removes the issue of obtaining illegal drugs from the lives of patients who ingest the drug in adequate dosages (1995).

Second, there is a belief that illegal methadone (stolen from clinics) leads novices to their first use of an opiate. Rosenbaum writes that this claim has proven to be completely unfounded. Rosenbaum's contention is persuasive, since novices are not likely to be attracted to a drug whose euphoric effects are slight compared with heroin or cocaine.

Third, during the fiscal austerity of the 1980s methadone became seen as a means to an abstinent end, rather than an end in itself. Patients were transformed into "clients." Methadone maintenance works well if those who are being maintained can count on a daily medical dose to function without the craving to procure illegal heroin. When dosage is cut—even with the well-intended aim of producing abstinence—addicts may revert to heroin use, with all its associated behaviors. Abstinence from dependence on opioids—including methadone—is an understandable ideal. Harm minimization, in contrast, is utlilitarian. It mediates between the polar division of social options into abstinence or heroin addiction, recognizing that the impracticality of the first choice, for many people, leads inevitably to the misery and danger of the second. It accepts something less than optimal psychic functioning, as diabetics on insulin accept suboptimal physical functioning. Those who see addiction as a moral failure are drawn toward the goal of abstinence. The harm minimization principle, however, advocates ameliorating symptoms, since the symptoms—crime, AIDS, poverty—are so harmful to self and to society.

A second way of implementing a harm minimization policy with respect to drug use is to explore alternative sanctions for those arrested for or convicted of drug offenses. Needle exchange and methadone maintenance are controversial because they imply an acceptance of drug addiction, but they do not necessarily alter the punishment imposed on convicted felons. Alternative punishments, as Joan Petersilia points out, are still punishment, but they reduce the severity of punishment in a manner that raises political difficulties of its own. The rationale for doing so, once again, is harm reduction. First, alternative sanctions, because they frequently incorporate treatment, offer a better chance of altering the drug-user's behavior, thus preventing further criminal activity once that person is released from the direct control of the criminal justice system. Second, these sanctions are often less expensive; when used for nonviolent offenders, they do not significantly increase the risk of harm for the citizenry in general, and they release resources for the apprehension and punishment of violent offenders. This would be an important step toward minimizing the harm from crime, since the current trend is in the opposite direction. The *Boston Globe* study cited previously concluded that "People convicted of violent crimes are getting dramatically lighter sentences." The *Globe* investigative team undertook a computer-assisted analysis of 1,054 court cases in Massachusetts's six largest counties—Suffolk, Middlesex, Essex, Worcester, Norfolk, and Plymouth. It showed a 28 percent drop in the average prison sentence given convicted armed robbers over the last ten years. Rape and aggravated rape sentences have similarly dropped 26 percent (Oneill, Lehr, and Butterfield 1995b). This is attributable to prison overcrowding generated by rising penalties for drug offenses.

Alternative sanctions for drug offenders include drug courts and the kinds of supervised probation programs discussed by Petersilia. Title V of the Violent Crime Control and Enforcement Act of 1994 (P.L. 103-22) authorizes the attorney general to make grants to states, state courts, local courts, units of local government, and Indian tribal courts to establish drug courts. This was done in response to the deluge of drug cases since the crack epidemic of the 1980s and the cycle of rearrest common to drug offenders. The idea is to use the authority of the court to reduce crime by changing the drug-using behavior of the defendants. According to a GAO report to the Senate and House Committees of the Judiciary, as of March 1995, there were at least thirty-seven drug courts operating nationwide, most of which had been fully operational for at least nine months (GAO 1995).

Drug courts view drug addiction as a disease. Some drug courts are diversion programs, that is, they are postarrest but preprosecutorial; others are postconviction. All of them require attendance at regularly scheduled status hearings where the drug court judge monitors the progress of the participant. Those who participate are required to submit to urine tests and various other requirements, such as counseling sessions and treatment, with the goal of becoming drug free. Drug courts recognize that relapses can occur. When participants fail to meet requirements, they are usually sanctioned in some way but not immediately terminated.

Whether drug courts reduce recidivism is not yet entirely clear, largely because the courts, although they share basic philosophies, vary in the quality of the judge administering the court and associated services. Most drug courts do claim, however, that they save the costs of incarcerating low-level drug offenders. The GAO concludes that although drug courts seem to be a positive innovation, careful evaluative research is needed, with control groups, to assess outcomes (GAO 1995; Robins, Davis, and Nurco 1974).

Supervised probation is amply discussed by Petersilia; as she points out, the most promising approach for drug offenders is to combine the supervision with a treatment program. It is sometimes argued that intermediate sanctions of this sort will not minimize harm because those who are in prison for drug-only offenses are in fact likely to be career criminals who have resorted to violence but were only apprehended and convicted for a drug offense. There is some evidence to support this, but, even if it is true, intermediate sanctions can still offer significant possibilities for harm reduction.

To begin with, an element of discretion can be built into alternative sanctions, so that inmates whose profile or behavior indicates a serious potential for violence need not be selected for the program. Second, although there are a large number of prisoners who have been convicted of drug-only offenses, the individual sentences for each prisoner are not particularly long. Even California's three strikes law, the most stringent in the nation, does not count drug use, drug possession, or the sale of drugs to an adult as a predicate offense (i.e., strike one or two). Thus, individuals convicted of drug-only offenses (other than sale of drugs to a minor) will never be subject to the three strike penalty, no matter how many times they are convicted. Apparently, the public, even in its most punitive moods, is not prepared to incarcerate nonviolent drug offenders for extremely long periods. These offenders will ultimately return to society. Time served in prison, as discussed above, is likely to make them more dangerous, rather than less so. Consequently, although the time of their sentence may seem like an opportunity to incarcerate them, and thus reduce the amount of harm they do, for a limited period of time, it might also be regarded as an opportunity to provide treatment for them, and reduce the likelihood that they will do harm for the longer period that they will be back on the streets.

In this sense, the fact that these individuals are imprisoned for a drug-only offense creates a window of public tolerance for alternative sanctions that can be used to implement sanctions that are less expensive and that crime policy experts conclude are more effective. The demand for punishment of offenders is much greater for those offenders who have been convicted for traditional *malum in se* offenses, rather than for using drugs. Moreover, the risks that decisionmakers incur in creating an intermediate sanctions program are less serious if the program is applied to drug-only offenders. In any such program, there is bound to be at least a few offenders who murder or rape someone when they could have been confined in state prison. If those persons were convicted of a violent crime, and could have been held for many years, the public outcry will be much greater than if the person was a drug offender who would have been released in a year or two.

None of this should be understood as a panacea, or even a second-best solution. Ultimately, the best way to minimize the harm caused by drugs lies in education and social reform, not in crime policy. There is some indication that this approach is returning to the political mainstream after its long banishment. The *1996 Drug Control Strategy* reveals a shift in priorities and a recognition that primary reliance on law enforcement is not as effective as it was thought to be by previous administrations.

When we educate about drugs we need to stress reality and health values, rather than scare tactics. Drug education often poses false polarities. Drugs are either harmless or will "fry your brain." The dangers of marijuana were overstated in the 1950s and 1960s. The absurd overstatements (that marijuana use leads to violent assaults) instead of discouraging use, encouraged false inferences in the opposite direction—that marijuana use posed no dangers. Many people can control their use of alcohol, cigarettes, and marijuana. Some can control their use of cocaine and even of heroin. In fact, drug effects and side effects are complex and vary according to the chemical properties of the drug, the setting in which it is used, the potency (unfortified wine vs. distilled spirits), the quantity used, the frequency of use, and the biological, psychological, and social circumstances of the user.

The social reform approach asks: Why do some communities produce street drug dealers and street violence while others do not? How do social, economic, and psychological conditions affect drug use and sale? To what extent do users ingest drugs to feel euphoric, to take one out of life's circumstances, to overcome despair, hopelessness, and low self-esteem? Such feeling states can occur to individuals within any social group, but they are heightened by joblessness, poverty, and neglect. Just as William Julius Wilson's research has found a clear relation between unemployment and crime, a clean and sober addict with a job will be less likely to relapse than one who is unemployed (Wilson 1995). The more satisfied and engaged people are with their lives and themselves, the less likely are they to be drawn—regardless of the consequences—to the euphoric feeling states of heroin, crack cocaine, and high alcohol dosage. And whatever the treatment modality, the more an addict can count on social support through family, friends, and therapy group, the more likely will therapy goals be achieved.

But the "truly disadvantaged" live in a world—often a housing project—without these supports, and that cues craving as they see drugs being sold and used all around them. Treatment for drug and alcohol addiction often isolates addicts, as in the Betty Ford clinic. But there are no Betty Ford clinics for the desperately poor. So we end up with a cycle of decline leading to jail and prison, at great cost to taxpayers and to society generally.

Conclusion

As all of the chapters in this volume have concluded, "crime" is not a unitary concept. They all distinguish between violent crime and lesser offenses and recommend a policy of harm minimization. Joan Petersilia's chapter carefully examines the range of crimes for which different and alternative sanctions might be appropriate. The Zimring and Hawkins chapter similarly concludes that the public fears violent crime and is most supportive of measures to stop it. Like Greenwood's chapter, it recommends early intervention to reduce violent crime. In this chapter, I have stressed the excessive costs and limits of a "War on Drugs" strategy to the drug problem and instead have advocated (as the *1996 Strategy* does) a move toward harm reduction measures. I have specifically recommended measures that lie within the realm of political acceptability at the present time—needle exchanges and methadone maintenance as prevention modalities, and drug courts and supervised probation as treatment modalities. All these measures fit within the crime-control model for drug policy that is presently in place. Ultimately, it is to be hoped that changes in public attitudes will allow us to move away from this model, which is expensive and demonstrably ineffective, and toward a different model that makes use of education, social reform, and nonpunitive treatment as our primary response to the problem of drug abuse.

References

American Academy of Pediatrics, Task Force on Pediatric AIDS. 1994. Reducing the Risk of Human Immunodeficiency Virus Infection Associated with Illicit Drug Use. *Pediatrics* December: 945–947.

Brooke, James. March 28, 1992. Yurimaguas Journal: Fighting the Drug War in the Skies over Peru. *New York Times.*

Center for the Study of Law and Society. 1988. Courts, Probation, and Street Drug Crime: Executive Summary and Conclusions. In Final Report of the Targeting Urban Crime Narcotics Task Force.

Covino. 1985. How the 69th Avenue Mob Maximized Earnings in East Oakland. *Califonia* (November).

Davis, Christopher, Richard Estes, and Vincent Schiraldi. 1996. *"Three Strikes": The New Apartheid.*

Dole, Vincent P. 1994. What Have We Learned from Three Decades of Methadone Maintenance Treatment? *Drug and Alcohol Review* 13:3–4.

Doyle, James. January 3, 1994. Drug Busts Slow Trade—But Not for Long. *San Francisco Chronicle.*

Ellickson, Phyllis L., K. A. McGuigan, V. Adams, R. M. Bell, and R. D. Hays. 1996. Teenagers and Alcohol Misuse in the United States: By Any Definition, It's a Big Problem. In *Addiction* 91(10):1489–1503.

Eranson, Laura, and Sam Whiting. July 30, 1996. Heroin's in Fashion—and Death Statistics Prove It. *San Francisco Chronicle.*

GAO Reports. May 22, 1995.

Hess, Henner. 1995. The Other Prohibition: The Cigarette Crisis in Post War Germany. Paper presented at the 47th Annual Conference of the American Society of Criminology.

Kaplan, J. 1983. *The Hardest Drug: Heroin and Public Policy.*

_____. 1992. "Chapter 12." In *Against Excess: Drug Policy for Results,* edited by Mark Kleiman.

Kleiman, Mark, ed. 1992. *Against Excess: Drug Policy for Results.*

L. A. Times. October 24, 1989.

Lee, Henry K. September 1, 1994. 46 Arrested in Sweep of East Bay Drug World. *San Francisco Chronicle.*

Mauer, Mars, and Tracy Huling. 1990. *Young Black Americans and the Criminal Justice System.* Washington, D.C. Sentencing Project publication.

_____. 1995. *Young Black Americans and the Criminal Justice System.* Washington, D.C. Sentencing Project publication.

Mill, J. S. 1982. *On Liberty* (Penguin English Library Edition).

Murphy, P., and T. Plate. 1977. *Commissioner: A View from the Top of the American Law Enforcement* 245.

Nadelmann, Ethan, and Jennifer McNeely. 1996. Doing Methadone Right. *Public Interest* Spring, 83–93.

Office of National Drug Control Policy. 1989. *1989 Drug Control Strategy.* Executive Office of the President.

_____. 1992. *1992 Drug Control Strategy.* Executive Office of the President.

_____. 1996. *1996 Drug Control Strategy.* Executive Office of the President.

O'Neill, Gerard, Richard Lehr, and Bruce Butterfield. September 24, 1995a. Small-Timers Get Hard Time. *Boston Globe.*

_____. September 25, 1995b. Accused's Assets Are Key Chips in Plea Bargains. *Boston Globe.*

Reuter, Peter. 1988. Can the Borders Be Sealed? *Public Interest* (Summer).

Reuter, Peter, and Robert MacCoun. 1995. Drawing Lessons from the Absence of Harm Reduction in American Drug Policy. *Tobacco Control* 4 (Supplement 2): S28–S32.

Robins, Lee N., Darlene H. Davis, and David N. Nurco. 1974. How Permanent Was Vietnam Drug Addiction? *Am. J. Public Health Supplement* 64:38–43.

Rosenbaum, Marsha. 1995. The Demedicalization of Methadone Maintenance. *Journal of Psychoactive Drugs* 27:145–149.

Rosenberg, Tina. November 27, 1989. The Kingdom of Cocaine: A Report from Columbia. *New Republic.*

San Diego Union-Tribune. September 26, 1995.

Schulhofer, Stephen J. 1994. Toward a Rational Drug Policy. *Univ. of Chicago Legal Forum* 222.

Skolnick, Jerome H. 1988. The Social Transformation of Vice. *Law and Contemporary Problems* 51(Winter): 9–30.

_____. 1990. A Critical Look at the National Drug Control Strategy. *Yale Law and Policy Review* 8:86.

_____. 1993. *Justice Without Trial: Law Enforcement in Democratic Society.*

Skolnick, Jerome et al. 1988. *The Social Structure of Street Drug Dealing.* California Department of Justice publication.

Specter, Michael. May 2, 1995. Highway of Drugs. *New York Times.*

Trujillo, Stephen G. April 7, 1992. Corruption and Cocaine in Peru. *New York Times.*

Wilson, William J. 1995. The Political Economy and Urban Racial Tension. *American Economist* 39(1).

Ziporyn, Terra. 1986. A Growing Industry and Menace: Makeshift Laboratory's Designer Drugs. *JAMA* 256 (22):3061–3063.

Comment: The Ambiguities of
Harm Reduction in Crime and Drug Policy

MARK A. R. KLEIMAN

The chapter under review points out that existing drug policies are not the ones that would minimize (nondrug) crime. Agreed. It further argues that those policies are built around the belief that drug use is bad in itself. That belief is attacked as both wrong and a source of bad policy. This analysis requires some unpacking.

First, it is worth reflecting on the odd way in which *drug* is defined, both in the chapter and in the broader public discourse, to include all of the current controlled substances, more or less on an equal footing, but to exclude alcohol and nicotine. If by *drug* one means all psychoactive chemicals, then the belief that drug use is evil in itself remains distinctly a minority view, except as applied to minors, since most Americans drink, at least a little, and aren't ashamed of it or worried about it.

One would never guess, either from the chapter or from the broader public debate, that alcohol is the drug most frequently involved in crime, and the drug that accounts for by far the largest number of user arrests (on charges of public intoxication, open container, minor-in-possession, and driving under the influence). Nor would one guess, from either source, the extent to which this widely used and socially accepted drug, freed from the moralistic meddling of the temperance forces by repeal and no longer subject to the adulteration of bootleg whisky, nonetheless manages to create other forms of harm: not only crimes, but also accidents, derelictions of duty in the home, workplace, and neighborhood, and health damage and the costs of treating it.

Although I do not, in Skolnick's phrase, "lie awake worrying" that someone out there might be drinking, I do lose some sleep about the estimates of binge drinking among high school and college students. More particularly, though, I lie awake worrying about drinking by some specific people. My circle of close friends—say, the people whom I would invite to use my guest room if they were to visit Los Angeles—is neither especially large nor especially hard-drinking. Nonetheless, among my friends I can count up two active alcoholics whose drinking makes them and those around them miserable and that will likely wreck their health if they don't get it under control soon and three people who have told me they are "in recovery" after long and painful battles. And those are just the ones I know about.

So though it is true that most people who drink do so with net benefit to themselves and no substantial cost to others, the costs of alcohol abuse to those who engage in it and those around them are almost certainly great enough to wipe out the consumers' surplus from moderate drinking and have a large social deficit left over. This is the situation—the bad results of the interaction between some human beings and ethanol—that the Volstead Act attempted to address. The Controlled Substances Act and related policies—"the War on Drugs"—attempt to manage the same set of potential problems with respect to other mind-altering chemicals. That the results of the current prohibitions are unsatisfactory no one can doubt. But that some more satisfactory result is straightforwardly available is much less obvious, and the instance of alcohol reminds us that there can be unsuccessful legalizations as well as unsuccessful prohibitions.

Now of course there is no valid logical step from the proposition "The widespread use of Substance X will create a surplus of damage over benefit" to the proposition "Substance X is evil, and so are the people who use it." Nor is it obvious that all of the substances covered by the Controlled Substances Act—"drugs" in political parlance—are in fact as dangerous as alcohol. Defining the harm profile of a drug is a complicated problem, with at least five components: physical toxicity, behavioral toxicity (i.e., frequency and severity of accidents, crimes, and derelictions of duty), "capture rate" to abuse (proportion of those who more than sample a drug who go on to a period of out-of-control use), severity of compulsive use in terms of damage to the user, and average duration of compulsive use (which can be thought of as a measure of the difficulty of quitting, but is not the same as the presence and strength of withdrawal symptoms). Of the substances currently banned (at least for nonmedical use) I would rank cannabis and the hallucinogens as less hazardous overall than alcohol, whereas heroin and the other derivatives and analogues of opium, refined cocaine, and methamphetamine seem to be at least as dangerous.

If the proposal were merely that we adopt new and less hostile policies toward marijuana and the hallucinogens, I would be for it, at least to the point of trying to determine whether such policies could actually be defined and implemented without too many undesired side effects. Since their risk profiles are quite different, with the damage from cannabis concentrated in the minority of users who become chronic, high-dose, high-frequency users and the damage from hallucinogens largely around the behavioral consequences and psychological sequelae of single uses gone wrong, the appropriate restrictive policies would presumably be different as well: Controls on cannabis would need to focus on frequency and quantity, and controls on hallucinogens could focus instead on the selection and preparation of the users, the conditions under which the drug is taken, and the availability of crisis intervention as needed during and after the experience.

But of course those drugs contribute relatively little to crime and absorb quite modest shares of enforcement resources, as it is. Unless one believes that there would be massive substitution away from more dangerous drugs, including alcohol—a plausible, but by no means well-established, proposition—then it is hard to foresee much of a crime-control contribution from any change in our cannabis and hallucinogen policies.

With respect to the illicit drugs that are the focus of the enforcement side of the antidrug effort and whose consumption and distribution are deeply implicated in serious crime—cocaine, especially in the form of crack; heroin; and methamphetamine—the case for a generalized softening of policy on crime-control grounds is much weaker. For the reasons suggested in the chapter and for some that it does not mention, I do not think that it would be possible to construct and implement a policy allowing the legal nonmedical use of heroin, cocaine, or methamphetamine that would outperform prohibition, all things considered.

But whatever one believes on that score, once the drugs are prohibited their use takes on a different social meaning. It makes the drugs expensive, and poor people addicted to expensive drugs are likely to support their habits partly by theft. Prohibition also creates illicit markets, which lure teenagers away from school and give young men both reasons and dollars to arm themselves. Thus inner-city residents do lie awake worrying that their neighbors may be buying heroin and cocaine, because they fear the theft of their possessions, the seduction of their children into dealing, and the sound of gunfire.

Thus I find it hard to offer a blanket assent to the assertion that the treatment of "drugs" as *mala in se* is irrational. The use of illegal heroin, cocaine, and methamphetamine in conditions of urban poverty may not be evil in itself, but it may be so closely associated with various evils as to make *malum in se* versus *malum prohibitum* a distinction without a substantial difference.

The chapter goes on to assert that a different set of policies—"harm minimization"—less hostile to drug use and drug users, would result in less crime. That depends.

We are told that the proposed new approach would also serve as a way-station to policies based on "education, social reform, and non-punitive treatment" that would be both less cruel and more effective in reducing the damage done by drug abuse than the current approach, because they would be free of what Skolnick takes to be the *malum in se* mistake. This is a case, it is said, where "crime policy analysts" have one (presumably correct) view and "real-world decisionmakers" and "the general public" a contrary one. I doubt it.

The actual picture is even more complex than the chapter makes it out to be and the details, as usual, are crucial. The crime-minimizing approach to drug abuse control would not necessarily be less hostile to drug use than the current approach, at least not for some drugs, though the mechanisms through which that hostility was expressed would be somewhat different. Moreover, the crime-minimizing approach would not necessarily be the one that produced the minimum of total social harm, since there are noncriminal harms associated with drugs. It might be worthwhile to accept somewhat more crime in return for somewhat less intoxication, less addiction, and less damage to health. (As Zimring and Hawkins have pointed out, those who regard drug policy as a subtopic of crime policy tend to have different views on this question than those who concentrate on drugs.)

The concept of "harm minimization" is less obvious than it appears, or rather it has two very different interpretations. One version is almost a truism: Given any problem, one should handle it in the way that minimizes aggregate social harm, net of benefits. The chapter is right to suggest that opposition to harm minimization, so construed, can only reflect some set of moral judgments taken as absolutes.

But the other version of harm minimization (also called in this context "harm reduction") focuses not on aggregate harm but on harm per use or per user. One formulation often encountered in the drug harm-reduction literature is that it entails reducing the damage done by drugs *without reducing the number of users or the quantities consumed*. Here the metaphor is less benefit/cost analysis than safety engineering: The job of an automotive safety engineer is to minimize the risks to each driver or passenger; reducing the total number of fatalities by encouraging people to take the bus, walk, or stay home is someone else's job.

Out of some mix of honest confusion and disingenuous rhetoric, proponents of "harm reduction" in the safety-engineering sense rely on the plausibility of aggregate harm minimization as an evaluative principle to promote policies directed solely at reducing the damage done by each user or dose: an entirely different proposition.

Perhaps a little algebra will clarify the distinction. Let H represent the aggregate social harm associated with drug-taking and drug control under some set of policies. Let h represent the average harm done by a given dose under those policies and D, the aggregate quantity consumed under those policies. Then by definition:

$$H = h \times D$$

Aggregate harm is the harm per dose (let us say "harmfulness") times the aggregate dosage. (This is not to assert that aggregate harm is a linear function of dosage; h and D are likely to covary in complex ways as policies and external factors change.)

To say that we would like to have policies that minimize aggregate harm, H, is not to say very much (except that the quantity of drug consumed or the number of users do not constitute independent objectives, separate from the damage done). But to say that we ought to have policies that minimize harmfulness, h, is to say quite a lot, and most of it almost self-evidently false.

A policy that reduced harmfulness by a little but increased consumption by a lot—that produced a small decrease in h but a large increase in D—would increase aggregate harm, and ought to appeal only to those for whom an *increase* in overall drug use seems a good thing: who regard drug-taking, or the freedom to take drugs if one wants to, as *bonum in se*. Although there are some people who more or less believe that about cannabis and the psychedelics, virtually no one is actually in favor of increasing the use of heroin, cocaine, or methamphetamine, though a few die-hard libertarians are still deeply invested in the defense of a *right* to smoke crack even though they sincerely wish that no one ever exercised that right. To pursue this approach in the name of harm reduction is to parade mere libertarian prejudice in the uniform of benefit/cost analysis.

The question, then, for drug policy generally, is whether there are policy changes that would reduce aggregate harm, either by reducing harmfulness without increasing consumption (or even while decreasing it) or by reducing harmfulness substantially while increasing consumption only slightly. Based on the empirical literature, that seems to be a reasonable view of the effect of some well-run needle-exchange programs: They reduce the risk of HIV infection for those heroin users who enroll in them, do not attract new users, and actually increase the desistance rate among current users by bringing them into contact with the treatment system.

Reducing the number of cocaine dealers in prisons would very likely be, on balance, a harm-reducing policy, whether considered from the narrow perspective of crime control or from a broader perspective incorporating other concerns about drug abuse. Although the demand for cocaine (and heroin, for that matter) is far more elastic than either popular mythology or the subject chapter allows, both the price of cocaine and its retail availability seem to be quite inelastic to changes in cocaine-related imprisonment around its current levels. Although enforcement still has value in keeping open retail markets from developing where they do not now exist, or as part of an attempt to eliminate them from specific neighborhoods, there is no reason to think that routine retail-level enforcement against the crack market pays its way either as drug abuse control or as a crime control. Although most of those in prison for cocaine dealing also commit nondrug crimes, on average they seem to be less active in predatory crime than the average nondrug prisoner, so shifting the composition of the prison population away from crack dealers and toward burglars would on balance tend to reduce the incidence of burglary.

Drug enforcement could also reduce aggregate harm by focusing on individuals and groups that engage in violence rather than simply those who are moving the most drugs or are the easiest to catch. Given the sheer volume of the trade in the inner cities, it is impossible for the police to arrest every dealer, but it is still possible for them to arrest any dealer, or set of dealers, they choose to focus on. This is particularly relevant when, as is now often the case, drugs are dealt by identifiable "youth gangs." Police in some gang-ridden areas of Chicago and Boston have explicitly told gang members that the full weight, not merely of the drug laws but of the laws against possessing weapons, driving unregistered cars, drinking in public, and violating probation terms, will be brought to bear on whichever group starts shooting, and the reported results have been dramatic.

But aggregate harm can be minimized by tightening control as well as by loosening it. Since the vast bulk of heroin and cocaine bought and sold is consumed by frequent, high-dose users rather than casual ones, and since most of the frequent, high-dose users of those drugs are arrested in the course of a year, a policy that enforced drug abstinence on parolees and probationers with frequent tests and automatic sanctions (a few days in jail) for each missed or "dirty" test could substantially shrink the heroin and cocaine markets without imprisoning a single additional dealer. It would also reduce user crime by effectively shrinking demand.

How effective such a program of "coerced abstinence" would be— what proportion of those subjected to it would repeatedly fail, or would abscond—remains to be seen, but a pilot test in the District of Columbia Drug Court suggests that testing and immediate sanctions has a powerful deterrent effect even compared with testing and deferred sanctions, cutting the frequency of drug use by approximately two-thirds. This approach, which departs substantially from current practice without departing at all from the hostility to the use of illicit drugs that characterizes current laws and policies, may well be the one politically and operationally feasible program that could actually make a serious dent in the costs of drug abuse and drug law enforcement.

It would be desirable for those who write and enforce the drug laws to adopt a less simplistic approach, one that made finer distinctions among drugs, among users, and among dealers. Politicians should disabuse themselves of the notion that large enforcement budgets and long sentences are, in and of themselves, beneficial in reducing drug abuse and controlling the related harms.

To the extent that the chapter asks for no more than this, it is well-justified. But to replace one set of oversimplifications with another—to suggest, in effect, that since a full dose of prohibition and enforcement has failed to bring about a cure we ought to try a homeopathic dose instead—doesn't really bring us any closer to sensible drug policies.

Comment: Breaking the Impasse in American Drug Policy

ROBERT J. MACCOUN

While I was recently thumbing through a psychology journal, an intriguing diagram caught my eye. It depicted a "cognitive-associative network," a spatial display of the degree of association among various words in the minds of the study's participants (Bushman 1996). Stimulus terms that represented unambiguously aggressive concepts were clustered near the center; for example, *hurt* was closely linked to *choke, knife, fight,* and *wound.* On the other hand, words chosen by the researcher for their ambiguity (*animal, rock, movie*) were arrayed on the outer periphery of the network, with one notable exception: The word *drugs* appeared smack dab in the middle, linked directly to the word *kill,* and only one link away from the words *gun* and *blood.*

There is indeed an intimate linkage between drugs and violence in the American mind, a linkage that makes Jerry Skolnick's chapter a particularly apt contribution to this volume. Unfortunately, I'm afraid we find it easier to perceive the link than to think about what to do about it. I suspect that if the participants in that psychology experiment were Western Europeans, any "drug-violence" association might have been much weaker.

Americans tend to think of drugs as a crime problem, but Europeans are more likely to view drugs as a public health problem (MacCoun, Model, et al. 1995). This makes harm reduction an easier sell in Amsterdam and Glasgow than in Los Angeles and Washington, D.C. Professor Skolnick's chapter is especially important because he illustrates persuasively that it is possible to extend the harm reduction philosophy from drug-related health problems to the drug-crime linkage in America.

Moral Philosophy and Drug Policy

In his chapter, Professor Skolnick argues that since the late 1980s, American drug policy has been rooted in a particular kind of moral justification for aggressive drug prohibition: the notion that drug use is *mala in se,* or "morally repugnant in and of itself"(also Husak 1992). I'm not sure this is entirely correct, yet it turns out to be wrong in a way that may underscore Skolnick's deeper point, that the defenders of our current punitive approach to drug policy have shown an almost visceral aversion to any serious debate about the ways our policies aggravate the problems they are meant to solve.

The *mala in se* interpretation implies that drug warriors are nonconsequentialist in their reasoning—they are morally opposed to drug use irrespective of its costs or benefits. Philosophers use the term *legal moralism* to refer to the notion that government has a moral obligation to ban an activity that is intrinsically immoral, regardless of the consequences of doing so. Like Skolnick, I'd long viewed the former Drug Czar William Bennett as the leading spokesman for legal moralist drug policy.

But I recently reread what Bennett actually wrote in his introduction to the first *National Drug Control Strategy* (Office of National Drug control Policy 1989, 7). He indeed argued that "drug use degrades human character." But in the next sentence, he offered what is clearly a consequentialist rationale: "Drug users make inattentive parents, bad neighbors, poor students, and unreliable employees—quite apart from their common involvement in criminal activity."

Similarly, James Q. Wilson's widely cited 1990 commentary article seemed to articulate the *mala in se* theory when he stated that "tobacco shortens one's life, cocaine debases it. Nicotine alters one's habits, cocaine alters one's soul."(Wilson 1990, 26.) But two pages earlier in the same essay, Wilson also made clear his consequentialist reasoning:

> The notion that abusing drugs such as cocaine is 'a victimless crime' is not only absurd but dangerous. Even ignoring the fetal drug syndrome, crack-dependent people are, like heroin addicts, individuals who regularly victimize their children by neglect, their spouses by improvidence, their employers by lethargy, and their coworkers by carelessness.

Bennett and Wilson eloquently and forcefully articulate the fears that many Americans have about drugs and their effects on others. It isn't that Bennett and Wilson simply view drug use as a manifestation of a "weakness of will" (although they no doubt believe that); they see it as a threat to human willpower and self-control. That proposition isn't invariably true, but there's little doubt that it is frequently true, especially with respect to the use of heroin, cocaine, and methamphetamines (not to mention alcohol).

Thus two of the most prominent advocates of what is thought to be the legal moralist position on drugs are actually invoking consequentialist arguments. I'd like to think that this bodes well for a reasoned discussion about the costs and benefits of our current policies. Frankly, while there's little doubt that drugs can contribute to morally unacceptable conduct, it's hard to think of any time-honored and widely accepted moral principle that might make drug use, per se, *mala in se* (Husak 1992, 64–68). It is even harder to imagine how such a principle might apply to the illicit drugs but not alcohol or tobacco.[4] But one of the problems with a legal moralist premise is that you either accept it, or you don't. If you accept the premise, there's nothing left to discuss. If you don't accept it, there's no one who will debate you except other like-minded individuals. So it is encouraging to discover that two of the leading advocates of our drug war frame their arguments in terms of consequences, rather than absolute moral imperatives.

The Taboo Against Examining Drug Prohibition

A consequentialist rationale for punitive drug policies implies an openness to a sincere desire to base our policies on evidence for their effectiveness in reducing unwanted consequences. Yet I think that the evidence suggests that the underlying thrust of Professor Skolnick's argument is correct. Drug warriors may talk like consequentialists, but they surely act like legal moralists. As Exhibit A, I'll offer the absolute ferocity with which former Surgeon General Joycelyn Elders was attacked for suggesting, in late 1993, the question of drug legalization was worthy of further study. She didn't call for drug legalization, she didn't say she favored it, she simply argued that, given the terrible violence associated with illicit drug markets, the notion was worth examining. Though this incident was not the only reason she lost her job, it was clearly a key reason. For Exhibit B, I'll offer the "Anti-Drug Legalization Act" (H.R. 135), a bill introduced in the 104th Congress by Representative Dick Solomon in January 1995. Its key section stated that "Notwithstanding any other provision of law, no department or agency of the United States Government shall conduct or finance, in whole or in part, any study or research involving the legalization of drugs." I noted these incidents with considerable interest, since they occurred while my collaborators (Peter Reuter, Tom Schelling, Jim Kahan, Karyn Model, and Joe Spillane) and I were already several years (and several publications) into a program of research and analysis on the drug legalization question, funded by a grant from the Alfred P. Sloan Foundation to RAND's Drug Policy Research Center (MacCoun, Kahan, et al. 1993). Neither the Sloan Foundation nor RAND had any legalization agenda; so far as I can tell, both organizations are genuinely agnostic about the issue. Our project was initiated in response to a growing body of support for drug law reform among leading judges, lawmakers, academicians, and policy commentators, as reflected by the considerable attention the topic has received in the op-ed pages of leading American newspapers. And attention to this issue has grown stronger, not weaker, over the past twenty years.

I'll confess that there is something beguiling about the thought of being an outlaw researcher. But seriously: What is this grave threat posed by drug legalization research? Why do we need a law to prevent it? If studying drug legalization were a self-evidently silly idea, it seems quite unlikely that any proposal to study the matter would survive peer review at NSF, NIJ, or NIH anyway. It is unfathomable that a program manager in any federal agency would hold such a proposal to a lower standard than competing proposals. If advocates of the status quo truly believe that a consequentialist analysis supports their position, why try to prevent research on the issue?

One explanation, which I explore elsewhere, is that discussions of drug law reform threaten deeply held but rarely articulated symbolic concerns, including the desire for social predictability, the aversiveness of value conflicts, the belief that drug users should suffer, and a visceral sense of disgust and impurity that the thought of drugs evokes in many people (MacCoun 1996). A second explanation, which is admittedly speculative, is that some of the hawks in the drug war simply fear that the facts aren't fully on their side.

Harm Reduction as a Middle Ground

Professor Skolnick (one of the nation's leading experts on policing and criminal justice strategy) makes a compelling case that our punitive drug policies frequently fail to rectify and sometimes even exacerbate the harms they are supposedly designed to eliminate. As illustrated by the research I described at the outset, Americans associate drug use with violence. Because we associate drugs with violence, we respond with punishment; when the violence doesn't abate, we further ratchet up the penalties, absent any evidence for their effectiveness. But Skolnick explains that the key policy concern is to identify why the drug-violence link exists and to be open to the possibility that our heavy reliance on criminal justice sanctions might sometimes be counterproductive.

But the irony of the intense opposition to drug law research is that the problems with prohibition don't guarantee that legalization would work better; indeed, under careful scrutiny, legalization has plenty of problems of its own. There are inherent tradeoffs in drug policy, and neither a Bennett-style drug war nor a Milton-Friedman-style free market can make those tradeoffs go away (Kleiman 1992; MacCoun, Reuter, and Schelling 1996). The central tradeoff is between reducing drug use and reducing drug-related harms. Our particular brand of prohibition is oriented almost exclusively toward reducing drug use; reducing harms is only secondary. Relative to the status quo, legalization would almost certainly reduce the average harmfulness per incident of drug use; in particular, we'd see a substantial reduction in black-market violence. Unfortunately, legalization runs the risk of increasing total drug use (Moore 1991; MacCoun 1993). Since total harm = average harm x total use, legalization might conceivably reduce average harm yet increase total harm (Reuter and MacCoun 1995; MacCoun and Caulkins 1996). We don't actually know whether this would occur, but the prospect does make legalization a risky proposal.

Yet the central insight of the European harm reduction movement is that it is quite feasible to implement harm reduction within a legal prohibition regime. This is illustrated quite clearly in the way national drug strategies are formed and implemented in Great Britain, The Netherlands, and Switzerland (the countries that pioneered harm reduction), and in Canada, Australia, and Germany (three countries that have recently begun adopting harm reduction approaches) (Reuter and MacCoun 1995; MacCoun, Model, et al. 1995). Each of these nations prohibits drugs like heroin, cocaine, and methamphetamines. Each nation is quite aggressive in policing and prosecuting drug traffickers and interdicting drug shipments. But during the past decade, each of these countries has increasingly emphasized a public health orientation toward drug problems, including drug prevention, drug treatment (frequently as an alternative to criminal sanctions), and interventions like needle exchange to reduce the harmfulness of addictive drug use. Harm reduction has not been a panacea; these nations still have serious drug problems, though no greater than those in the United States. But they have been able to significantly reduce many of the social costs associated with drug use.

These nations have discovered that reducing total drug-related harm requires an integrated package of use reduction and harm reduction interventions. Adopting harm reduction measures has not required them to curtail their use-reduction efforts. Unfortunately, the American drug policy debate has sadly become polarized around a false dichotomy. We act as if anyone who doesn't enthusiastically support an ever-increasing escalation of criminal sanctions against drug users must favor brand-name cocaine in the neighborhood supermarket. The tragedy is that this bifurcation has blinded us to the many opportunities to reduce some of the terrible costs that drug abuse (and sometimes, drug policies) causes to families and neighborhoods. Professor Skolnick's chapter is a refreshing call for a reasoned consideration of the wide array of options in the middle of the policy continuum.

Notes

1. To give another example, a Central Asian police chief, in a town (Osh) noted for drug trafficking, told Michael Specter that he hand picked twenty good, honest men. But since they earn $45 per month and have families, "You can figure out the rest."

2. This, of course, occurred when Prohibition ended. Conversely, prohibition of alcohol or cigarettes would likely lead to an enormous black market in those products, with the same socially deleterious features as the current drug market (Hess 1995).

3. I have used the term *harm minimization*, rather than *harm reduction*, because the latter originally seemed associated with a predominantly antiprohibition stance. However, harm reduction proponents, notably Ethan Nadelmann, who heads The Lindesmith Foundation, has been advocating less-comprehensive measures, such as those proposed here (Nadelmann and McNeely 1996).

4. On the other hand, libertarianism is a coherent nonconsequentialist position against drug prohibition, but I for one find it similarly unpersuasive.

References

Bushman, Brad J. 1996. Individual Differences in the Extent and Development of Aggressive Cognitive-Associative Networks. *Personality and Social Psychology Bulletin* 22 (8): 811–819.

Husak, D. N. 1992. *Drugs and Rights.*

Kleiman, Mark, ed. 1992. *Against Excess: Drug Policy For Results.*

MacCoun, Robert J. 1993. Drugs and the Law: A Psychological Analysis of Drug Prohibition. *Psychological Bulletin* 113:497–512.

_____. 1996. "The Psychology of Harm Reduction: Alternative Strategies for Modifying High-Risk Behavior." Wellness Lectures, California Wellness Foundation and University of California publication.

MacCoun, Robert J., and Jonathan Caulkins. 1996 "Examining the Behavioral Assumptions of the National Drug Control Strategy." In *Drug Policy and Human Nature: Psychological Perspectives on the Prevention, Management, and Treatment of Illicit Drug Use,* edited by W. K. Bickel and R. J. DeGrandpre, 177–197.

MacCoun, Robert J., James Kahan, James Gillespie, and Jheeyang Rhee. 1993. A Content Analysis of the Drug Legalization Debate. *Journal of Drug Issues* 23:615–629.

MacCoun, Robert J., Karyn Model, Heide Phillips-Shockley, and Peter Reuter. 1995. "Comparing Drug Policies in North America and Western Europe." In *Policies and Strategies to Combat Drugs in Europe,* edited by G. Estievenart.

MacCoun, Robert J., Peter Reuter, and Thomas Schelling. 1996. Assessing Alternative Drug Control Regimes. *Journal of Policy Analysis and Management* 15:1–23.

Moore, Mark H. 1991. Drugs, the Criminal Law, and the Administration of Justice. *The Millbank Quarterly* 69:529–560.

Office of National Drug Control Policy. 1989. *1989 National Drug Control Strategy.* Executive Office of the President.

Reuter, Peter, and Robert J. MacCoun. 1995. Drawing Lessons from the Absence of Harm Reduction in American Drug Policy. *Tobacco Control* 4 (Supplement 2): S28–S32.

Wilson, James Q. 1990. Against the Legalization of Drugs. *Commentary* 89.

About the Editor
and Contributors

John J. DiIulio Jr. is a professor of politics and public affairs at Princeton University. He is the coauthor (with James Q. Wilson) of *American Government* (Houghton-Mifflin, 1998), *Improving Government Performance* (Brookings, 1993), and a dozen other books and selected volumes. He directed the Bureau of Justice Statistics project that resulted in *Performance Measures in Criminal Justice* (BJS, 1992). He is winner of the American Political Science Association's Leonard D. White Award in Public Administration and of the Association of Public Policy Analysis and Management's David N. Kershaw Award for cumulative contributions to the field. He now directs several programs that study and assist faith-based programs for inner-city youth.

J. Mark Eddy is a researcher at the Oregon Social Learning Center (OSLC) in Eugene. Prior to his current position, Eddy worked as a researcher and a therapist at the Western Psychiatric Institute and Clinic at the University of Pittsburgh Medical School. Since its founding in 1994, Eddy has served as director or co-director of the Early Career Preventionists Network (ECPN), an internet-based group of over 300 early career researchers. He is a member of the Board of Directors of the Society for Prevention Research, and was the recipient of the 1998 Society for Prevention Research Early Career Scientist Award. Eddy is the author of *Conduct Disorders: The Latest Assessment and Treatment Strategies* (1996).

Peter W. Greenwood is the director of RAND's Criminal Justice Program. His areas of research have included violence prevention strategies, police investigation practices, prosecution policy, criminal careers, selective incapacitation, juvenile justice, and corrections. He is currently directing several evaluations of preventive and correctional interventions for high-risk juveniles. Dr. Greenwood is a member of the American Society of Criminology, the Homicide Research Working Group, the Los Angeles Violence Prevention Coalition, and is a past president of the California Association of Criminal Justice Research. He has served on the faculties of the California Institute of Technology, the Claremont Graduate School, the RAND Graduate School, and the University of Southern California.

Gordon Hawkins is a senior fellow to the Earl Warren Legal Institute at the University of California–Berkeley. From 1961 to 1984 he was a professor at the University of Sydney Law School, New South Wales, Australia, and served as director of the Sydney Institute of Crime. He is the author of *The Honest Politician's Guide to Crime Control* (1970); *The Prison: Policy and Practice* (1975); and of nine other books written in collaboration with Franklin Zimring.

Mark A. R. Kleiman is a professor of policy studies at UCLA, lecturer on Public Policy at Harvard Medical School, and cochair of the Drugs and Addictions Working Group at Harvard University. He is the chairman of BOTEC Analysis Corporation and the editor of the *Drug Policy Analysis Bulletin*. His past positions include director of Policy and Management Analysis for the Criminal Division of the U.S. Department of Justice and deputy director of the Office of Management and Budget for the City of Boston. He is the author of *Against Excess: Drug Policy for Results* and *Marijuana: Costs of Abuse, Costs of Control*.

Robert J. MacCoun is a professor at the Richard and Rhoda Goldman School of Public Policy at the University of California–Berkeley. Trained as a social psychologist, from 1986 to 1993 he was a behavioral scientist at the RAND Corporation. Professor MacCoun has collaborated with economist Peter Reuter on studies of street-level drug dealing in Washington, D.C., comparative research on European and American drug policies, and analyses of the effects of drug laws on drug use and drug-related harms. They are completing a book tentatively titled *Beyond the Drug War: Learning from Other Places, Other Times, and Other Vices*, to be published by Cambridge University Press. Professor MacCoun has also published studies of jury decisionmaking, tort litigation, bias in the interpretation of research results, and the likely effects of sexual orientation on military cohesion. In 1996 he was selected as Distinguished Wellness Lecturer by the California Wellness Foundation and the University of California for his theoretical work on harm reduction.

Mark H. Moore is the Guggenheim Professor of Criminal Justice Policy and Management at the Kennedy School of Government. He was the founding chairman of the Kennedy School's Committee on Executive Programs and served in that role for over a decade.

Norval Morris is the Julius Kreeger Professor of Law and Criminology, Emeritus at the University of Chicago Law School. He was appointed to the faculty of law at the London School of Economics in 1949. Subsequently he practiced law as a barrister in Australia and held academic appointments at Melbourne and Adelaide Universities in Australia, and at Harvard, Utah, Colorado, and New York Universities. Immediately before going to Chicago, Professor Morris directed a United Nations crime prevention institute in Japan. He has served and presently serves on numerous federal and state government and scholarly councils and commissions. Professor Morris is a Fellow of the American Academy of Arts and Sciences. He has written extensively on the criminal justice system, his last four books being *Madness and the Criminal Law* (1982), *Between Prison and Probation* (1990) with Michael Tonry, *The Brothel Boy and Other Parables of the Law* (1992) and *The Oxford History of the Prison* (1995) with David Rothman.

Joan Petersilia is professor of criminology, law, and society in the School of Social Ecology, University of California, Irvine. Prior to joining UCI, she was director of the Criminal Justice Program at RAND. She has directed major studies in policing, sentencing, career criminals, juvenile justice, corrections, and racial discrimination. Dr. Petersilia's current work focuses on the effectiveness of justice interventions, including prisons, probation, and parole. She also has expertise in policy analysis, program design and implementation, and statistical evaluation. Dr. Petersilia has served as president of both the American Society of Criminology and the Association of Criminal Justice Research in California. She is a Fellow of the American Society of Criminology and received its Vollmer Award in 1994 for her overall contributions to crime and public policy. She currently serves as vice-chair of the National Research Council's Committee on Law and Justice, member of the NIJ *Crime and Justice* editorial board, and consultant to several organizations, including the State of California and RAND. Dr. Petersilia is the author of numerous books and articles.

John B. Reid is executive director of the Oregon Social Learning Center, a nonprofit research institute that specializes in basic and clinical research in the areas of the conduct disorders, child abuse, delinquency, and violence. The eight principal investigators and staff of 140 have been funded continuously by federal and private agencies since the late 1960s. The group has published over 250 scientific articles and a dozen books on the development, treatment, and prevention of conduct problems and delinquency. Reid is also the director of one of four Prevention Research Centers funded by the National Institute of Mental Health (NIMH) and has conducted several large randomized trials testing theory-driven intervention models targeted at youngsters and their families at various points in the life course. He serves on several standing research committees at the NIMH and is on the board of directors of the Society for Prevention Research.

Albert J. Reiss Jr. is the William Graham Sumner Professor of Sociology, emeritus, at Yale University. He is a past president of The American Society of Criminology and of the International Society of Criminology. He has served as the chair of the U.S. National Research Council's Panel on the Understanding and Control of Violent Behavior and as a member of the Panel on Criminal Careers and Career Criminals. He has published several major studies on crime and on policing and currently is a member of two major study teams—on human development in Chicago neighborhoods and on community policing in Indianapolis, Indiana. He has contributed to our understanding of co-offending, delinquent careers, the organization of law enforcement, and the exercise of discretionary enforcement of law. He has contributed to our knowledge of community variation in crime, the development of observational methods for studying behavior, and of longitudinal designs. Among his major contributions are *The Police and the Public* and *Communities and Crime*.

Edward L. Rubin is professor of law at the University of Pennsylvania Law School. Until September, 1998, he was Richard W. Jennings Professor of Law at the University of California School of Law, Berkeley. He joined the Berkeley faculty in 1982 after clerking for Judge Hon O. Newman and practicing at Paul, Weiss, Rifkind, Wharton, & Garrison. Professor Rubin teaches and writes in the areas of administrative law, constitutional law, legal theory, and financial services. He is the author of *Judicial Policy Making and the Modern State: How the Courts Reformed America's Prisons* (1998) (with Malcolm Feeley) and *The Payment System* (2d ed. 1994) (with Robert Cooter). He has also served as a consultant to the governments of Russia and the People's Republic of China.

Jerome Skolnick came to New York University School of Law after taking early retirement from the University of California, Berkeley, where he was Clair Clements Dean's Professor of Law, Jurisprudence, and Social Policy, a chair he now holds as professor emeritus. For ten years he was director of the University of California's Center for the Study of Law and Society. At NYU Law School, Skolnick teaches seminars on the police and on the regulation of vice and is co-director of the Center for Research in Crime and Justice. Among his best known books are *Justice Without Trial* (1994), a study of police in democratic society; *The Politics of Protest* (1969), written as director of the Task Force on Violent Protest and Confrontation of the National Commission on the Causes and Prevention of Violence; *House of Cards* (1978), a study of the regulation of casino gambling; *The New Blue Line* (1988), analyzing community oriented policing (with David Bayley); and most recently, *Above the Law* (1994), a study of police use of excessive force (with James J. Fyfe). He also enjoys writing occasional pieces for newspapers and magazines. Professor Skolnick served as president of the American Society of Criminology (1993–1994), was elected a fellow of the ASC, and has recently (1997) completed a three-year term as chair, The National Academy of Science/National Research Council's Committee on Law and Justice.

Robert Weisberg is the Edwin E. Huddleson Professor of Law at Stanford University. He clerked for Judge Skelly Wright and for Justice Potter Stewart and joined the Stanford faculty in 1981. Professor Weisberg is the author of *Criminal Law: Cases and Materials* (3d ed. 1996) (with John Kaplan and Guyora Binder) and of a forthcoming book on law and literature (also with Binder). He teaches criminal law, criminal procedure, and commercial law.

Franklin E. Zimring is the William G. Simon Professor of Law and Director of the Earl Warren Legal Institute at the University of California–Berkeley. His major fields of interest are criminal justice and family law, with special emphasis on the use of empirical research to inform legal policy. Professor Zimring is best known for empirical studies of the determinants of the death rate from violent attacks, the impact of pretrial diversion from the criminal justice system, and attempts to measure the deterrent and incapacitative effects of criminal sanctions. He has authored or coauthored books on deterrence, the changing legal world of adolescence, capital punishment, the scale of imprisonment, and drug control. His most recent books are *Crime Is Not the Problem: Lethal Violence in America* (1997), written with Gordon Hawkins, and *American Youth Violence*, to be issued in late 1998.